WORD OVER ALL

Also by Eric James:

Judge Not: A selection of sermons preached in Gray's Inn Chapel, 1978–1988

(available from Christian Action, St Peter's House, 308 Kennington Lane, London SE11 5HY; price £4.95)

WORD OVER ALL

Forty Sermons, 1985–1991

ERIC JAMES

Foreword by Trevor Huddleston

First published in Great Britain 1992
SPCK
Holy Trinity Church
Marylebone Road
London NW1 4DU

British Library Cataloguing in Publication Data

A catalogue record for this book
is available from the British Library

ISBN 0-281-04596-8

Printed in Great Britain by
Mackays of Chatham plc.

CONTENTS

Contents

FOREWORD

The title of this collection of forty sermons is highly significant. As Eric
James says in his own Preface: "There are few more powerful words in any
language than the word 'word' itself....That most lovely verse in Matthew's
Gospel, 'Lord, I am not worthy that thou shouldest come under my roof, but
speak the *word* only, and my servant shall be healed', may have a meaning
that is simple and direct — 'Say the word!' — but after two thousand years
of Christian history, worship and prayer, those words are alive with
meaning ..."

The remarkable thing about these sermons is that each one of them is
"alive with meaning" because their author is able to use each subject, each
occasion, each place, to interpret that word with such freshness and
immediacy. In reading these sermons there is never the feeling that one has
"heard it all before". Always there is the stimulus to make one wonder how
one has missed the truth when, presented like this, it is so compelling. Just
because the preacher has such facility, it is easy to imagine that his sermons
are simply the result of a special gift. In one sense this is undoubtedly true:
in the sense that "he gave gifts unto men ... some apostles; and some,
prophets; and some, evangelists; and some, pastors and teachers .... for the
building up of the body of Christ." What is often forgotten, however, is that
every sermon, if it is to reach the hearts and minds of its hearers, is itself a
creative act. That creativity is an agony that requires an intellectual,
emotional and spiritual labour if the "word over all, beautiful as the sky" is
to be heard. Look at the variety of subjects, events, people, places and truths
covered by these forty sermons. Imagine for a moment what the preacher
himself has to imagine: the kind of congregation he is preparing to address;
the circumstances in which they will be gathered together in front of him:
more especially, the mood that is likely to prevail. A memorial service is

distinct from a service for the consecration of a bishop; a congregation of judges from a congregation of students at the beginning of a new academic year; Good Friday from Ascension Day — and so on. To be the kind of preacher revealed in these sermons you also have to be the kind of person — parson — who is always in touch with the challenges and the problems confronting those to whom he preaches. Eric James, as I know very well, *is* that kind of person. These sermons reveal a preacher whose pastoral concern is deep enough to embrace not just the individual and his or her spiritual needs but the individual living in a society that itself has to be understood. There is no doubt that Eric James's experience as a broadcaster, capable of reaching an audience of millions nation-wide and of expressing religious truths — *the word* of God — within a four minute "slot", has given him a great control of language. At the same time, his experience as Director of Christian Action, "a fellowship of men and women who work to translate the teachings of Christ into practical action in local, national and international affairs", keeps his vision as wide and as catholic as humanity itself. Because he has used his opportunities for travelling across the world, he has a vision of human affairs which transcends the narrow, restricted and parochial concerns of the Church of England "as by law established". And because in his ministry he has been a diocesan missioner, he understands the meaning of "mission" itself. He knows, for instance, that the discipline of study involves reading widely and not only academically. Contextual Theology and Liberation Theology are not strange to him, rather they are an essential part of his understanding of the "word over all".

If I had to choose *one* of the forty sermons as expressive of the heart of the matter in this collection, I would choose the sermon "For the Consecration of the Reverend Richard Harries as Bishop of Oxford" delivered in St. Paul's Cathedral on Ascension Day, May 28th, 1987. It begins with a literary allusion: "Only connect ..." — an epigraph coined by E. M. Forster for his novel *Howard's End*, which, after eighty years, is undiminished in its power to convey the profoundest of truth about human relationship itself. "*If* you can connect ... if *only* you can connect .... all you bring together will be exalted." I think any reader who decides to begin with this sermon will immediately recognise the unique quality of Eric James's preaching. It is addictive because, like all the best exposition of the word, it combines truth and understanding, light and warmth, intelligence and empathy.

I only wish I could deliver even half as many such sermons in such a short space of time (1985—1991) and with such consistent quality. "Only connect ..." and the sermons will do the rest.

☩ Trevor Huddleston CR

PREFACE

It was at the beginning of the Second World War, at Southwark Cathedral, where, years before I was ordained, I was learning the organ under Dr. E.T. Cook, that I first heard Vaughan Williams' *Dona Nobis Pacem*, sung by the Southwark Cathedral Special Choir. The work was barely three years old; and, in those first months of the War, *Dona Nobis Pacem* was a heartfelt cry. But the words I most remember from that cantata were from the poem "Reconciliation" by Walt Whitman, which Ralph Vaughan Williams had skilfully and beautifully woven within the work:

> Word over all, beautiful as the sky,
> Beautiful that war and all its deeds of carnage must
>   in time be utterly lost....

It is surely not surprising that for a preacher — and a broadcaster — those three words "Word over all" have continued to vibrate and resonate in all the years that have been given me.

There are few more powerful words in any language than the word "word" itself. Few words, for instance, had more meanings in Greek than the word *Logos*. It could mean a banking account or a treasurer's ledger; the account one must give of oneself, or, metaphorically, a penalty. It could be a kind of concern. It might be a measure: an item could be of little or no *logos* or value. It could be the relation of one subject to another: the ground, the explanation, or the reason. In logic — itself, of course, derived from *logos* — it could be a proposition; in philosophy, the life-force bringing the world to birth. Sometimes it could mean a story, a speech, or a saying; a treatise, or a talk; an order, or a command. No word has richer resonances. And more words have probably been written on the meaning of *logos* in St. John's Gospel than on any other word in all the bible: "In the beginning was the Word....and the Word was made flesh and dwelt among us."

That most lovely verse in Matthew's Gospel (viii.8; Luke vii.7) "Lord, I am not worthy that thou shouldest come under my roof, but speak the *word* only, and my servant shall be healed" may have a meaning that is simple and direct — "Say the word!"; but after two thousand years of Christian history, worship and prayer, those words are alive with meaning — not least because worshippers have so often used them before they have received the Holy Communion: "Lord, I am not worthy that thou shouldest come under my roof: but *speak the word only....*"

Four remarkable lines of poetry are ascribed to Queen Elizabeth I:

'Twas God the word that spake it,
He took the Bread and brake it;
And what the word did make it;
That I believe, and take it.

But, in the course of forty years as a preacher, I have often found the phrase "Speak the word only" — admittedly taken out of its context — a direct, if humbling, command, as I have prepared to preach: a command that sometimes seems to come from the congregation, but, more often, from the Lord himself, who "gave the word" — and gives it.

Of course, these sermons are *not* "the Word only". Indeed, the book might have been called *My word*! This ambiguity has been with the church since — and before — its foundation. I sometimes shudder when, after, say, the reading of a passage from St. Paul — or even some passage from the Gospels — the reader proclaims: "This is the word of the Lord", and am tempted to shout out: "But it isn't!"; for we never have "the Word only"; it is always mediated through "earthen vessels". Yet, George Herbert wrote:

Judge not the preacher; for he is thy Judge.
    If thou mislike him, thou conceiv'st him not.
God calleth preaching folly. Do not grudge
    To pick out treasures from an earthen pot.

And when all is said — and done; when the Last Word has been uttered, it is, and will be 'Word over all'.

I am particularly grateful to Bishop Trevor Huddleston C.R., for his Foreword to this volume — and honoured by it. Few can have spoken the word more powerfully to the church and to the world in our time.

I am also grateful both to the Council of Christian Action — and especially its secretary, Mrs. Jane Spurr, who has prepared this manuscript with her customary care and skill — and to the Treasurer and Masters of the Bench of Gray's Inn, who have done so much in this last decade and more to support and sustain me in ministry.

Eric James
Feast of the Transfiguration
1991

ACKNOWLEDGEMENTS

The author and publishers are grateful to the following for permission to reproduce copyright material:

David Bolt Associates for "In the Church of St Ouen" by Siegfried Sassoon from *Siegfried Sassoon: A Poet's Pilgrimage* by Dame Felicitas Corrigan, published by Victor Gollancz in 1973 (ch.7).

Cambridge University Press for the extract from "Theology and Self-Awareness" by H. A. Williams in *Soundings: Essays Concerning Christian Understanding* edited by A. R. Vidler, published in 1962 (ch.25).

Church House Publishing for "In Search of a Round Table" by Chuck Lathrop from *The Good Wine* edited by Josephine Bax, published in 1986 (ch.30).

Darton, Longman and Todd Ltd for the extract from the Foreword by H. A. Williams from *Only Connect: Worship and Liturgy from the Perspective of Pastoral Care* by Robin Green, published in 1987 (ch.8).

Doubleday for extracts from *The Friendship Game* by A. M. Greeley, published in 1971 (ch.27).

Faber and Faber Ltd for the extract from "Little Gidding" from *The Four Quartets* by T. S. Eliot, published in 1942 (ch.22).

David Higham Associates for the extract from *The Power and the Glory* by Graham Greene, published by Heinemann Publishers in 1940, © Verdant S. A. 1940–1968, 1971 (ch.33).

Janet Morley for extracts from *All Desires Known* by Janet Morley, published by the Movement for the Ordination of Women and Women in Theology in 1988, new and expanded edition published by SPCK in 1992 (ch.25).

George Sassoon for "They", "The Redeemer", "A Mystic as Soldier", "Deliverance" and "Everyone Sang" from *Siegfried Sassoon: Collected Poems 1908–1956*, published by Faber and Faber Ltd in 1947 and for the extract from *Siegfried's Journey 1916–1920* by Siegfried Sassoon, published by Faber and Faber in 1945 (ch.7).

SCM Press Ltd for the extract from *The Body: A Study in Pauline Theology* by John A. T. Robinson, published in 1952 (ch.5).

The Tablet for extracts by John Todd from his review of *A New Vision of Reality: Western Science, Eastern Mysticism and Christian Faith* by Bede Griffiths, published in the issue of 23/30 December 1989 (ch.24).

1

ASH WEDNESDAY AND COAL

King's College, London;
Ash Wednesday February 20th 1985

ASH Wednesday this year seems to have a special significance.

It's as though another element had been "given" us, to be set at the very heart of our spirituality this Lent: a lump of coal. Coal this year seems to provide the Ash for Penitence; and, indeed, to provide for all of us the raw material of theology and spirituality.

"Coal", the Coal Board's prospectus confidently states, is "the United Kingdom's greatest natural energy source". It's important, therefore, to start our theology there: with nature; with, if you like, the Doctrine of Creation: "First that which is natural" says St. Paul. We need to start our theological digging and excavation there.

On Shrove Tuesday I 'phoned a friend who's a vicar in a town that is dominated by its colliery; and I asked him what comment and contribution he thought coal had to make to our keeping of Lent this year.

"Well, Eric" he said "first I'd have to say that the Church here has been out of touch with the pit-men for a very long while, not just today but for generations. You'll know" he said "we're better with managers than with men."

Raw material there for penitence.

The Miners' Strike began, you'll remember, in response to the decision of management to close certain pits, and it has been dominated by a phrase: "The right of management to manage".

There is, I think, some need of theology there. I have found myself wondering whether somewhere along the line the old terms of "employer" and "master" and "management" have got confused.

1

In the complex process and long-term management of an industry I have been wondering what is the place of the worker. I have the feeling that a false doctrine of man may lie behind this simple division into management and managed: a doctrine that is, of course, worked out in difference of life-style, income and experience. Just as in Christian doctrine every man's a king, so, surely, every man's a manager.

The sad scenes on television of scuffling at the pit-head which we've seen so often in the last months, spell out some aspects of the sins of our society: the too easy resort to violence, of course. But we can too easily think that is the heart of the matter. We need to dig deeper into the subject. We worship a God who from the beginning of time has been bringing Order out of Chaos. Order and Law are very important subjects to Christians and Jews. But Law must be the reflection of our underlying conception of Justice. Justice towers above our Laws. Archbishop Temple said: "Justice is the first requirement of Love". Law must reflect an order which evidently springs from Justice. That Justice will protect the weak from the powerful; the poor from the depredations of the rich. It will put limits and constraints upon the powerful, whether the powerful are Trades Unions, Employers, Government, or this individual or that.

I spend most of my time at the moment working with the Archbishop's Commission on Urban Priority Areas; and almost each week I meet with the unemployed in places like Liverpool. Very many of the unemployed, I have to tell you, have ceased to think of Britain as a place which is greatly concerned with justice for them. They think of it, with some reason, as a place where the rich are getting richer, and the poor, poorer, and where the employed are not overmuch concerned with them, the *un*employed.

Order and Law mean our having a theology of authority and power.

I have found myself this last year wondering what Christian teaching on authority and power we Christians have succeeded in conveying to members of the Police Force. I have many friends in the police. They are all under pressure. The present Head of the Hendon Metropolitan Police Training Centre is a good friend of mine. He was a churchwarden in South London. The Dean of the Southwark priest-workmen is also in the Police Force.

Yes; but what theology of authority and power have we Christians to pass on to our police? I don't mean only to those battalions of police drafted in to mining areas but to those also in positions of command and authority.

There are, of course, some very special Christian insights into authority and power given us by Christ Himself. They are not easily and immediately applied to this situation and that. But we need to know them, and need to have wrestled with them if we are to help, say, the police understand them.

Christ says very special things to his followers, not least from the Cross itself, about power and powerlessness; indeed, about the power of powerlessness.

Another important word in the strike has been the word "Economic". Sometimes it has sounded rather simple: "No man in his senses would keep an uneconomic pit going".

Yes, but I noticed that in the Vale of Belvoir, in Leicestershire, recently, the Coal Board was not given permission to dig up coal as cheaply as it could wherever it could. It was said that that beautiful environment was more important than just "economics". It helped, I've no doubt, that it was a Duke who was defending that particular argument and who won his case. But it does signify that few of us would say that economics are all important.

Indeed, the cost of defeating the strike and of financing redundancy is probably greater than the cost of sustaining many uneconomic pits for quite a while — which reveals that we may have other priorities.

Christians, certainly, have to take economics very seriously. But our faith should help us to set economics in a wider perspective.

There is another major word which has dominated the strike: the word "community".

"The Trades Unions must not be allowed to hold to ransom the rest of the community" said one eminent politician.

But another said: "This strike, if the miners lose, will mean the destruction of many mining communities".

"Community" is a slippery sort of word. But St. Paul has clarified it for Christians a good deal, and we use his phrases in our liturgy week by week. Community and Communion can never be separated. We proclaim that "though we are many, we are one body: members one of another."

Of course, the words can be treated simply as rhetoric. But I am saying this morning that just as *Bread* brings the word "Community" to life — "One Bread: One Body" — so too does *Coal*.

Managers and men: all one Body.

McGregor and Scargill: members one of another. Men, women and children, in pit villages — and with us here today in King's — all one Body.

Polish miners and British miners: all one Body. And, when you think of the chemical products that modern research and technology have turned coal into, there's a whole family, world-wide, which is thus made members one of another.

There is one more phrase which has been heard a great deal over the last year, when fruitless attempts were made to bring the strike to an end, and which has much theological and spiritual content to it. We heard many times last year of *"Conciliation Procedures"*: ACAS "Conciliation Procedures".

Now "conciliation procedures" are surely what the church is centrally about: "God and sinners re-conciled".

There is no power to re-concile unless you are willing to be a man-in-the midst — which is a very priestly position. But this is no ritual

3

reconciliation. Unless you are willing to get involved — and also, paradoxically, unless you can remain detached and objective — unless you are involved, first, by patient listening and understanding, and then seeing exactly what both sides have to say, and why — unless you are willing to participate deeply and also in some way remain transcendent — and willing to get hurt in the process — you have little hope of leading all together towards justice and reconciliation. It is a very theological God-given task, and therefore very down to earth.

I had never thought till this year and this strike, of the Incarnation of Christ and his Triumphant Suffering on Calvary as a "Conciliation Procedure".

And what need there is now of conciliation procedures in those pit villages where not only villagers but families have been divided.

There's much more I could say of the theology and spirituality which I believe this Coal Strike has, so to speak, *brought to the surface*: about, for instance, the Gospel of Creation and Technology; about the Gospel and change and decay — and change and renewal; the Gospel that helps us to face change: face death and resurrection; face being laid aside in unemployment and sickness; about the Gospel and Sin: sin in Government; sin in Management; sin in Trades Unions; sin in Local Communities; sin in the church: for the power of the church to reconcile is severely limited by its sinful past and its sinful present.

But I have said sufficient, I hope, to make you see why *Ash* Wednesday this year has a special significance for me. And why I see *Coal* as a kind of God-given element that must be at the heart of all our spirituality this Lent.

And I shall end what I have to say simply by giving you a text — from that most wonderful passage in the Prophet Isaiah, in the sixth Chapter:

"Then flew one of the seraphims unto me, having a live coal in his hand, which he had taken with tongs from off the altar".

What a difference it would make to our church — what a difference it might make to our nation — if this Lent we each one of us saw a seraph, a messenger of God, setting a lump of coal at the centre of our church life; at the centre of our spirituality; at the centre of our national life.

Who knows? By Easter the Church and the Nation might have risen together to new life.

2

IN MEMORIAM: ERIC SYMES ABBOTT, DEAN OF WESTMINSTER

Lincoln Theological College; June 5th 1985.

"He hath made us accepted in the beloved": Ephesians 1.v.6.

I shall always associate that particular text with Eric Abbott. It meant much to him. He made it mean much to me — and to hundreds of others: through his own personal ministry, not least in this place. That single fact lies at the heart of our commemoration today.

I would have to say that no one made "acceptance in the beloved" — the divine acceptance, in and through Christ — more living and powerful to me than did Eric. And he did that primarily through the strength and quality of his personal friendship.

Eric taught you the paramount importance of knowing yourself to be "accepted in the beloved". And he taught you that friendship, the ministry of friendship, ministry through friendship, is central to this.

Just as we look back to the days of Christ's flesh as "history" — events in the past which nevertheless have their repercussions in the present — so I look back on the days when I was first 'accepted' by Eric, and knew that acceptance to be sacramental of the acceptance of Christ, thirty-five and more years ago, as events in the past which go on having their repercussions in my life even today.

Eric taught you that the raw material of friendship — letters and postcards; going for a walk, or a holiday, together; simply spending time together, and talking, and so taking your opinions, taking you, seriously; birthdays and other anniversaries — all these Eric taught you are the "matter" of the sacrament of acceptance.

5

Many of you will know that I was allowed to spell all this out at length in an hour long lecture in Westminster Abbey on the day that the memorial stone was placed over Eric's ashes. Because I have already said all that — and stay with it, without withdrawing or countering anything I said then — I want to go a little deeper today, not least because this chapel, so loved by Eric, is a more intimate ambience than the Abbey; and also because I think Eric probably loved Lincoln, and his time at Lincoln, and this place in particular, more than he loved any other place or time in his life. The Scholae Cancellarii, as he loved to call it, was the sort of size he could "manage": a place in which he felt and experienced acceptance; whereas he was conscious that King's, and Keble, and Westminster, and the volume of personal ministry he had by then to sustain, put utterly impossible pressures and demands upon him.

When I first met Eric, I was overawed by him. He was always immaculate, and it only gradually occurred to me — and only gradually did I have the confidence to believe — that why Eric spoke so often and so much about "acceptance" was not only because he knew it to be so important; not only because he knew he himself so desperately needed it; but because he found it so difficult to receive, or to believe in when he received it. And this difficulty lasted to the end of his life, and made itself most potently manifest in his last years and months.

There are, of course, various aspects of our knowledge of our "acceptance"; and I think it is important for us to recognise that because "He has made us" psycho-physical organisms — indeed, socio-psycho-physical organisms — acceptance will rarely, if ever, be mediated to us "simply spiritually". As Eric would often say, quoting St. Paul (rather out of context!): "That was not first which is spiritual, but that which is natural".

Eric was a born physician of the soul. The work came to him so "naturally"; but I think he never took fully seriously what help psychology might have been to him personally. Though there were many "psychological" novels, so to speak, on his shelves, there was not one book of psychology, strictly speaking. Of all pastors I have known, it could be said more truly of E.S.A. what was said of our Lord: "He knew what was in man". He was, to use the words he loved of Bishop Ken, "Deep in the Study of the Heart immers'd". Yet Eric would often quote with feeling, as he applied them to himself, the words of the crowd at the cross: "He saved others; himself he cannot save". Although all his ministry he "went to Confession" — indeed, for many years he saw regularly the then renowned spiritual director, Reginald Somerset Ward, "The Author of the Way", as he was known, and after R.S.W.'s death saw regularly Norman Goodacre — I think is is true to say that no one ever got to the "heart of the matter" where Eric's own problems were concerned. Not least because he rather shunned psychology, his inability to know himself accepted remained, and his ministry, marvellous as it was — so marvellous that it may seem strange even to mention its limitations — had, nevertheless, certain limitations. Perhaps I can best illustrate what I mean by a comparison.

Twenty-one years before Eric won his scholarship to Nottingham High School, a somewhat different boy also won a scholarship to that same school: David Herbert Richards Lawrence.

D.H. Lawrence, and, later, E.S.A., received probably as fine an education at Nottingham High School as was available anywhere at that time.

Both E.S.A.'s father and mother were schoolteachers. Lawrence's mother was a schoolteacher. His father was, of course, a collier, though he, like his wife, had a bourgeois background.

Lawrence was as attached to his mother as E.S.A. was to his. Lawrence said what E.S.A. might have said: that his own 'malady' was his own deep attachment to his home and his mother. Indeed, E.S.A. might have written what Lawrence wrote: "Nobody can have the soul of me. My Mother had it, and nobody can have it again. Nobody can come into my very self again and breathe me like an atmosphere".

From early childhood, Lawrence and E.S.A. were both brought up on the Bible. No one can deny that Lawrence was consistently one of the most religious men who ever wrote. It was Lawrence, not E.S.A., who wrote: "I shall always be a Priest of Love". He wrote it soon after he had completed his first major novel, *Sons and Lovers*, and added: "I shall preach my heart out, Lord bless you." And he did, but in, of course, a very different way from E.S.A.

Lawrence retained a love for the Nottinghamshire that surrounded the Eastwood Urban District of his upbringing. "That's the country of my heart" he wrote. When it was time to leave the Midlands, we are told "he looked like a man under sentence of exile", though he soon threw off his provincial shackles. Eric virtually turned his back on Nottingham when he went to Cambridge, which captivated and captured him. Lawrence, before he was thirty, was introduced to Cambridge, and there to Bertrand Russell, Maynard Keynes, E.M. Forster and G.E. Moore; but he did not much enjoy the meeting. By then, Lawrence was into the social problems of the world that was shaped like the Nottingham he knew so well, and thus into socialism. Professor Vivian de Sola Pinto puts Lawrence into the long line of the great prophets of English literature, from Langland in the 14th century, through More and Latimer, Bunyan and Blake, Carlyle and Morris, to the present day. "Lawrence" he wrote "is the latest, but by no means the last figure in that line."

"I suppose we are prudes, but standards were different then" wrote Lawrence of his earlier life. E.S.A. would undoubtedly have said the same. But Lawrence was always escaping from his prudery: indeed, from the imprisoning standards of his early life. So was Eric, but much more gradually.

To the author of the story "You Touched Me", touch was the quivering sensitive way Lawrence had of entering into the understanding of things, whilst E.S.A. was to his last hours somewhat afraid of the body and indeed of the erotic, however kind and compassionate he was to those for whom the erotic was the means of their downfall.

In the realm of sexuality, as well as social thought, Lawrence was undoubtedly a prophet; by which we do not necessarily mean we agree with all he said, but that he had the psychic courage to look at his experience openly and afresh, and respond with honesty and integrity.

Harry T. Moore, the biographer of Lawrence, has this to say: "Authors often try to shake off burdens of the past by writing about it. Sometimes the process is conscious, sometimes not: its effectiveness usually depends upon the strength and depth of the feeling involved. In religion, confession leading to absolution requires a painful searching of the spirit; in psycho-analysis, the patient who is uprooting a neurosis must relive in agonizing memory, the causal traumatic experience; and in literature, the process is somewhat similar".

I have made the comparison between those two Nottingham High School boys: Lawrence, born, mark you, twenty-one years before Eric, and Eric, the Dame Agnes Mellers Scholar at the High School — Lawrence, of course, used the name Mellors in *Lady Chatterley's Lover* — because it seems to me important not only to say how marvellous Eric was in his ministry — that I have done and will go on doing to my dying day — but also to press the question: "What was it that limited Eric in his ministry?": What was it that limited him socially, so that this Nottingham schoolboy became the very personification of the B.K. Cunningham concept of the priest as "an English gentleman in Holy Orders"?

What was it that blocked Eric's ability to know himself "accepted in the beloved" — *body*, soul and spirit?

The question is important, for if I was right to say in Westminster Abbey — and I believe I was — that "when the history of the training of the clergy of the Church of England comes to be written there can be no shadow of doubt that Eric Abbott will have within it one of the highest places of honour — in the number alone of clergy for whose training he was directly responsible, at Lincoln and King's, he is without equal..."— then the failure of the Church of England to produce priests who are prophets as well as pastors, who proclaim a profoundly embodied spirituality, who would understand the politics of spirituality, and assist the articulation of a spirituality emanating from and appropriate to our inner cities and urban priority areas — must also to some extent be ascribed to the limitations of Eric's ministry. He himself was aware, and often said as much, that the Church of England, which is so proud of its title the Via Media, could so easily become the Via Mediochre.

8

The question is important in another respect. We are met here not least to launch, in thankful memory of Eric, a lectureship on spirituality. For a definition of spirituality, Eric would probably have pointed us to the Baron Von Hügel, who "distinguished without dividing" the mystical-emotional element in religion from the historical-institutional element and from the intellectual-scientific element. Von Hügel maintained that these three elements needed one another, both as complements and correctives.

As I have reflected thankfully on the life of Eric Symes Abbott, I have come to the conclusion that the mystical-emotional element needs to include the psycho-sexual, and the historical-institutional element needs to include the social and sociological. "Acceptance in the beloved" needs always to involve all of this trinity, because we are socio-psychophysical organisms. And I hope my fellow trustees of the lectureship on spirituality founded in memory of E.S.A. — including your Warden — will be willing to pay due regard to this "lesson", so to speak, that I believe we learn from the life of Eric: from his limitations as well as his gifts.

But there is one other aspect of "acceptance in the beloved" about which I must speak before I end, and without which this address could be gravely unbalanced.

"Acceptance in the beloved" is not only about what we feel and know, it is about what God does. And one of the primary manifestations of God's acceptance of us is the way he uses us, in spite of our limitations, with our limitations, through our limitations.

You had only to go to Westminster Abbey on the day of Eric's memorial service to know beyond a peradventure that it was the memorial to one who was "accepted in the beloved". I began this address by talking of Eric's acceptance of me. But the Abbey was packed from end to end that day with individuals, almost every one of whom had personal reason to be grateful for Eric's personal ministry; and present there that day were only a fraction of those who wanted to be there and had real and personal reason to be there. Eric had been a great Warden of Lincoln; a great Dean of King's College London; a great Warden of Keble; a great Dean of Westminster. He had been a great servant of the Church of England. No one's counsel was ever more widely sought and valued. He refused bishopric after bishopric. He knew that his personal ministry was the heart of his vocation. I have never known, and never shall know, any one more fully used by God than Eric. And, as I say, one of the primary manifestations of God's acceptance of us is the way He uses us.

Eric was very fond of Julian of Norwich. He would quote passage after passage of her *Revelations of Divine Love*. But there was one phrase of the Lady Julian he loved above all other: "All our wounds are seen afore God not as wounds but as worships". There is surely no greater sign of our "acceptance in the beloved".

And I have no doubt that Eric now sees his wounds afore God "not as wounds but as worships". And thus has He made both him and us all "accepted in the Beloved".

3

HOLY, HOLY, HOLY

The Ordination Service, Blackburn Cathedral; June 30th 1985

At the beginning of this year, a cyclone devastated several of the islands in the South West Pacific. They are islands remote from us here in Britain; but I know that many people in this Diocese keep close links with that area, not least because one of your previous bishops, Bishop Baddeley, was bishop out there before he became Bishop of Blackburn.

I am one of the "Commissaries", the agents in England, to the *Archbishop of Melanesia* (as he now is), and I have to go out there from time to time. I went out last just after another cyclone had devastated some of the islands. I particularly remember February 25th 1972.

I awoke at 7.00 in the morning aboard the *Southern Cross*, the seventy-foot boat of the Archbishop, by which he visits some of the thousand islands of the whole diocese. I turned over in my bunk, looked out of the porthole, and got my first glimpse of the island of Espiritu Santo, and of the little port of Santo where we were just about to dock.

At half-past eight, I walked along the burning hot unsheltered road from the wharf into the town, past some oil-storage tanks, a night club, a few shops and a couple of banks: one English and one French. I was on my way to meet Harry Tevi — a tall black Vanuatu priest, who is in fact now Bishop of one of the dioceses of the Province of Melanesia.

And I'm not surprised; for that morning, my diary reminds me, I had this conversation with Harry:

"What's your favourite aspect of theology?"
"The Old Testament, without a doubt."
"Why?"
"Because our society here is so like the society described
    in the Old Testament — but you can see what a difference
        the *New* Testament would make to it."
"Who has most helped you to love and understand the Old

11

Testament?"
"The German theologian Gerhard von Rad."
"Who is the character you most like in the Old Testament?"
"Isaiah. He makes me think so often of *Holy, Holy,*
   Holy and of doing something about this world around
      me."

That conversation took place as we walked towards Harry's school, to look at the remains of the classrooms which had been almost entirely destroyed by the cyclone — alas! that school has been destroyed yet again by a cyclone this year.

That evening, at the Holy Communion in Harry's church — a church of bamboo poles and a roof woven of sago palm leaves — I can remember seeing above the altar the words *TAMBU — TAMBU — TAMBU*, in large letters, written beautifully in vegetable dye on tapa cloth, beaten bark; and during the service, I remember the crowded church — more men than women, the tall black men with hair like lawyers' wigs of black — I remember them singing with reverent nasal voices: *Tambu — Tambu — Tambu.*

Although I recognised they were singing *Holy, Holy, Holy,* it didn't occur to me for a quite a while that that word *Tambu* was our English word *Taboo* — or, rather, that our English word *Taboo* is really their word *Tambu.* We picked it up in the last century from the South Pacific.

There are relatively few words in the pidgin English of the South West Pacific, and when the first English missionaries began to teach the people of those islands, the best word in the local vocabulary they could find to translate our word *Holy* was *Tambu.*

But when I went on from Espiritu Santo to the Solomon Islands, further north, and fetched up at the chief island, made famous during the Second World War for its land and sea battles, Guadalcanal — and made even more famous by John Wayne after the war — a shock was waiting for me in the new and lovely Cathedral. There again were the words *Tambu, Tambu, Tambu,* above the altar; and in the Communion it was those same words that the people sang. But when I went to the Bishop's vestry it had on the door *Tambu* — Private! Keep Out! And — if you'll allow me to mention it in this Holy Place — when I went to the "loo", there, too, on the door was *Tambu.*

Now in some religions the Holy is simply what is taboo. In the Old Testament the Holy is quite often "Forbidden Ground": something you're not to touch — on pain of death. God Himself is often portrayed not only as awe-some and awe-inspiring but as unapproachable — only to be approached in a cloud, or with veiled face.

But the coming of Jesus radically altered all that. The Holy for the Christian is never simply the taboo. It's never simply the shrine and the sanctuary: the place set apart that only the few can penetrate. It's never

12

simply the holy day as distinct from the everyday. It's never simply the "holy" man as distinct from everyman in his ministry — and every woman.

Jesus, for the Christian, is the supreme revelation of the Holy: born in a stable; a carpenter's son; crucified as a criminal.

He was born and died not on days which *were* holy, but on days which were *made* holy by the way he lived and died on them.

Jesus did not live in *the Holy Land*. The land was *made* Holy by the way *he* spent his day-to-day life there.

It was from the raw material of the everyday and the ordinary that Jesus fashioned holiness.

And for ever after, for the Christian — wherever we are; whoever we are; whatever the time and the day — that moment presents us in our decisions and responsibilities with the raw material of holiness — out of which the holy has to be fashioned in response to God.

Now why do I say all this to you here — and now?

Because when Harry Tevi was consecrated Bishop of Vanuatu, he was commissioned and empowered — for life — to work away at the Holy, and to help others to work away at the Holy. In fact, one of his priests, Walter Lini, is not only a priest, he is Prime Minister of Vanuatu. He had only just been ordained priest when I met him, but now he is exercising his priesthood as he seeks to bring justice to his nation, and food, and roads, and drains, and schools, and hospitals; and all this he sees as intimately connected with the Holy.

It could be tempting here — and now — to envisage a primarily shrine-centred idea of the Holy.

It could be tempting here and now, in the Cathedral of St. Mary the Virgin, the day after St. Peter's Day — to say "Ah, yes, St. Mary and St. Peter — *They* were holy."

But the whole point of the New Testament is that each one of us is called — in our own way, our own life, our own locality, with the raw material of our temperaments — to be Holy as God is Holy; not with an untouchable holiness, a keep out, keep away, unapproachable holiness; a holiness of taboos; but with a warm, compassionate, tender, strong, welcoming, accepting, disciplined, sacrificial, purified, passionately loving, practical, down-to-earth holiness: the holiness of Jesus.

And those who are being made deacons or priests here today have been called to help fashion holiness in our bit of the world: to help us in our homes and parishes, and places of work — and to help not least those who have no work: to help us all work at holiness "seven whole days, not one in seven". Whenever we work at holiness we must be mindful of its mystery and of the need to be consecrated and committed to the task: so that heaven and earth — the whole wide world — shall be full of God's glory. And at this time in our nation's history, the need for holiness to be worked out in terms of social justice, health, education, employment, is as great as it ever was.

And who is the One who will really empower us in this working away at holiness?

Oddly enough it is He who has a name I mentioned in the first minute of what I've been saying: Espiritu Santo — which I imagine you well know is Portuguese for Holy Spirit — God in Person; God in Action; God who is Holy with the Holiness He revealed supremely on this earth in Jesus Christ our Lord.

I learnt only recently that in Portugal there's a *bank* of Espiritu Santo — *Banco Espiritu Santo E Commercial De Lisboa.* And rightly so; for either banking is of God or it's not, and we ought not to be using banks. What we do with our money is an important part of our holiness. It's the symbol of what we all do here today: we offer ourselves to God for him to bless, saying:

Come Espiritu Santo — Holy Spirit —
our souls inspire —
our bishops inspire —
those to be ordained inspire —
our Prime Minister and Government inspire —
all of us — all God's people inspire,
so that the whole world shall be full of his glory.

4

REMEMBER THE POOR

St. Paul's Epistle to the Galatians 2 v.10;
Gray's Inn Chapel; July 14th 1985

This week's riots at Handsworth, Birmingham will have disturbed, dismayed and saddened us all. *The Times* carried the report of a market analysis firm which said "There are few places in England and Wales that would exhibit worse indices of urban deprivation". There is 30% overall unemployment. For young people the figure is even higher; and for young black people it is far, far higher: 55% of those between nineteen and twenty-four are unemployed. It is on this Sunday-after-Handsworth that I think we should hear again St. Paul's words: "Remember the Poor".

Most of you will know that during the last two years I have spent much of my time visiting areas like Handsworth — what are now called Urban Priority Areas — as I have worked alongside the Archbishop's Commission on Urban Priority Areas, which, curiously, was having its last meeting last Monday while the Handsworth riot was taking place.

It would be no exaggeration to say that in these last two years I have had to think, or re-think, what theology has to say about those areas — and, indeed, what should be our attitude to them — and to frame my conclusions as concisely and cogently as possible.

The call of Christ to show compassion to those in need finds an immediate response in the hearts of Christians (and not only Christians), and requires no "theology" to drive it home; indeed, theological reflection may sometimes have the result only of introducing complications and qualifications which make the demands of the Gospel easier to evade.

When St. Paul argued that the Churches he had founded should "remember the poor", he did not need to mount a theological case to show that this was a demand of the Gospel. Only when certain congregations were slow to respond did he resort to arguments that would stimulate their generosity. The principle itself has never been in dispute. It is impossible to be a Christian without responding in some way or other to the neighbour who is in need. The Church has a long tradition of encouraging this response through charitable giving, support of welfare work among the poor, hungry, and homeless, at home and overseas — most recently, through bodies like Christian Aid. Throughout its history it has acknowledged its obligation to "remember the poor".

In this country we have been witnessing an aggravation of poverty, in the form of "multiple deprivation", particularly concentrated in our inner cities and urban priority areas; caused to a great extent by circumstances beyond the control of those who are affected by it. There is a clear Christian duty to respond to this situation and "remember the poor" in our UPA's; but it can hardly be said that in the last decade either church or state have made this a high priority. The church, like the nation, appears for the most part to be pursuing its concerns and managing its life as if these "patches" of acute need ought not to trouble us overmuch.

In theory, a Commission, like the one with which I have been associated, should simply sound an alarm: tell the nation what we have now seen, and heard, and know — of the concentration of human suffering on our doorstep, of which the great majority of church members, like the majority of our fellow citizens appear to be unaware — and then, at least those who call themselves Christians will come to the aid of those who have fallen so far behind the relative prosperity enjoyed by the rest of us. No further "theology" is required. The command "remember the poor" is clear.

Yes. But what sort of aid is required?

It is here that we enter an unavoidable area of debate.

The question at issue is whether the acknowledged Christian duty to "remember the poor" should be confined to personal charity, and service directed to individuals, or whether it can legitimately take the form of social and political action aimed at altering the circumstances which appear to cause poverty and distress.

For myself, I believe that these are "false alternatives", and that a Christian is committed to a form of action which embraces both. What is at stake is the degree of priority which should be accorded to each of them, and, to determine that, we need to look at the strengths and weaknesses of each approach.

Jesus addressed the greater part of his teaching to questions of personal behaviour and belief. His most characteristic illustrations are drawn from the relationships and personal choices of individuals. Yet his proclamation of the Kingdom had radical social and political implications. It was to be embodied in a community in which the normal priorities of wealth, power and respectability would be overturned. It was doubtless the fact that he pointed out these implications that was one of the main causes of his rejection, suffering and death. This does not mean that Jesus was primarily a social reformer, or that he was a violent revolutionary.

16

He was deeply concerned that any child should realize their potential and become what he proclaimed them to be: an infinitely valuable child of God. The church has consistently followed him in stressing the theory of the inalienable dignity and worth of every individual and the absolute equality of all — of each and every one — before God. (This is, of course, a matter of the greatest contemporary relevance, given the racial prejudice still manifest in many parts of our society, and even, at times, within the church itself.)

Never was this personal emphasis more necessary than now.

Modern society seems so often to deal with individuals as "anonymities"; and even the services from which the most personal attention might be expected — the health and welfare services — seem sometimes to reduce their clients to the status of "cases" or "applicants", with little concern for the ways in which individuals may differ in their need: a need which is only discovered in patient, personal dealing. The positive side of this is, of course, that the provision of social benefits demands an impartial and even-handed approach to all — like the administration of Justice. And the church has the full authority of the Gospel to protect the God-given dignity of every individual, and must do all it can to defeat the trend and tendency towards "impersonality".

But it is at this point that I have often heard in the last years the voice of protest. It is not an unreasonable voice: indeed, it is not seldom bland and urbane. It says something like this:

"Yes: The church has a clear mandate to give high priority to moral and spiritual values. We live in a society in which material values are openly proclaimed; in which economic doctrine rather than social and ethical concern is allowed primarily to regulate public policy; in which social and collective action is regularly justified by appeal to self-interest. By becoming prominently involved in social action the church may at least appear to be giving priority to a material standard of living rather than to the non-material values at the heart of its message. Only if the church addresses a personal challenge to every individual and confronts him or her with a call to personal repentance and to a new life of prayer, witness, and service, can the church be said to be keeping to the priorities of the Gospel."

I have learnt to look closely and carefully at the arguments of those who call for an emphasis on these priorities.

There can be little doubt that members of the Church of England have generally found it more congenial — even more convenient — to express their discipleship by helping individual victims of misfortune or oppression rather than by working to rectify injustices in the structures of society. And there are a number of reasons for their preference for what may be called "ambulance work".

No one minds being cast in the role of protector and helper of the weak and powerless: there is no threat there to one's superior position and one's power of free decision. But to be a protagonist of social change may involve challenging those in power, and, indeed, risking the loss of one's own power and the security of one's own way of life. Helping a victim or sufferer seldom involves conflict; working for change in the structures of society can hardly avoid it. Direct personal assistance to an individual may seem relatively straightforward, uncontroversial and rewarding; involvement in social issues implies choosing between complicated alternatives, and accepting compromises which often seem remote from any clear moral position.

Christians have tended to assume that keeping the peace and avoiding conflict are one and the same. We have no tradition of initiating needful conflict and coping with it creatively. We are not at home in the tough secular milieu of social and political action.

Yet I have to say that a glance at the history of Christianity is sufficient to show that the very notion of a private religion, without social and political implications, is a relatively recent one. In the early centuries, if Christians had been concerned only with personal salvation and piety, they might well have been able to keep their heads down and avoid exposing themselves to persecution.

In the Middle Ages, it was taken for granted that the whole political and economic life was an appropriate sphere for the concern and influence of the church.

For a time, it is true, philosophers thought of a "soul" with which religion is concerned in a body with which it is not, or should not, be concerned. But that time is now long since past. Modern philosophy, in fact, gives us some encouragement to return to the Biblical way of thought, according to which God — if he addresses us at all — addresses our whole person, body and soul, complete with the social relationships amid which we live. Modern social sciences insist that no analysis of the human person is adequate which does not take into account the influence upon the person of social conditions and culture. The suggestion that religion is an entirely individual affair — the flight of the alone to the Alone — is surely untenable and unacceptable.

The impossibility of identifying a "soul" independent of material circumstances has always been particularly obvious to missionaries working among people who are starving or are deprived of the basic conditions of life: ministry to them clearly cannot be divorced from concern for their material needs. And the same is true today — not least of those long unemployed — in, say, Handsworth.

In the last two years I have seen areas in this country where unemployment, poor housing, and the threat of criminal violence have reached such proportions that they are like a plague; they so dominate people's thinking, feeling, and existence, that no presentation of the Gospel is possible which does not relate to their material deprivations. In these circumstances, everything tells against the notion that there is a "soul", quite independent of social and economic conditions, to which an entirely individual gospel may and should be addressed.

That God has a concern for the just ordering of society is a conviction which runs right through the Bible: through the Old and New Testaments, and on into a long line of Christian social theorists, from St. Augustine to the present day. Moreover the New Testament adds its own values to those offered by the Old. Jesus' teaching on the Kingdom reveals a pattern of human relationships which can be fully realised only in the New Age, but which can be at least partially experienced in the present; and other values, such as freely given mutual service, care for the weak, and the overcoming of racial, social, and sexual barriers, are so prominent in the Epistles that they can claim a place in any Christian social thinking. The elaboration of these elements into an actual system of social and political life has occupied the minds of English Christians from Thomas More to the present day. No single blue-print has emerged; and to consider anything like a blue-print for action is not my purpose this morning. My purpose this morning has been more simple: to say to you, as I say to myself, "Hear again the words of St Paul: 'Remember the Poor'." Remember the poor of Handsworth, and reflect that individual action alone will not deal with that situation. There is no way in which our Christian remembrance of the poor can evade more corporate, collective and social action.

5

THE CHURCH, THE BODY OF CHRIST

St. Paul's Knightsbridge;
Ash Wednesday February 12th 1986

Today there has been the voting on the future of the Westland helicopter company; and everyone knows that the lives of the workers of that company are caught up in a complex network of forces — known and unknown shareholders; international merchant bankers; politicians; Sikorski's in the United States; and so on.

It would be nice for the Westland workers in rural Yeovil to imagine they are simply individuals with independence. But economics, politics, the power structure and the class structure, are harsh realities of the world.

It is easy to think that this is a new situation. But let me quote from a marvellous study of St. Paul written more than thirty years ago:

"Paul starts, as we do, from the fact that man is bound up in a vast solidarity of historical existence which denies him freedom to control his own destiny or achieve his true end. This is the 'body' of sin and death, in which he is involved at every level of his being, physical, political and even cosmic. The great corporations of modern society are expressions of this all-embracing solidarity. The temptation of Western man is to seek salvation by exalting the individual *against* such collectives or by seeking withdrawal from the body of socio-historical existence. Paul saw that the Christian gospel is very different. For the body is not simply evil: it is made by God and for God. Solidarity is the divinely ordained structure in which personal life is to be lived. Man's freedom does not lie in the fact that he is not bound, nor his individuality in the fact that he is not social. Both derive from an unconditional and inalienable responsibility to God, which is not denied by the solidarities of the body and can indeed be discharged only in and through them. Christians should be the last people to be found clinging to the wrecks of an atomistic individualism, which has no foundation in the Bible. For their hope does not lie in escape from collectivism: it lies in the resurrection of the body — that is to say, in the redemption, transfiguration, and ultimate supersession of one solidarity by another. This is Paul's gospel of the new corporeity of the Body of Christ, which itself depends on the redemptive act wrought by Jesus in the body of His flesh through death.

One could say without exaggeration that the concept of the body forms the keystone of Paul's theology. In its closely interconnected meanings, the word *soma* knits together all his great themes. It is from the body of sin and death that we are delivered; it is through the body of Christ on the Cross that we are saved; it is into His body the Church that we are incorporated; it is by His body in the Eucharist that this community is sustained; it is in our body that its new life has to be manifested; it is to a resurrection of this body to the likeness of His glorious body that we are destined. Here, with the exception of the doctrine of God, are represented all the main tenets of the Christian Faith — the doctrines of Man, Sin, the Incarnation and Atonement, the Church, the Sacraments, Sanctification, and Eschatology. To trace the subtle links and interaction between the different senses of this word *soma* is to grasp the thread that leads through the maze of Pauline thought."

The concept of the body is the key to the unity of the whole of St. Paul's theology. It is also the most striking mark of its distinctiveness. No other New Testament writer gives the word 'body' the doctrinal significance Paul gives it. His development of the theology of the body is characteristically his own. And with it you can say, without fear of contradiction, is bound up most of his particular contribution to the thought and practice of the early church.

In my lifetime there have been three great studies of this Pauline doctrine of the Body of Christ.

The first was by the Jesuit theologian at Louvain, Emile Mersch, who was killed in an air raid in 1940. His great book, published in English in 1938, *The Whole Christ*, in its French title had the *Body* of Christ more clearly at its heart: *Le Corps Mystique de Christ*.

The second was published in 1941 by the Mirfield monk and theologian Fr. Lionel Thornton: *The Common Life in the Body of Christ*.

The third, from which I have already quoted, was a little masterpiece, not least of compression — Bishop John Robinson's study of less than a hundred pages, *The Body* — published first in 1952, when he was beginning to rise to the height of his theological powers.

Its first chapter is called "The Body of the Flesh", and goes back to the Old Testament anthropology which lies behind St. Paul's thought — the relation between flesh and spirit: Hebrew ideas that were so different from the Greek ideas of the body-spirit relationship in which there was a very negative attitude to the body.

The second chapter is on "The Body of the Cross" — the body that dies; the body that is open to sin; Christ's body that was crucified, dead and buried through the sin of man.

The third chapter is on "The Body of the Resurrection" — which enables us to speak of the Church as "The Extension of the Incarnation" and to associate intimately with God, Christ, the Church and indeed humanity itself.

That theology of the Church as the Body of Christ has now become so much part of our thinking in the last fifty years, through what we call the Liturgical Movement, that the phrases of St. Paul which have now been put at the very heart of our liturgy can trip off our lips almost too lightly. I mean those great proclamations:-

> "We are the Body of Christ: In one Spirit we were all baptised into One Body: Let us then pursue all that makes for peace and builds up our common life.
>
> We break this bread to share in the Body of Christ: Though we are many we are one Body, because we all share in one bread — one loaf."

In the Report *Faith in the City* — which I hope you who here rejoice in the name of "St. Paul's" will feel it particularly your Christian duty to read — you will find many references to St. Paul's theology of the Body of Christ and to the essential idea of membership one of another. "The quality of the relationship between the Urban Priority Areas and the wider church" it says "is a supreme test of the life of the whole Body".

At this point I could spend hours illustrating from my last two years' work alongside the Archbishop's Commission on Urban Priority Areas, for the central testimony of that Report is to the very opposite of "membership one of another" and of our being "all one body"; it is to the reality of *alienation* — thousands alienated from the church and from society; young and alienated, black and alienated; unemployed and alienated.

I think of a magistrate in Liverpool, in his sixties — a very responsible and respectable man — saying equally sadly "I never thought I should live to be on the side of those who are brought before me as shoplifters — not all of them, of course, but many of them".

I think of the Liverpudlian, who'd been unemployed for years, who said "When you get to forty here you only have to sign on every three months 'cos you're finished".

I think of the black teenagers in a youth centre in Hackney who laughed at the very idea that they should vote in the next election — "There's no point in *us* voting" they said — as did almost every teenager I met with in youth centres.

I think of the head teacher in Tower Hamlets who took me through his class register in his primary school, giving me the reasons why his children have so little chance in our society — and describing the pressures on the schoolteachers — who get paid so little in comparison with our police.

But I will not give you more illustrations, I will simply quote one paragraph from *Faith in the City*:

> "It is only when the Church itself is sensed to be a community in which all alienation caused by age, gender, race and class is decisively overcome, that its

mission can begin to be authentic among the millions who feel themselves alienated, not only from the Church, but from society as a whole. The challenge this presents to the Church of England in many aspects of its life and organisation is a challenge also to give this corporate, or 'community', aspect of our Christian understanding a high place among our theological priorities."

6

THE PEOPLE HAD A MIND TO WORK

Industry Year Service, Bedfordshire
Nehemiah 4.v.6
Luton Parish Church;
May 4th 1986

It was the year 445 BC. Nehemiah held high office at the court of the Persian King, and he heard for the first time of the desolation of Jerusalem, the city of his fathers. A hundred and fifty years had gone by since Nebuchadnezzar had sacked the city, and in the years that intervened it had been impossible to rebuild it. The walls that were intended to protect the city from looters from without no longer stood. Plundering neighbours invaded the city from all sides. And if any man was rash enough to set about the job of restoring order out of this chaos, he was either prevented from so doing or his work was soon destroyed.

Nehemiah, on hearing the news, was unable to remain inactive; and the Persian King found himself persuaded to give Nehemiah leave to travel to his old home. There he succeeded in mobilising everybody to help rebuild the city: every single person, without distinction: the old and the young; the priests and the laymen; the skilled craftsmen and the peasants. And not only the people from Jerusalem, but their neighbours too: from Jericho, from Thekra, from Mizpah and other surrounding towns.

Soon, the walls began to rise. One section followed another. And the higher the walls rose, the greater grew the pleasure of the people in their work. In the end, even those who had set themselves to the task hesitantly and with little enthusiasm found themselves bound up in it body and soul. And the sentence which ends the report on their achievement rings out like a song of triumph: *"The people had a mind to work"*.

That story, I find — like so many of the stories of the Bible — has a remarkable power to pose questions relevant to today — and not only to pose questions; it has power, I believe, to rekindle our vision, and produce possible answers.

The first question which that story poses for me — and makes me want to ask you, as we gather here to mark this Industry Year, is: "What is it that gives you a 'mind to work'?" Is there something of Nehemiah in you?

I am bound to recognise something certainly of Nehemiah in me and in the job which — under God — I have been privileged and called to do, working as I have done these last two and a half years alongside the Archbishop's Commission on Urban Priority Areas, and I recognise this Nehemiah-like call in many different people in different places as I have gone about the country — and indeed the world: when I have visited this hospital and that school; this parish and that project; this laboratory and that factory — making, say, laser-beam cables. I find myself often alongside people who — thank God — have a 'mind to work'. We could, I'm sure, spend several hours today celebrating what gives people the 'mind to work' in industry and manufacturing, in agriculture and fisheries, in jobs which have been done for many years, and year in year out, and in jobs recently created.

And it is right that we should thus celebrate our industry and commerce, for our standard of living is greatly dependent on our manufacturing base and achievements. Our industries, large and small, provide the taxes and the cultural patronage which sustain our families and the fabric of our society. They provide our housing, our education and our hospitals. Our industry provides, too, the means to renew our decaying industrial areas and inner cities, and to develop new technologies essential for our future. Without industry's profitable performance, we should not be able to give significant help to those millions in our own country and in the world at large who are still in thrall to poverty, illiteracy and disease.

But there is a second question which this story of Nehemiah evokes and provokes in me which I want to share with you, whose responsibilities enable you in some way to represent here today the Industry of Luton.

Nehemiah appealed to his fellow countrymen. He compelled no one. And in this freedom, "the people had a mind to work".

As I pondered that story I found myself contrasting in my mind the times of old when work, skilled and unskilled, was often a bitter "must"; and other times when work of one kind was regarded by others as too degrading for them to undertake. Then there were the occasions — and some are still with us — when there was work to be done, but the reward was too little. And I thought of the places where each worker was told where he must work and what he must do, and forced to do it: the slave societies of the ancient world and of the modern world, with their labour camps. And I thought of the importance of those whose work in society, whose industry

25

brings them no financial reward — like, most notably, those who worked with Nehemiah.

But, at the end of my mental review it was the thought of today's unemployed, particularly in our own country, that occupied my mind — with every political party agreeing that their plight is of huge importance; and — however we may disagree on the numbers of unemployed there are likely to be — having to face the fact of large scale and considerable long term unemployment in our country whatever the government. And it was at this point that the second question formed in my mind, which has come to me often as I have gone round the country: Have those of us in Church and State — in the voluntary, the statutory sectors of our society, or in any of the political parties — yet thought radically enough about the plight of our unemployed? — particularly of the many young people who have little or no prospect of employment when they leave school yet have "a mind to work"?

There are two simple facts: the huge number of jobs in this country which even now cry out to be done, and the huge number of unemployed. And our society — which has succeeded in some ways beyond all imagining — is, in spite of all efforts, signally failing to bring together the unemployed and those jobs which cry out to be done.

In the course of my ministry I have often been called to visit other countries. A young bishop in Sri Lanka had become a particular friend of mine. Less than three years ago that young bishop died an untimely death. He had been a curate here, in England, in Poplar, before he became a bishop in Sri Lanka. He was a Nehemiah if ever there was one. He, as a Christian, gave great support in Sri Lanka to a movement which owed much to the influence of Gandhi in India and to the Buddhist culture of Ceylon. The movement is called *Sarvodaya*. In each local community, each town and village, groups are called together to refashion their locality. It means hard labour and sacrifice. It means also the awakening of many individuals to their gifts and capacities. It means sharing time, thought, energy, skills — and wealth — for the welfare of all. It puts an end to much misery in many localities. It is concerned not least with scientific and technological advance, and it is a profoundly spiritual movement. *Sarvodaya* workers freely share their time, thought and labour, and see themselves as dedicated agents of change.

Bishop Lakshman Wickremesinghe, Bishop of Kurunegala — to give him his full name — was as concerned that the movement should make itself felt as much at the national as at the local level, for, in a country so full of tragic tensions, the *Sarvodaya* workers bridged gaps between classes, religions and races. "The people had a mind to work" — together. They literally worked together, building, for instance, drains and the walls of dams.

26

I recognise that the *Sarvodaya* movement cannot simply be transplanted to our complex Western society. But the West, at such a time as this, may well have much to learn from the East. We in England can often learn from the wider family of man, not least from our Commonwealth.

Some of you will be aware of the investigation into the scope for community service by young people in this country carried out under the auspices of "Youth Call" by Professor Marsland of Brunel University. That investigation established that in England and Wales now there are well over 300,000 openings in the statutory social services, in health and in education. To these may be added the opportunities for useful work in other fields such as conservation, urban renewal and energy saving.

The idea of a "nationwide community service of a non-compulsory character" is supported by the great majority of our population and by leading members of all the main political parties. Of course, it would need to be very clear to professional workers that the expansion of community service in this way is designed not to replace but to reinforce their efforts. But I believe that organisations like Community Service Volunteers have amply demonstrated that by their work there is benefit both to the community, by an improvement in the quality of life, and to young people themselves, by the opportunity for real and personal development.

I raise therefore the question whether it might not be a significant way of marking Industry Year for the discussions and debates about this "nationwide community service of a non-compulsory character"to be taken now to the next stage, by the establishing of pilot schemes in certain fields and localities. There is a real possibility that such schemes would give many more people "a mind to work" — and an opportunity; and we dare not at the moment neglect any such opportunities.

In this land of ours we are fond of singing Blake's "Jerusalem", and of "building Jerusalem in England's green and pleasant land". On such occasions we rarely link Blake with Nehemiah. But Nehemiah could not have been far from the mind and heart of Blake when he penned those words.

I have suggested that Nehemiah still has power in this Industry Year to provoke in us some of the right questions — which will certainly highlight the complexity of our problems. He may even suggest to us some of the right answers, or the direction in which some of the right answers may lie. Above all he has power, I believe, to renew and rekindle our vision.

7

SIEGFRIED SASSOON AND REMEMBRANCE

Gray's Inn Chapel;
Remembrance Sunday November 9th 1986

It was a hundred years ago this September that Siegfried Sassoon was born: surely one of the greatest of the Great War poets.

There are other reasons why it is appropriate that he should be the subject of a sermon on a Remembrance Day in this particular place.

It was in February 1913 that, at the instigation of Sir Edmund Gosse, Sassoon sent a sheaf of his poems to Sir Edward Marsh, who, a year later, found Sassoon a vacant top flat in this Inn, in 1, Raymond Buildings, close to where, of course, he himself lived, and where Master Stone and his family now live, and it was there that Sassoon met Rupert Brooke and many other literary figures of the day.

Sassoon was descended from jewelled Jewish ancestors who had been bankers in Baghdad and Bombay; but he was baptised a Christian and confirmed in St. Paul's Cathedral at sixteen. He was a born contemplative, and essentially religious, so that when the Great War came, and the Gehenna of the Somme, he was one of the most deeply religious of all the War poets — though his religion was anything but conformist and conventional: witness, for instance, his deeply cynical and satirical poem about the Church of England at home:

> The Bishop tells us: 'When the boys come back
> They will not be the same; for they'll have fought
> In a just cause: they lead the last attack
> On Anti-Christ; their comrades' blood has bought
> New right to breed an honourable race.
> They have challenged Death and dared him face to face.'

'We're none of us the same!' the boys reply.
'For George lost both his legs; and Bill's stone blind;
Poor Jim's shot through the lungs and like to die;
And Bert's gone syphilitic: you'll not find
A chap who's served that hasn't found *some* change.'
And the Bishop said: 'The ways of God are strange!'

Sassoon often saw the situation on the Somme as a kind of Calvary —
with Christ present in person. For instance, the poem "The Redeemer"
which he wrote in 1915:

Darkness: the rain sluiced down; the mire was deep;
It was past twelve on a mid-winter night,
When peaceful folk in beds lay snug asleep;
There, with much work to do before the light,
We lugged our clay-sucked boots as best we might
Along the trench; sometimes a bullet sang,
And droning shells burst with a hollow bang;
We were soaked, chilled and wretched, every one;
Darkness; the distant wink of a huge gun.

I turned in the black ditch, loathing the storm;
A rocket fizzed and burned with blanching flare,
And lit the face of what had been a form
Floundering in mirk. He stood before me there;
I say that He was Christ; stiff in the glare,
And leaning forward from His burdening task,
Both arms supporting it; His eyes on mine
Stared from the woeful head that seemed a mask
Of mortal pain in Hell's unholy shrine.

No thorny crown, only a woollen cap
He wore — an English soldier, white and strong,
Who loved his time like any simple chap,
Good days of work and sport and homely song;
Now he had learned that nights are very long,
And dawn a watching of the windowed sky.
But to the end, unjudging, he'll endure
Horror and pain, not uncontent to die
That Lancaster on Lune may stand secure.

He faced me, reeling in his weariness,
Shouldering his load of planks, so hard to bear.
I say that He was Christ, who wrought to bless
All groping things with freedom bright as air,
And with His mercy washed and made them fair.

Then the flame sank, and all grew black as pitch,
While we began to struggle along the ditch;
And someone flung his burden in the muck,
Mumbling: 'O Christ Almighty, now I'm stuck!'

The contemplative in Sassoon was always there. That is clear from the poem he wrote in March 1917 in the Church of St. Ouen:

Time makes me be a soldier. But I know
That had I lived six hundred years ago
I might have tried to build within my *heart*
A church like this, where I could dwell apart
With chanting peace. My spirit longs for prayer;
And, lost to God, I seek him everywhere.

Here, where the windows burn and bloom like flowers,
And sunlight falls and fades with tranquil hours,
I could be half a saint, for like a rose
In heart-shaped stone the glory of Heaven glows.
But where I stand, desiring yet to stay,
Hearing rich music at the close of day,
The Spring Offensive (Easter is its date)
Calls me. And *that's* the music I await.

That same year Sassoon had written a poem called

A Mystic as Soldier

I lived my days apart,
Dreaming fair songs for God;
By the glory in my heart
Covered and crowned and shod.

Now God is in the strife,
And I must seek Him there,
Where death outnumbers life,
And fury smites the air.

I walk the secret way
With anger in my brain
O music through my clay,
When will you sound again?

Sassoon had fought with such conspicuous gallantry that he received the Military Cross and was recommended for the VC. He was given the nickname "Mad Jack".

In July 1917, with courage equal to any he had shown in action, he made a public statement which he sent to his C.O.:

I am making this statement as an act of wilful defiance of military authority, because I believe that the war is being deliberately prolonged by those who have power to end it.

I am a soldier, convinced that I am acting on *behalf* of soldiers. I believe that this war, upon which I entered as a war of defence and liberation, has now become a war of aggression and conquest. I believe that the purposes for which I and my fellow-soldiers entered upon this war should have been so clearly stated as to have made it impossible to change them, and that, had this been done, the objects which actuated us would now be attainable by negotiation. I have seen and endured the sufferings of the troops, and I can no longer be a party to prolong these sufferings for ends which I believe to be evil and unjust.

I am not protesting against the conduct of the war, but against the political errors and insincerities for which the fighting men are being sacrificed.

On behalf of those who are suffering now I make this protest against the deception which is being practised on them; also I believe that I may help to destroy the callous complacence with which the majority of those at home regard the continuance of agonies which they do not share, and which they have not sufficient imagination to realize.

The War Office tried — with some success — what we would nowadays call a 'cover-up'. A Medical Board was hastily convened — and rigged — and duly found 2nd Lt. Sassoon in need of medical care and attention; and he was despatched to Craiglockhart War Hospital. There he was in the care of the brilliant neurologist Dr. W.H.R. Rivers, who wrote:

The patient is a healthy-looking man of good physique. There are no physical signs of any disorder of the nervous system. He discusses his recent actions and their motives in a perfectly intelligent and rational way, and there is no evidence of any excitement or depression. He recognizes that his view of warfare is tinged by his feelings about the death of friends and of men who were under his command in France. At the present time he lays special stress on the hopelessness of any *decision* in the war as it is now being conducted. His view differs from that of the ordinary pacifist in that he would no longer object to the continuance of the war if he saw any reasonable prospect of a rapid decision.

I have always myself coveted the courage of Sassoon. It has reminded me again and again — and does to this day — that we must be as courageous for peace as for War. On the way to Craiglockhart, Sassoon flung his Military Cross into the Mersey.

At Craiglockhart there occurred a strange meeting: one of the great creative meetings of history. Among Sassoon's fellow patients was Wilfred Owen, some seven years younger, who already knew Sassoon by repute, and was a fervent admirer of his poetry. One day he appeared in Sassoon's room with several volumes of his verse under his arm, which he asked Sassoon to sign for him and for some of his friends. He then admitted that he wrote poems himself and shyly asked Sassoon to look at them. Sassoon was impressed by them and they became close friends. Under Sassoon's influence and gentle criticism, Owen began that series of poems which made his fame: an *annus mirabilis* between that summer of 1917 and his death in action on 4th November 1918, only seven days before the Armistice.

Thirty years later, when I was a student at King's College, London, I spent a year at our college in the country at Warminster in Wiltshire. I had to preach sometimes at Heytesbury in the Wylie Valley. The squire at

Heytesbury House was Siegfried Sassoon. He never came to a service in the Church, but he would often be seen on the cricket field, which was the large lawn in front of his house on which we students played. Cricket was one of the loves of his life — not least village cricket — the cricket of *his* village. I saw Sassoon only once more, when I was Chaplain of Trinity College, Cambridge. He was the guest at dinner of Monsignor Gilbey, the Catholic Chaplain to the University. I remember Sassoon's eagle-like features by candlelight across the table. He had just been received into the Catholic Church, at Downside Abbey, in August 1957. He wrote eight lines of verse to mark the occasion:

> No comfort came until I looked for light
> Beyond the darkened thickets of my brain.
> With nothingness I strove. And inward sight
> No omen but oblivion could obtain.
>
> He spoke. He held my spirit in His hand.
> Through prayer my password from the gloom was given.
> This Eastertide, absolved, in strength I stand.
> Feet firm upon the ground. My heart in heaven.

The last decade of Sassoon's life was a period of deep peace, the fruit of "spiritual battles won".

He wrote, just before he died:

> "It has been a long journey,
> And my last words shall be these —
> that it is only from the inmost
> silences of the heart that we know
> the world for what it is, and
> ourselves for what the world has
> made us."

Appropriate thoughts, I think, for a Remembrance-tide sermon, as we remember, thankfully, Captain Siegfried Louvain Sassoon, and all who have died that we might live; and as we reflect upon our own responsibilities for peace in this world of ours, and of the importance we each one of us need to give to our spiritual journey.

But I don't think the last words of a sermon in memory of Siegfried Sassoon should be prose.

His war poetry ended with a triumphant cadence. One evening in the middle of April 1919 — a sultry spring evening — after sitting for about three hours after dinner, he was taking himself off to bed, when suddenly some words flooded into his head as though from nowhere. He wrote down the poem in a few minutes; a thankfulness for liberation from the years of war, but also a deeply religious poem of Hope and *trust in*

Resurrection — which has given hope and trust to thousands more in the sixty-seven years since he wrote it:

> Everyone suddenly burst out singing;
> And I was filled with such delight
> As prisoned birds must find in freedom,
> Winging wildly across the white
> Orchards and dark-green fields; on — on —
>   and out of sight.
>
> Everyone's voice was suddenly lifted;
> And beauty came like the setting sun:
> My heart was shaken with tears; and horror
> Drifted away....O, but Everyone
> Was a bird; and the song was wordless; the singing will
>   never be done.

8

ONLY CONNECT

For the Consecration of the Reverend Richard Harries
as Bishop of Oxford; St. Paul's Cathedral;
Ascension Day May 28th 1987

"Only connect..."

At your Consecration, Richard, the preacher will surely be forgiven for beginning, and not only beginning, with a literary allusion.

"Only connect..." The power of that epigraph, which Forster set at the front of *Howard's End*, four years before the beginning of the First World War — is undiminished. Indeed, a book bearing that title, by Robin Green, on "worship and liturgy from the perspective of pastoral care" has been published this year; and, last year, Professor Leslie Houlden intentionally echoed it in his book *Connections*. And the more I have thought on the role of a bishop, the more that phrase has seemed to articulate and express it: "Only connect".

As an aside, let me say that at Cuddesdon this last Holy Week a student vouchsafed to me — with all the authority of a Cuddesdon ordinand — that the Oxford interregnum had revealed that the only task left to a Bishop of Oxford now is to connect: to connect the work of the area bishops.

But Forster's word "only" did not mean "only" in that belittling sense. It meant, of course: "*If* you can connect.....If *only* you can connect....all you bring together with be exalted."

And that word "connect", which sounds so deceptively simple, as the phrases of great literature so often do, also needs definition. Even my "Scrabble" dictionary relates it to a "body or society held together by a bond"; and, without realising how near to great theology it is treading, it adds: "ligaments, membranes, cartilages", and throws in one or two interpretative words for good measure: "that which gives coherence"; and then treads even holier ground: "to associate with others in relationship; to enable two or more *disjecta membra* to become one; to unite."

But if to connect and to unite have so much in common, then we are met here today not simply for some occasion of church order; we stand within the holy of holies; we draw near to the mystery of the Atonement itself: to the mystery of at-one-ment; and therefore to the mystery of our humanity, of sin and of grace, and to the very Person and Work of Christ.

And that is so; for Forster did not perhaps sufficiently recognise how corrupt and destructive as well as how glorious and exalting our connections can be, in church as well as state.

The Great War, that great slaughter, which began, as I've said, just after *Howard's End* was published, occurred, surely, because men had made most terrible and terrifying connections, as they did again a quarter of a century later, and still do now.

The phrase "well-connected" shows how snobbery and connections are connected; and the religious connection has its own corruption, not least in ecclesiasticism, hierarchy, pietism, prelacy, and our own peculiarly Anglican forms of arrogance and snobbery.

My own mentor and friend, Eric Abbott — a revered predecessor, of course, of yours, Richard, as Dean of King's College — used to say to me: "Boy, if you are to be ordained, you must have almost as high a doctrine of corruption as you have of glory: corruption in church as well as state."

When we have "almost as high a doctrine of corruption as we have of glory", we can face afresh our past, not least our Anglican past: we can face, for instance, the Oxford Anglican connection: "Soapy Sam", Stubbs, Paget, Gore, Strong, and so on.

Yes. But when we connect "connecting" with the Atonement itself, we begin to see the pain and the price of connecting: that no bland Anglican sleight of hand will do. At-one-ment is achieved often only at cost and with costly confrontation.

It is, of course, dangerous to suggest at the consecration of a Bishop of Oxford, bishop not least of St. Aldate's and St. Ebbe's, that he has a part to play in the Atonement; but it would only be more dangerous to suggest he has no part to play in it. And perhaps for the avoiding of error we might remember P.T. Forsyth's pithy dictum that "the real successor to the apostles was not the episcopate but the New Testament." Most of us are only here today because we believe in the New Testament connection with what we are doing.

"Only connect..." The University of Oxford, they tell me, tends to keep its bishops at arms length; but Oxford remains one of the great symbols and centres of scholarship and research. It will be no mean achievement, Richard, if you can strengthen the connection between scholarship and the church, not least in the pulpits and pews of your diocese. But the Gospel has within it truth that is hidden from the wise, and at this time the challenge to a Bishop of Oxford is not least to ensure that those who read and those who teach theology connect with the realities of life; indeed, that theology rises out of the realities, the often cruel realities, of life — not least the realities of what we have come to call the urban priority area.

"Only connect..." What resonances of that phrase throb through the Church and the world today! I wonder, Richard, how you will help the rich Oxford commuters to connect with the poor of, say, Cowley; and the decision makers of the Chilterns to connect with those whose destinies they control in the North East and North West; how you will help the employed of Oxford to connect with the unemployed: the white people to worship with the black, and to grow in understanding the Sikhs, Hindus and Muslims, in say, Slough.

"Only connect..." In these last months and years, it has thankfully become abundantly clear that the Church has not lost all its ancient power to connect with and speak to the soul of the nation, and to recall it at such a time as this from an uncaring absorption in sectional avarice to concern for justice and compassion.

"Only connect..." Church and State. Your own appointment, Richard, is — for better, for worse — part and parcel with that connection. But in your time as bishop it is urgent that a connection between Church and State be forged and fashioned afresh that better reflects the realities of the religious and social situation of England today — and of the Church of England — and above all the priorities of the Gospel.

"Only connect..." May you never be content, Richard, to be a bishop in the Church of England, representing simply that section of Christendom according to whose Use you are being consecrated. A bishop, wherever he is, is called to represent the wholeness of the Catholic Church to its divided parts, to be a creative force of its coming unity. "Only connect..."

Some of those who come from far to take part in your Consecration today, Richard, personify some of the pains, as well as the glories, of our inter-connecting. I suppose apartheid, from one point of view, is the very opposite of connecting. But from another it is the very incarnation of connecting based on that fear, racial prejudice and self-concern, which is to be found not only in South Africa.

"Only connect..." Richard *Oxon* and Richard Harries: a man, a husband, blessed with a wife and family; and Richard, the private person, and Richard, the media man. "Only connect..." the intellectual Richard and the "feeling" Richard, and "both will be exalted".

Harry Williams, in a characteristic preface to Robin Green's *Only Connect* has written: "Christian writers have often spoken of our humanity being taken up into God. What in fact they have meant is the repression in the sub-conscious of a great deal of what we are, so that only half of us — the respectable pious half — is offered to God to make His own, while the stinking darkness is left to itself to fester unseen and work its evil spell upon us, disguised in this or the other religiously acceptable form." If our

Gospel be true, a Christian bishop should know a lot about connecting "the beast and the monk" within — to use Forster's marvellous metaphor — and about helping others, clergy and laity, to make that connection.

"Only connect..." Recognise the masculinity and femininity in yourself, and you will want to see that masculinity and femininity in yourself recognised by the church in the women and the men who present themselves to you for ministry in Christ's church.

"Only connect..." Your ministry will often feel lonely and be lonely, but you will not be alone. *Episcope*, like priesthood and ministry, is a function of the whole church. Every member of the church will have a share in your *episcope*. "Only connect..."

Richard, you will know well that I have a small shelf of books by you on prayer, signed with your love and good wishes. We are not here today to speak much about prayer, but to pray with you and for you. But let me just say this: that last Good Friday, immediately after I had conducted the Three Hours, a kind Cuddesdon student drove me into Oxford simply to look at a field of fritillary in bloom in a water-meadow near Magdalen Bridge. As Housman said:

> to look at things in bloom
> Fifty Springs are little room

But in that half hour, as we wandered along Addison's Walk, I could not forget that you would be coming to be bishop of that place — that City, that University, that Diocese — but secondly, that the God who would empower you had revealed himself both in a Man who hung on a Cross the first Good Friday and cried "My God my God, why?" and in that field of frail and vulnerable fritillary. "Only connect..." He will be alongside you as you pay the price and bear the pain of at-one-ment and connecting.

"The head that once was crowned with thorns is crowned with glory now." Ascension Day is a feast of glory, and a most marvellous day for your Consecration, Richard. The hands that will soon be laid upon you — "only connect" — will say in what we now call "body language" that "He who ascended is the same also as He who descended — that He might fill all things" — which He does still.

Still

> "Christ our God to earth descendeth
> Our full homage" — a word with peculiarly English episcopal resonances! —
> Our full homage to demand."

9

THE SAME NIGHT HE WAS BETRAYED

Diocesan Eucharist:
Liverpool Cathedral;
Maundy Thursday March 31st 1988

This morning of Maundy Thursday, I take, not a text, but a phrase from the Eucharistic Prayer:

"The same night that he was *betrayed*, he took bread and gave you thanks."

When I sat down to prepare what I had to say to you today, I was conscious of being several people, in a way that I am not often thus conscious.

The first person I am conscious of being — and in this I imagine I may represent something in you as well — is a person who this day feels particularly close to the first seven words of that phrase I have taken, and to the person who focuses them, Judas Iscariot: *"The same night that he was betrayed.......Jesus took bread and gave you thanks"*.

I could not myself come to this Maundy Thursday Eucharist, and to this renewal of commitment to ministry, without knowing myself to be a person with a great deal in common with Judas Iscariot. And no matter how much I take refuge in those lines of the Irish poet "A.E.", that:

> In the lost childhood of Judas
> Christ was betrayed

— that is to say: no matter how conscious I am that most of my particular forms of betrayal have a long and complex history, longer even than the thirty-six years since my ordination, I can only come here admitting, owning, and confessing my betrayals.

That's one person I know myself to be this particular morning. Maybe so do you.

Yet, mercifully, that phrase I've taken: "The same night that he was betrayed..." though it begins with betrayal, does not end there. Indeed, the point and the power of it, is that, though it takes betrayal seriously, it indicates that our betrayals are taken up and used as part of our redemption: that the Lord takes even our betrayals and transforms them. "The same night that he was betrayed...": on the very occasion of his betrayal, "he took bread and gave you thanks". At the worst time, he did the best deed. That first Maundy Thursday Jesus revealed the creative possibilities even within our capacity for betrayal, and, indeed, even in our actual acts of betrayal.

I expect many of you will know that wonderful inscription carved above the west door of the church at Staunton Harold in Leicestershire:

In the yeare 1653
When all things sacred were throughout ye nation
Either demolisht or profaned
Sir Robert Shirley, Barronet,
Founded this church;
Whose singular praise it is,
to haue done the best things in ye worst times,
and
hoped them in the most callamitous.

So the second person I am, as I come here today, is one conscious of the way that Christ has used even my betrayals, and my capacity for betrayal, over the years. And I've no doubt many of you would also want to echo that.

But the third person in me is one who knows he does not come here alone. I come here, as do most of you, as a representative person: I, as an ordained member of a church which has perhaps this Holy Week particular reason to be conscious of our corporate betrayal.

When I was ordained at King's College, London (all those years ago!) Eric Abbott, the Dean, who was also my closest friend, said to me, shortly before my ordination: "Boy, you're a romantic; and you won't survive unless you have a high doctrine of corruption — almost as high a doctrine of corruption as you have of glory: corruption in Church as well as State."

That corruption of the Church seems to surface more strongly at some times than at others; and it seems to have surfaced quite a bit in the Church of England since last Holy Week. But "surfaced" is the operative word; for that betrayal, that corruption, I believe, still needs to be known and faced at depth — not least in areas like the corruption of faith, which seems unable to face, for instance, the complex truths of our human sexuality;

and still needs to face afresh the complex truth of God's self-revelation, and not to resort to false and faith-less simplifications.

I come here as a person conscious of corporate betrayal.

Last Maundy Thursday, Jim Thompson, the Bishop of Stepney, when he preached at a similar service to this, for the ministers of his East London episcopal area, said:

> "It is strange that of all the services I am involved in during the year, this Maundy Thursday service is by far the most difficult to plan, on the day when we remember the institution of the Sacrament of Unity....One part of the Church makes it clear they won't come if there is a concelebration; another part of the Church makes it clear they won't come if we don't have a concelebration; and others say they won't take part if there is a woman taking a liturgical role. And, so the sacrament of unity suffers. My sadness about these divisions has made me go back to the original Last Supper, where Jesus, looking at the small group who were to be the springboard of the universal Church, prayed that they would find the unity which had been demonstrated in His relationship with the Father. The reason for this unity was 'that the world might believe'. Yet James and John argue about who will be the greatest in the Kingdom of Heaven; Peter betrays his Lord, to whom he has sworn his allegiance and his life; Thomas was filled with doubt; and Judas betrayed Him with a kiss. I wonder how Jesus was able to contemplate both taking on the world and also the painful divisions of His own small band of followers."

And the Bishop ends:

> "I must make it clear that I don't know how to satisfy everyone in this Maundy Thursday service."

I think that those words of the Bishop of Stepney accurately indicate the fact of corporate betrayal, and indeed the sense of the corruption of the Church, which the third person I am carries with me this morning: a corruption to which, of course, I have made and make my own contribution.

But, again, that phrase in the Eucharistic Prayer comes to my aid. Jesus did more than "contemplate both taking on the world and also the painful divisions of his own small band of followers". "The same night that he was betrayed he took bread and gave you thanks." Pained beyond words he undoubtedly was; but he was not crushed by the betrayal of Judas, and James, and John, and Peter, and the rest of the disciples, when they forsook him and fled. The darkness did not overcome Him. The bread which he took was not some rarified purified bread. "The same night that we was betrayed, he took bread"...people like us; disciples like us; a church like ours — "and gave thanks." Not all the betrayal of the Church in embryo, or that lay ahead, could divert or deflect him from finishing his strange work, or eradicate that thankfulness to his father which lay at its heart.

Paradoxically, thankfulness, gladness and joy are at the heart of the fourth person in me who joins with you in your Diocesan Eucharist today.

For nearly five years, since *Faith in the City* was launched, I have been privileged to see a good deal of your diocese; and being allowed also to be close to Bishop David and Archbishop Derek when they wrote *Better Together* has meant I have seen and shared a bit more; and I think that I am probably in a position today, in a way few others in the whole Church of England can say, with a full heart, "Thank you, all who are in the Church in this Diocese of Liverpool, for the imaginative inspiration you have been and are to the rest of the Church of England."

"The same night that he was betrayed, he took bread *and gave you thanks.*" The fourth person who I am, here today, is someone who is here solely to give thanks, to make Eucharist, for Christ's ministry in parish upon parish, and ministry upon ministry, which I have seen up and down this land in the last five years; and nowhere more imaginatively, more faithfully, more vigorously, and more gloriously, than in your Diocese.

When the BBC decided to devote its *Panorama* Programme for the Monday in Holy Week this year to the Church of England, it had a magnificent opportunity to portray the ministry of Christ that we know — and Christ knows — goes on week in week out in our Church. But the temptation to sensationalism and over-simplification was too great; and the result was an opportunity missed, tragically missed. I, who have had much opportunity to know the Church of England in these last years could hardly recognise the heart of the Church of England as I have come to know it. I could hardly recognise in that programme what I come here so gladly to give thanks for on the day that Christ was betrayed: come gladly to Him who "takes bread", takes us and our lives, and "gives thanks". Who would have thought last Monday evening that that programme was about a Body aware — at least in part — of its betrayals, but aware also of Him who takes Bread, takes His body, takes us and gives thanks? Who would have guessed from that programme that in this cathedral church, and in many another cathedral today, there would be hundreds upon hundreds of those who come to renew their vows, knowing that their Lord has forgiven their betrayals, knowing that he has taken them and used them, and will use them, and gives thanks for them? Who would have known from that programme that thousands are deeply fulfilled in that ministry to which Christ has called them?

Which leads me to the fifth and last person I am who comes here with you today to renew my vows.

I came North last Friday, and spent the day in sight of Liverpool and its Cathedrals. I spent the morning going round Cammell Laird's and lunching with workers there. In the afternoon, I went round some Birkenhead parishes and projects seeking help from the Church Urban Fund, and spent the evening with Frank Field, MP for Birkenhead. It was clear from the people, nearly thirty of them, queuing up with their problems for Frank Field to attend to, the kind of problems that many of you have to confront in your ministries this side of the Mersey: problems of housing, social security, poverty, health provision, and so on.

Since last Saturday I have been privileged to spend Holy Week with the Padgate Team Ministry. Yesterday afternoon I visited the Atomic Energy Authority Laboratories at Risley with the Industrial Chaplain. I could not imagine a week's more helpful preparation for preaching to you this morning. I can envisage the shape of the ministry to which many of you are called, and for which you have come now to renew your vows: some of you still at the beginning of your ministry; others, like me, nearing the age of retirement. Wherever our ministry is set; whatever stage we have reached in that ministry, I have little doubt that phrase in the Eucharistic Prayer has something to say to each one of us today: "The same night that he was betrayed, he took bread and gave you thanks."

There is in fact one other person in me who comes here today — whom I will briefly mention in conclusion — for I suspect that person may have been particularly responsible for my choosing to preach to you on this Eucharistic phrase. Some of you will know that I wrote recently the biography of Bishop John Robinson. In coming to Liverpool I have not been able to forget that Ruth, John's wife, came from Anfield, and went to Holly Lodge High School, and that John and Ruth first held hands on a Liverpool tram.

I was privileged to be close to John Robinson when he died. Indeed, when he preached his last sermon, on "Living with Cancer", in the Chapel of Trinity College, Cambridge, he asked me to come to Cambridge, to sit next to him and take over if he could not get through what he had written. He was determined to preach that evening if he could — and he did. He wanted to preach not least to "Christen", as he called it, the pulpit lectern he had given to the chapel in thankfulness for his ministry, which humanly speaking he knew to be nearing its end. He had caused only two words to be inscribed on that pulpit lectern — *in eucharistia*.

In the end, I suspect that everyone of us here this Maundy Thursday would want those two words to be written over our ministry: *in eucharistia*: in thanksgiving.

"In the same night that he was betrayed, he took bread and gave you thanks".

10

THE THREE WISE MEN
Gray's Inn Chapel; January 22nd 1989

The Second Chapter of St. Matthew's Gospel: the first verse:
"Wise men came from the East to Jerusalem".

The story of the Wise Men is undoubtedly one of the most fascinating in all the Scriptures. In contrast to the story of the shepherds, it's very much a "top people" sort of story.

Jerusalem was, of course, the historic fortress city: set high, the capital city, the erstwhile royal residence, the place of pilgrimage, with, at the heart of it, the Temple. "Blessed City, Heavenly Salem": idealized, yet undeniably a place of transcendent beauty.

There's nothing surprising about Wise Men coming from the East and fetching up there; but it may help to compare that magnetic city with what we so often simply call "the City".

When I was a boy, there was magic in those two words "the City". I can still remember when my Mother first said: "Your Father's taking you up to the City tomorrow". And there was the Mansion House, the Stock Exchange, the Bank, the Old Bailey and St. Paul's to be seen. It was, that day, *my* Jerusalem.

But it wasn't long before I began to think of the City as also in some way mysteriously threatening. I soon began to see it — when I went out to work as a boy of fourteen — as a centre of massive, impersonal, autonomous power; with its own rules, rituals and energies; with its experts, who were in control — most of the time — often to the great advantage of themselves and of their patrons; with a kind of private language that mystified outsiders and outwitted rivals. It was the centre of that market which, I saw with my own eyes, so often and so plainly operated to the disadvantage of the disadvantaged. Yet there were those who trusted the City and saw in it Salvation. It was *their* Jerusalem.

So when I read of Wise Men going to Jerusalem, I'm not surprised. Indeed, I remember in 1957, the Cohen Council on Productivity, Prices and Income being called "The Three Wise Men". As, then, a Cambridge College Chaplain, I knew one of them well, as a Fellow of the College, the economist Sir Dennis Robertson.

So I'm not surprised when I read that the Wise Men in the Scriptures quickly made contact with those in power. The network was, of course, well aware of them, and they knew the network. Élite met élite.

But those Wise Men may well not have been Wise Men. The word in the Greek New Testament "magos" means more often: "expert in astrology, interpreter of dreams and other secret arts, sorcerer". *Magos* is of course close to our word magic. And there are some nasty specimens of *magoi* in the experience of the apostolic church: Simon Magus, for instance.

Well, the story that Matthew recounts is that these sorcerers left their power-base in the East, like some diplomatic delegation, with the intention of getting in first with an alliance with a new political authority, of whom "Intelligence" had given them advance warning.

They came to do homage, and understandably assumed that they would find what they were looking for at the headquarters of the existing political authority. That authority — not entirely surprisingly — co-opted, (or, should one say, seduced?) the established religion, whose task was to keep the state secure and to give warning of any threats of rival authority. As a result of these negotiations, the sorcerers were sent off in a quite different direction. And they found their prince, not in a place of conventional power, but in a poor, refugee household which had only just avoided being a one-parent family. Mercifully, their guiding-star re-appeared, and they were delighted to know they had reached their journey's end, even in such unexpected surroundings. And they opened their treasures: their forms of wealth which they had managed to keep tightly shut in other environments of political, economic and religious power. So gifts which were brought to adorn a palace became play-things for a child born in poverty.

The gifts of the Magi represent their various interests. Gold is their economic interest: the wealth gained by their sorcery and secret powers from the credulous and gullible, from those whom they had serviced and from those who had no power of themselves to help themselves. Incense and myrrh are some of the tools of their dubious trade. Incense represents the religious vested interest which can so easily be corrupted into occult fatalism; myrrh represents the preservative interest — which seeks at all costs to keep things in place and conspires on behalf of the status quo against the new, or what Christians call the "risen" life. They hand over these symbols of their interests, surrendering them to the newly arrived Lord of Heaven and Earth. Finally, they sever their contract with Herod. They no longer need to depend either on their own arcane science or on political patronage: the will of God has access to them, as it did to Mary and Joseph, through the subconscious and the subliminal. And they go home another way. Wise men often do — especially the security conscious. The Wise Men were "street-wise", we would say.

The "magoi" are clearly different from the Christmas card image of "wise men" or "benign kings". But it wasn't long before Christian communities had opted for the wise men interpretation rather than that of the sorcerer and the magician. Indeed, Ignatius of Antioch was soon writing: "Magic crumbled before this star: the spells of sorcery were all broken, and superstition received its death blow". And Justin Martyr wrote: "The magoi, having been carried off as booty for all manner of evil deeds, by coming and adoring Christ are shown to have gone away from that power which had taken them captive.."

Well, I have to say, that I know of no biblical scholar of repute who would vouch for the historicity of the story of the wise men. But it is marvellous myth and most lovely legend. And myth and legend can, of course, be bearers of the most sublime and profound truth.

It is surely not without significance that the earliest writers of the Christmas story wished to surround it with such a tale of recognition and deliverance. The surrender of the powers which hold the human spirit in thrall is still one of the most joyous themes of the Gospel, especially, for instance, in contemporary Africa.

But is there a message here for those of us who seem in our day to be so captive, so in thrall, to that apparently superhuman power called the City of the Market? Can economic power also be seen to yield to that poor Child who is the Son, the revelation of God? Can that captivating power be reclaimed as the servant of truly and deeply human choices, be subject to moral control and freed from being the capricious scourge of the already disadvantaged?

That is one of the unavoidable, inescapable challenges of the Gospel. Perhaps, to face that challenge, we need to think more about those three strange mythical figures: those *magoi*. However dark and evil we may reckon them to be, they at least got there. They got there before the seemingly holy and righteous. They acknowledged and worshipped the new-born Son of God.

They offered gifts of gold.

If we were they, I suppose we might today bundle all our credit cards together, indeed, all our credit, all the sanctification of greed with which we are so familiar and are so bound up — and simply cast it at the feet of the Christ-child. That could have its effect.

And frankincense — the representation of all that we willy-nilly worship and deeply desire. That too, recognised, offered, surrendered, and consecrated, would make untold difference.

And myrrh — that symbol of our fragility and mortality: that we "can't take it with us": that symbol of all those fears which are so soon awakened by every disaster: that the bell that tolls for others will soon toll for us; all our anxiety at our mortality — our recognition of our transience; were we to hand that over to Him who is the very revelation of the only love which can cope with what we bring to Him — in our strength and frailty — that too would be transforming.

> They all were looking for a king
> To slay their foes, and lift them high
> Thou cam'st a little baby thing
> That made a woman cry

That baby is neither myth nor legend. He is the very centre of the Christian faith: its power to change and transfigure us and our world.

Yet, I am suggesting, the myths with which we have surrounded and decorated that cradle still have much to say to each one of us in our age and in our need.

11

THE ROLE OF THE WATCHMAN

Gray's Inn Chapel; January 29th 1989

There are several occupations which have considerably changed their nature during the course of history. I suppose the role of the watchman is as good an example as any.

Some of you will no doubt be all too familiar with being instructed to keep a "watching brief". Others of you may have been officers of the watch in earlier years, on board ship, or even, indeed, have served in the Black Watch. In your leisure hours, others of you may have been sent in as night watchman, to protect a more expert batsman than you from having to face the bowling at the end of the day. Near me in Kennington there's a local authority site which always has a couple of Alsatian watch-dogs on guard. It's a place which as a priest I have no hesitation in passing by on the other side. The Watch Night service I listened to this year, in bed, from St. Martin-in-the-Fields, still reminds one of the ancient division of the night into watches. Most of us have opportunity these days to join the local Neighbourhood Watch.

In our Old Testament lesson this morning, the prophet Ezekiel, in spite of his bitterness and dejection, is lifted up by the Spirit and summoned to dwell with the exiled Israelites on the banks of the river Cherbar. At first, he simply sits among them: identified with them, saying nothing. Then he hears the voice of the Lord saying:

> Son of Man, I have made you a watchman
> for the House of Israel.

He is called to a very difficult ministry. It's certainly one of identification with the plight of his people and with their sufferings. It's one of comfort and support; but it's also one of prophecy: of denunciation and warning.

The role of the watchman is made even clearer in the words of the prophet Habbakuk, who is also called to minister to the Israelites in exile. Habbakuk not only identifies with and challenges the people, he argues with God, articulating the people's anxiety in their predicament and plight, and in their despair. At the end of his passionate psalm of complaint he says:

> I shall stand at my post:
> I shall station myself on my watch-tower,
> watching to see what he will say to me:
> what answer he will make to my complaints.

> Then the Lord answered me and said,
> 'Write the vision down,
> inscribe it on tablets
> to be easily read'.

The role of the prophet as watchman is undoubtedly a difficult one. Despite his divine commission, he will not always be listened to.

That was Jeremiah's situation.

> I set watchmen over you, saying Hearken.
> But they said: We will not hearken...

Sometimes the prophet-watchman is the victim of another's wickedness. That was the case with Hosea.

Ezekiel had a sense of being chosen from among the people; but he found it a heavy responsibility to denounce evil and proclaim what is to be.

The message Isaiah was called to deliver was unwelcome:

> I stand continually upon the watchtower, and behold,
> there cometh a chariot of men with a couple of horsemen...
> And he answered: Babylon is fallen, is fallen.

Then he hears someone calling to him:

> Watchman, what of the night? And
> the watchman says: The morning comes, but also the
> night....

In the book of Lamentations, the people are summoned to cry out during their watch: to pour out their hearts in the presence of the Lord; to raise their hands to him for the plight of the children and of the hungry.

So the watchman embodies the doubts and the hopes, but above all the experience, of the people.

In the Psalms, too, the watchman looks for the signs of the dawn:

> My soul fleeth unto the Lord:
> before the morning watch, I say, before the
> morning watch.

The prophet-watchmen were odd people: "Odd men out": often seemingly insignificant and marginal; set at an angle to society; often they were 'awkward cusses'. Yet they had a divine vocation.

In the New Testament, this idea of "watching" is given a new importance and urgency. It all begins "while shepherds watched...." Jesus is constantly recorded as telling his hearers to watch, to be on their guard, and alert; to stay awake. And, of course, in Gethsemane, He sadly asks the disciples: "Could ye not watch with me one hour?"

In St. Luke's Gospel, there is a group of women at the Cross, and in St. John's Gospel, Mary, in particular, watches Christ die, from the foot of the Cross.

Not surprisingly, this image animated and inspired artists, writers and musicians, from Jacopone da Todi's *Stabat Mater Dolorosa*.

I don't know if any of you have ever stayed in a monastery or in a convent and been present for the night office.

When I've done that, I've often felt like a watchman: watching, for instance, with the sick who are not able to sleep, beyond the confines of where I was staying. Again: I remember so well an all-night Prayer Vigil for Racial Harmony held in St. Margaret's, Westminster. When the dawn came up, it flooded the great East Window with light, which surrounded the head of the Crucified Christ; and that triumphant light became a marvellous symbol of hope.

Sometimes I see my own job, as a priest, as having much in common with the Old Testament prophets, called to be present with people who are being marginalised. That is why I try to spend much of my time in the inner cities. This may involve my being close to teachers, social workers, and so on; and often to people with whom seemingly at first sight I have little in common.

Recently, I've been having a good deal to do with a group with whom I could hardly have less natural connection. I have been having to get involved in the crisis in the maternity service. In the inner city, one thing has become painfully clear: that the midwifery service is in crisis. Between 1985 and 1995 the birth rate is expected to rise by 14%, whilst in London there is already a shortfall of 40% in practising midwives; and, as at three quarters of all births the midwife is the most senior person present, this is a very serious situation: for mothers, and, of course, babies.

This week I've spent some time in Tower Hamlets where last year a third of the teachers resigned for one reason or another.

But I see my own job as a priest not as isolated: the priest, in my judgment, ought not to see himself as a lone watchman, but as one who reminds the whole of the Church — and indeed the whole of humanity — that to be truly human is to be a watchman.

I'm particularly fond of this Biblical image, because it so marvellously combines contemplation and action. It combines simple presence where you ought to be, and where you're needed — standing, say, alongside and amongst the homeless — and prayer. Prayer and Presence: Presence as a form of prayer.

Lastly, let me just make the simple observation — and I underline that word "observation": A watchman is someone who has his eyes open. Perhaps he has *had* to have his eyes opened. "Then shall the eyes of the blind be opened" says the prophet Isaiah.

One of the best Christmas presents I received this year was one of the smallest: a book, available from the Friends' Bookshop in the Euston Road, called *The Quiet Eye: A Way of Looking at Pictures*. That kind of watching is so important. But it's important, too, to have a way of looking at people, and a way of looking at society.

When I was a child, my mother and father used to sing together a duet written at the turn of the century: "Watchman, what of the night?" I suspect I owe to them my very first drawing to this particular Biblical image; but, over the years, it has come to mean more and more to me. Without watchmen, what is best in our country, in our world, in our humanity, could so easily perish. But the grace of God is always reminding us through the Scriptures — and through its images like the image of the watchman — of the true and deepest meaning of our humanity; and that same grace empowers us to bring that image alive, not only in ourselves but in others.

12

FAME IS THE SPUR

Gray's Inn Chapel; February 5th 1989

I don't suppose the centenary of the birth of the novelist Howard Spring will be celebrated by many; but it falls this week; and I think it's worth celebrating.

Howard Spring was really a journalist, who worked on the *Manchester Guardian* and the *Evening Standard*. He was born in Cardiff. His first best-seller, some of you will remember, was *My Son, my Son*, published in 1938; but his greatest claim to fame was undoubtedly *Fame is the Spur*, published in 1940, and made into an absorbing film, by the Boulting Brothers, in 1947, with Michael Redgrave playing the lead, as the up-and-coming Labour politician, and with people like Bernard Miles and Sir Seymour Hicks in the cast.

Members of this Inn will not be surprised to hear that it was thought wise to change the name of the politician, from Shawcross — which it was in the novel — to Radford, for the film. Between the book and the film — in 1945 — Master Shawcross* had become Member of Parliament for St. Helens.

I can see my mother, who loved what she called "a good read", snatching some time to read *Fame is the Spur*, when it first came out, in the midst of looking after us four children. And that must be nearly fifty years ago. But I can also remember Bishop Mervyn Stockwood asking me one day whether I'd read *Fame is the Spur*, and adding: "It's the best book on ambition that I know". And that would be all of twenty years ago.

So I got hold of it again a couple of weeks ago, to celebrate the centenary, and read it from cover to cover, and couldn't put it down. It's as good as new.

---

*Hartley William Shawcross, Baron Shawcross of Friston, P. C., G. B. E., Q. C.,
   M. P. St. Helens 1945-58
   Attorney-General 1945-51

It's, I think, a marvellous title:

Fame is the spur that the clear spirit doth raise
(That last infirmity of noble mind)
To scorn delights, and live laborious days.

That's, of course, from Milton's *Lycidas*.

But the book is more than a good title. Lurking behind the title is the question whether to be ambitious is good or bad.

Sometimes people say: "The trouble with that lad is he's got no ambition." No "get-up-and-go" is the way they put it now. While they say of others: "Of course, it was his ambition which was his downfall."

Shakespeare was invariably negative about ambition. "Fling away ambition" is his advice to Cromwell. "By that sin" he says "fell the angels". He speaks of "thriftless ambition that will ravin up thine own life's means", and of "vaulting ambition" — what a wonderful adjective! — "vaulting ambition which o'erleaps itself". He says "the substance of the ambitious is the shadow of a dream". And there's that wonderful passage in *Julius Caesar* which virtually contracts the whole of *Fame is the Spur* into a span of seven lines — when Brutus says:

'Tis a common proof
That lowliness is young ambition's ladder
Whereto the climber-upward turns his face;
But when he once attains the upmost round
He then unto the ladder turns his back,
Looks in the clouds, scorning the base degrees
By which he did ascend.

In *Fame is the Spur*, Howard Spring's young politician starts at the bottom of the ladder, with ambition to serve, and to right wrongs: the poverty stricken conditions of a northern mill town; and there can't be much wrong with that. Fame wasn't his spur at the beginning; but in no time, fame in serving becomes an end in itself; and those who need to *be* served, who need wrongs righted, are forgotten. Prosperity and status cause him to sacrifice his friends and his ideals. By the time he is old and titled, he is unable to draw from its sheath the rusted sabre of Peterloo, which had been his inspiration from the days of his youth.

This week does not only hold within it the centenary of the birth of Howard Spring. Tuesday is Shrove Tuesday, and Wednesday, Ash Wednesday; so it's the week of all weeks of the year for having another look at ourselves: for getting to know more the springs of our motivation. Part, at least, of the trouble with the hero of *Fame is the Spur* is his lack of self-knowledge: having begun life as a good Methodist, he had ceased to hold his motivation up to the light: certainly he had ceased to look at it in the light of Christ. You feel he'd come to assume he'd rather grown out of all that.

One of the good things about a novel like *Fame is the Spur* is that although it's what one might call "episodic" — you see John Hamer Shawcross, alias Radford, beginning his battles, falling in love, and so on — the acid of ambition eats away at him gradually: and it's the whole canvas of his life that enables you to see what becomes of the man and how it happens.

I was not surprised, when I looked up "Ambition" in my Dictionary of Christian Ethics, to find nothing directly under that particular subject, but to be referred to a dozen other subjects; for ambition often grows on something else, feeds on it: it's a kind of cancer.

Perhaps the desire for, even the genuine need for, money may foster ambition: ambition for that position which will bring with it wealth. But "Nothing is ever enough" said Epicurus "to the man for whom enough is too little".

Ambition feeds on envy, pride, hubris, self-love — and indeed self-loathing. The man who does not properly love himself is always wanting to sit next to someone who may seem to give him what he lacks in himself, just by proximity. It's the man who has no confidence in his own name and nature who's always dropping the names of others.

Ambition is a form of expansionism which grips and forces into service all its wants.

I find myself wondering how many of the take-overs of today are really necessary for efficiency and good, and how many are actually the product of a kind of ambition euphemistically designated "enterprise".

Sir Philip Sidney, whose portrait will confront us ere long in Hall, said: "To be ambitious of true honour and of real glory and perfection of our nature is the very principle and incentive of virtue; but to be ambitious of titles, place, ceremonial respect and civil pageantry is as vain and little as the things are that we court."

Fame is the Spur is basically a biography in fiction. And it has made me turn to the biographies on my bookshelves and compare and contrast them, in relation to ambition — for instance, David Livingstone and Cecil Rhodes. Both men had dreams for Africa; and noble dreams they were. Both men had elements of nobility of character and deep, passionate loyalties; but by the standards either of purity of motive or of spiritual achievement there can be no possible comparison between them.

Lockhart's *Life of Cosmo Gordon Lang*, Archbishop of Canterbury, is one of the most treasured books on my shelves. Son of the manse and Fellow of All Souls, he assumed his career would be a natural progress, via the Bar, to Parliament and beyond. Within two years of his ordination as priest he playfully signed himself "C.G. Cantuar". The whole subsequent story is an admirable illustration of an imperfectly sublimated sense of ambition — which is probably why the biography ends in such sadness.

53

The same may be said of an even more revealing autobiography: Lord Reith's *Into the Wind.*

For the Christian, there are antidotes to ambition which I believe we discard only at our peril.

The first is time regularly set aside for reflection. Fame would not have increasingly become the spur to John Hamer Radford had he made time for some kind of spiritual "audit", so to speak, with discipline and regularity: weekly, monthly, yearly.

And that regular self-examination for the Christian is also regular review of life in the light of the Cross of Christ and the Kingdom of Heaven.

In that light, and in that power, our primitive and pugnacious urges, which, if perverted, lead to the extravagances and cruelties of "vaulting ambition", can be sublimated and directed aright.

The Christian accepts his task, his work, his vocation, from God, upon his knees, and gives it back to God, and receives it back from Him, and gives it back to Him again, so that fame is never the primary spur.

But one subject to which my Christian Ethics Dictionary referred me from the word Ambition was, significantly, sloth. If we are slothful and slovenly about the life of the Spirit we provide the vacant soil in which the weed of ambition can riot.

There's one other difference between the secular man of ambition and the Christian, and that is to be seen in how we deal with our fellow human beings. When ambition seizes a man — or woman — or when he disguises his ambition, under whatever pretext, the true nature of his motives and ends most often reveal themselves in the callousness of his methods and his lack of sensitiveness to the needs and claims of his fellows. This is particularly where power tends to corrupt. But when the Cross of Christ, and the Kingdom of Heaven, and the Glory of God, are the spur to our existence, naked ambition has no depth of soil in which to root.

Well, as I've said, this week is, of all weeks, with Shrove Tuesday and Ash Wednesday at its heart, full of opportunity to confront our motivation; and, may I add, most of us need some friend of our soul to help us face ourselves. We cannot do it simply alone. Fame may or may not be our spur, but it is crucial that from time to time we face just what is, in the light of Him whom Milton calls in *Lycidas* "All-judging Love".

13

WHO IS THIS?

The Chapel Royal, St. James's Palace;
Palm Sunday March 19th 1989

"When he entered Jerusalem, the whole city went wild with excitement. 'Who is this?' the people asked."

"Who is this?"

That question from the Gospel is one which each one of us needs to have on our hearts and minds each day in Holy Week.

Some of you may have read the small Penguin book *Night* — an autobiographical fragment by the Hungarian Jew Elie Wiesel, who was deported with his family to Auschwitz when he was still a boy, and then to Buchenwald.

A Rabbi who teaches Elie to pray as a youth explains to him that every question possesses a power that does not lie simply in what seems the obvious and immediate answer. "Man raises himself toward God" he says "by the questions he asks him". "Man questions and God answers. But we do not understand those answers."

"I pray to God within me" says the Rabbi "that he will give me the strength to ask Him the right questions."

"Who is this?" the people asked that first Palm Sunday. It was the right question, but I wonder how many of them stayed for an answer.

Holy Week affords us opportunity to press that question "Who is this?" and to stay with it.

When the Archbishop of Canterbury was Bishop of St. Albans and I was his Canon Missioner, he despatched me one day to stand in for him at the preview of that spectacular television film directed by Zefferelli: *Jesus of Nazareth* — which by now will have been seen by crowds of people. At that preview there was only a handful of us in Lord Grade's — Lew Grade's — private film studio off Oxford Street.

Professor Geoffrey Lampe, I remember, was there — alas, now dead; then a Cambridge theologian. Lord Grade told us that within six months

300 million people would have watched that film in the United States and Europe. Quite a crowd! — a kind of modern Palm Sunday crowd.

I remember Lew Grade — a modern Jew — taking his cigar out of his mouth and putting down his glass of brandy, in a pause between one part of the film and another, and saying slowly: "Well, whatever you say, that Jesus is a magnificent man..."

I found myself thinking that I was only in a position to criticize that film's idea of Christ because I knew in my own mind what my answer was to that question "Who is this?" — and why.

Each Holy Week enables us to reflect more deeply upon our answer to that question. It enables us to stand with the crowd in the Temple on Palm Sunday, and watch while Jesus overthrows the tables of the moneychangers and the seats of those that sell doves; and, as we watch, we can say to ourselves "Who is this?"

We can enter the Upper Room on Maundy Thursday and watch while Jesus washes his disciples' feet: "Who is this?" we can ask.

And when the disciples sleep in Gethsemane we can watch with Him, as his sweat falls down to the ground as great drops of blood, and we can ask "Who is this?"

And when Judas betrays his Master with a kiss; and when eventually Jesus is nailed to the Cross, like a rat to a barn door, we can ask "Who is this?"

And we can bring our answer to that Palm Sunday question with us on Easter Day.

But I think that each day in Holy Week our answer to that question needs to be related to our own needs; and that means that part of our entry into Holy Week requires that we shall spend some time in thinking what our needs are, and how they relate to Jesus being crucified.

In December 1961 I married Herbert to Jane. Herbert was a former undergraduate of mine at Trinity College, Cambridge. Jane has always written to me each Christmas, a letter with the family news. This year's arrived after Christmas — written on December 21st. It told me of the progress of the three children. "Flora" Jane said "flies to Boston this evening at 6.p.m., so will not be with us at Christmas...you can't really hang on to them." Flora was just about to get her doctorate in Neurology here in London. She was flying to see her boy-friend in the States. But by the time that letter arrived I knew that Flora had been killed in the Lockerbie disaster.

For the last three months Herbert and Jane have been asking the agonised question: "Who is this?" What sort of a God is He?

"Man raises himself to God by the questions he asks Him".

Tomorrow morning I have to take the funeral of Tatiana Pond, a young barrister who has been a member of our choir at Gray's Inn Chapel where I'm what's called "The Preacher". She was a girl as full of zest for life as

Flora Swire. But only last week-end she went on a parachute jump and was the victim of a ghastly accident. Tomorrow I must try to help Tatiana's parents, and her boy-friend, get some sort of answer to that question they too are desperately asking this Holy Week: "Who is this?" Who is the God who lies behind our sort of world?

In Holy Week, I am comforted particularly by one fact: the fact that Jesus himself, when He hung upon the Cross, when there was darkness over all the earth, cried out with a loud voice: "My God, My God, why?"

What was that cry but Jesus' own question "Who is this?"

"Man raises himself to God by the questions he asks Him."

The Man Jesus raised Himself to His Father by the question He asked Him.

I do not really want to give you my answer to that question "Who is this?" this morning. I want to encourage you to ask that question yourself this week, and to try to find your own answer — or to find an answer at a new depth.

Most of us have had, or will have, some reason to cry out in our pain at some stage in our own life "My God, My God, why...?" "Who is this?"

And when, in our darkness, we ask that question, some light usually comes, even if it only comes slowly. Flora's parents, as they have thought about their daughter, her zest for life, her gifts of friendship, her skills as a neurologist — and so on — know that — though her death had all the elements of an anarchic chaotic world about it — that cannot be the whole truth about the God who created such a wonderful person as their daughter.

When the Memorial Service to Flora Swire was held in her village church, I was privileged to be allowed to read some lines from T.S. Eliot's "Little Gidding". Her parents had told me that T.S. Eliot had meant much to her and had done much to provide her, as a thinking neurologist, with depths to her faith.

A few days after that service, I went into the newly decorated Lambeth Palace Chapel. It had taken seven back-breaking months for the artist Leonard Rosoman to paint the vaulted roof of the Chapel with marvellous figures and designs in glorious colours. But what caught my eye was the new Lenten frontal on the altar. Across the very dark frontal — contrasting with the colours of the roof — were written nine words of T.S. Eliot:

"We thank thee that darkness reminds us of light."

Quite often our questions come out of darkness, but, in time, through them we discover light.

No one can go through Holy Week and not encounter darkness — within the world at large: within the Gospel narratives of the Passion: within ourselves.

No one can go through Holy Week asking "Who is this?", pressing the question each day till Easter itself, and not discover eventually some Light.

57

We are all invited in Holy Week to undertake a kind of pilgrimage: a journey with Christ Himself — simply by asking, pressing, that question of the Palm Sunday crowd: "Who is this?"

14

THE DEDICATION
OF A MEMORIAL TO
MICHAEL UNDERHILL Q.C.

Gray's Inn Chapel; April 16th 1989

No verse in the whole hymn-book could be more apt and appropriate to our purpose today than that so familiar verse of George Herbert:

> A man that looks on glass,
> On it may stay his eye;
> Or, if he pleaseth, through it pass,
> And then the heaven espy.

But the purpose of the mirror the architect Sir Edward Maufe saw fit to place on the wall of our Chapel has hitherto been more functional and mundane. It has been to enable those who sit opposite the Benchers to espy not heaven but the Preacher!

Yet George Herbert anticipated our problems, and wrote another poem, on Preachers and Glass:

> Lord, how can man preach thy eternall word?
> He is a brittle crazie glasse,
> Yet in thy temple thou dost him afford
> This glorious and transcendent place
> To be a window, through thy grace.
> But when thou dost anneal in glasse thy storie,
> Making thy life to shine within
> The holy Preachers, then the light and glorie
> More rev'rend grows, and more doth win;
> Which else shows watrish, bleak, and thin.

Doctrine and life, colours and light, in one
     When they combine and mingle, bring
A strong regard and aw; but speech alone
     Doth vanish like a flaring thing.
     And in the eare, not conscience ring.

Well; *now* that "brittle crazie glasse" opposite has been marvellously embellished by David Peace, and whoever now looks at that glass may stay their eye on that most lovely text, which he has so skilfully engraved on it, in memory of the much loved Michael Underhill — who was, what Chaucer, and later, Shakespeare, called "the mirror of courtesy".

Few worshipped more regularly in this Chapel than Michael, and in my mind's eye I can see him now, sitting with his back to the wall and to the mirror. Michael loved beauty, and of one thing I'm sure: he would have delighted in his memorial. He would have delighted particularly in its reticence; and he would have loved the words that Rosalie and the family have caused to be engraved in his memory.

Those words — from St. Paul's great Hymn of Love — are so familiar to us in the Authorised Version, and are such a gem of English literature, that we are sometimes tempted to treat them simply as a thing of beauty; as a most lovely necklace of words, so to speak. In fact, every phrase and almost every word in those two verses is worthy of a separate sermon.

"For now we see through a glass, darkly: but then face to face: now I know in part; but then shall I know even as also I am known. And now abideth faith, hope, charity, these three; but the greatest of these is charity."

St. Paul was a good preacher, and he knew that for anything to be real it must be local; and he had an eye and an ear for the metaphor that matters locally. Corinth was a place famous not least for its mirrors. They were made and bought and sold there. They were, of course, made of metal.

"Now" says St. Paul "it's as though we looked at life in one of your Corinthian mirrors — darkly." Most metal mirrors were never as good as glass, unless they were polished and polished. Quickly, the clarity of the image dulled and darkened.

What Paul actually said was "Now we see *en ainigmati* — enigmatically — in a riddle, darkly, in a mirror. Then the mirror will have been removed, and we shall see face to face."

Human beings, I find, are sharply divided into those who find the idea of Another World Than This and of an After Life something they can easily and immediately accept and those to whom such an idea is either intellectually or psychologically impossibly difficult.

I went recently to the new production of *King Lear* at the Old Vic. Surely, one of the most moving moments in *Lear* — if not the most moving — is when Lear bends over the lifeless body of Cordelia and simply says:

Thou'lt come no more

and then five times says the single word:

Never, never, never, never, never.

Even for those whose faith and hope is in an afterlife and a meeting again with those they love, in this world that word "never" holds within it all that we mean by bereavement. "Thou'lt come no more" in this life is bereavement enough, and in this life the next has some darkness for all: is to some degree enigma.

But St. Paul is very confident. "Then we shall see face to face". It is a phrase which betokens confidence — we speak so often of "face-to-face relationships": but almost as if he had suddenly had a second thought — that we see quite a lot of people face to face yet hardly know them — St. Paul uses an even stronger metaphor:

"Now I know in part; then shall I know even as also I am known".

Many a time I saw Michael Underhill here face to face — admired him and held him in great affection — as did all of us; but it was that very face to face knowledge of him that made me aware he was a very private, reserved and reticent person. It will have been the privilege of Rosalie and the family to have known Michael and to have been known by him at far, far greater depth. But every one of us is an island.

When St. Paul says "Now I know in part..." there is no doubt he is talking primarily about knowledge of God. And when he talks of knowing "even as also I am known" he means "as God knows me".

There's no greater knowledge of us than that: greater far than our knowledge of one another.

Edmund Spenser wrote:

Faire is the heaven, where happy soules have place
In full enjoyment of felicitie
Whence they doe still behold the glorious face
Of the divine eternall Majestie

Some people find the idea of God's knowledge of them frightening: that terrible All-Seeing Eye that used sometimes to be put up on the wall of Victorian bedrooms.

But it is the last verse of this great passage which holds its secret and has power to remove all fear.

St. Paul says our knowledge of God is partial. Our faith, in this world, always has an element of risk in it and of uncertainty. Our hope has always an element of the unknown about it. Sometimes it even has to be blind — as blind as our faith. But Charity — the Charity of God — the Charity that God is — there is no reason for fear when Charity is the very nature, the unchanging nature of God, revealed in Jesus; so that the more we know

61

of Him the more we discover of Charity itself — Himself: and growth in the knowledge of God is growth in the knowledge of his love.

It is that Charity which created us, brought us to life, from which, St. Paul wrote to the Romans, neither death nor life shall be able to separate us.

One of Michael Underhill's relatives, Evelyn Underhill, Fellow of King's College, London, and a great authority on mysticism, wrote a book called *The School of Charity*. Like others of her books, it introduced her readers to the mystics, particularly the English mystics.

When I think of those words "the greatest of these in Charity" my mind immediately adverts to the most popular of English mystics, St. Julian of Norwich, who lived in the 15th Century, in the anxious days of the Black Death. Evelyn Underhill introduced a good many to St. Julian's writings. And there is one passage at the close of her *Revelations of Divine Love* which epitomises, as I say, the words of St. Paul: the final words of our engraving: "the greatest of these is Charity".

Julian of Norwich wrote:

> Would'st thou witten thy Lord's meaning? Wit
> it well: Love was his meaning. Who shewed
> it thee? Love. What shewed he thee? Love.
> Wherefore shewed it he? For Love. Hold thee
> therein and thou shalt witten and know more in the
> same. But thou shalt never know nor witten
> therein other thing. Thus was I learned that
> Love was our Lord's meaning.

It was His meaning in the making of Michael Underhill — and of his little grandson, who was born on the day of his burial and will be baptised here in this Chapel this afternoon. It was His meaning in the making of us all.

15

AN IMAGE OF ANXIETY

Hampstead Parish Church;
Whitsunday May 14th 1989

"The doors were shut, where the disciples were assembled for fear...."

The Gospel today, the good news for Whitsunday, begins with a curious kind of ikon: an image, the very image, of anxiety.

Behind locked doors, the caged and cowed disciples were assembled: unhappy men, bereft and bereaved of him in whom they had hoped and trusted, him whom they had loved — heads down and dejected, you feel; the room itself, it is difficult to imagine other than in gloom; the disciples, trapped in their fear like animals whom fear has immobilised.

But into that room came Jesus, free of all that would fetter him: the grave, the grave-clothes, fear. No walls could confine Him. He is all Love — and, therefore, Life — and, therefore, Light. And He says to them: "Peace be unto you".

The older I get, the fewer dogmatic assertions I am willing to make; but after thirty-eight years as a priest I will share with you one conviction that I hold more certainly as the years go by: that fear and anxiety are the most destructive weapons in the devil's armoury — if you will allow that old-fashioned phrase.

Whenever I hear confessions these days — formally in a church, or more often informally in an armchair — I find myself almost always first asking myself what anxiety, what fear, lies behind and beneath this confession, this particular guilt or shame or sin, or supposed sin; and I find myself wanting to know what does that particular person think is the root of their fear and anxiety.

Anxiety, I think, has a great deal to do with its German cousin "angst". Anxiety is most often unconscious fear: fear, the origins of which have not really been identified. Anxiety usually has an indefiniteness about it, a lack of object. It arises within our deep past, and from the remote future, and from what lies mistily about us. "Feeling anxious" lies deeper than

63

"feeling afraid". Anxiety — or fear — in the singular — gives rise to fears, in the plural, and to what often turn up as sins.

Anxiety — the elemental fear of insignificance — of having no significance — of death, if you like — lies behind and beneath so much human behaviour. It lies behind so much proud behaviour; behind so much pretentious talk: the man who talks as though he's pretty well always right; or about the wonderful people he's in touch with. It's fear of being nothing that makes people grab at symbols — and more than symbols — of something: in the hope that they will be what they possess. It's behind much materialism and consumerism. It's fear, often, that makes people pompous and prickly. It's fear, often, that makes us talk as though we were confident and unafraid. It's fear, often, that makes us criticise others — to give ourselves some brief significance and superiority. It's fear, often, that makes us make excuses, and tell petty lies — and sometimes not such petty lies. It's fear, in church circles, that makes us over-dogmatic. It's habitual fear that makes us habitually uncharitable. It's fear which lies at the root of so much sexual disorder. It's fear which puts each one of us sometimes "behind locked doors", in this relationship and that, professional and personal. It's fear that lies behind so much seeming racialism — fear of the unknown: not only of the unfamiliar colour, but of the unfamiliar cooking-smell and way of life. It's fear which generates much of the generation gap: "I don't know what's become of young people these days" we say — and we don't. It's fear that occasions a great deal of vandalism — fear that if you don't make your mark this way — visibly, violently — you'll never make it at all.

It has always interested me how often falling in love and marriage removes, almost at a stroke, the anti-social tendencies of teenagers. They have made their mark with someone. A don't-care-society has suddenly revealed its care, in and through one person; and anxiety has suddenly been assuaged.

I can expect in Hampstead, of all places, that some of you will have read Freud, Fairbairn and Winnicott, and will therefore have no difficulty in believing that the fear of the disciples originated not in that Upper Room but more probably in their infancy and childhood. And that is no novel idea: the Psalmist says: "Even from my youth up thy terrors have I suffered with a troubled mind".

It was Freud who said: "Anxiety in human beings is originally nothing other than an expression of the fact that we are fearing — or feeling — the loss of love: the love that assures us we are valued and valuable." It is not therefore surprising that St. John says quite simply: "Perfect Love casteth out fear". Nor is it surprising that when He who had revealed Himself to the disciples as Perfect Love — Almighty, Suffering Love — stood suddenly in their midst, and said to them "Peace be unto you", they were released from fear into His Love, and Life, and Service. They were set free.

Now, what the Bible brings us — the Gospel of the Divine Love and Life — is not to be thought of as some magical action. It's about what happens when Divine Love, Divinely Human Love, confronts, is allowed to confront, our human anxiety and fear, and all that springs from it. And we have to let that Love go to the depths of our being.

At the moment, I have no idea what your particular anxiety may be: your particular fear — of death, or of what bits of life. Neither do you know mine. I only know that to be human is to be anxious, and the Christian Gospel is about allowing our anxiety, whatever it may be, however deep, to meet up with the Love that Jesus revealed God to be.

That Love of God is very rarely experienced directly and immediately. It's usually experienced through some other person or persons.

This week I have been in Cleveland. A judge of Gray's Inn, where I do a little "moonlighting" as Preacher, asked me if I could come and sit with him in Court. I felt that to be a very great privilege. It was also, I have to say, quite painful.

The case before the judge in Middlesbrough, Cleveland, you'll not be surprised to hear, was a harrowing case of child abuse.

A pregnant mother of twenty-four sat before us: the mother of four other children. The young man beside her was the accused. He was the father of the child she was expecting. They now live together. He was accused of abusing sexually the four year old daughter of the mother — by a previous husband — her fourth child.

The pregnant mother sat there anxious. The accused was the person who was closest to her, and you could see her anxiety that if he was sent to prison she would have her baby alone and unsupported. And there were the other children, too, to care for.

The accused young man also looked hopeless — he was denying the charge; but the evidence against him was very considerable.

He has, alas, a speech impediment: indeed he was unable to speak in court at all, and had hardly been able to speak to any of the officials outside the court except in monosyllables.

The judge, who in this Family Division case purposely did not robe in his wig or judge's robes, made it clear that the abused child must be his first responsibility — and, indeed, the unborn child and the younger children than the one who has been abused must also be his particular care. But he suddenly said — to everyone's surprise — to the pregnant woman's and to the father's alongside her: "I want to come to your house tomorrow. I want to hold the court in your home." "I want you" he said to the father "to be able to speak where you'll feel best able to speak."

I had to leave Middlesbrough before that visit took place. But I could see how surprised the court officials were at the judge's decision, and I could see how astonished the woman and the man were. They had come only in fear and anxiety of the judge, and they had met with someone who spoke kindly to them and wanted to say "Peace be unto you" and to work out what might be the next step in caring for the children and the mother — and the father — and enabling their capacity to love and support one another to be restored. The guilt or innocence of the father was of course still important to the judge and, walking in the grounds of the Judges' Lodgings, outside Durham, that evening, he said to me: "I wish I knew more about that young man's speech defect: when you can't communicate naturally the pressure to communicate unnaturally could be huge."

That accused father had been the very image of anxiety: his mouth closed for fear: the door of speech shut. The court itself was at first a kind of upper room of anxiety. But you'll not be surprised that I found that judge's decision to leave the court and go to the home, in one of the most depressed parts of Cleveland, a kind of image of today's Gospel, which reflected and refracted, so to speak, the message of the Gospel that makes us say:-

> Come down O Love Divine
> Seek thou this soul of mine
> and visit it....

and is also an example of how we can shed the Love of God abroad.

In the end, we all have to learn that God's judgment is the judgment of His Love:

> "the flame of the Everlasting Love" — Newman says — "doth
> burn ere it transform"

Our Prayer at Whitsuntide

> "Come down O Love Divine"

is a request also for judgment. And we all need to learn to love our Judge.

16

ON CHINA

Gray's Inn Chapel; July 8th 1989

Since we last met here in Chapel three months ago, much has happened in the world at large — and I mean that literally: "the world at *large*"; for China's population alone, of one billion and one million — itself justifies that phrase. Every fourth or fifth person in the world is Chinese.

I don't suppose any of us will forget for the rest of our life the figure of that brave young Chinese man standing in front of the procession of tanks heading down the Cangan Boulevard on Monday morning a month ago, in front of the Beijing Hotel. We shall forever retain the memory of tanks swerving a little, and then coming to a halt, and that young man crying and pleading in front of them, then climbing onto the first of the tanks, and — incredibly — trying to have some sort of conversation with those within; and then literally climbing down, and allowing the tanks to continue on their way.

I think it is worth reflecting, meditating, on that incident here in Chapel. It's an eminently appropriate thing for us to do here; and I simply want to offer some thoughts that may assist us to do just that.

Of course, we know very little about that young man for certain. We don't even know his age. We don't know whether he was a student. There are reports that he was, and that he has since been executed; but there is no certainty of that. We don't know whether his action was sudden and impulsive or premeditated. We don't know whether he was by himself or whether he was supported, and spurred on, by others. An Associated Press photograph of the incident I have says the man was pulled away by bystanders. We don't know whether he was beside himself — perhaps to the point of madness — or whether what he did, though impassioned, was fully rational. We don't know the resources he brought to his action from family upbringing, or studies, or religion. We don't know whether he was petrified beyond words.

Yet all that we *don't* know can never take away from what we *do*: that it was a memorable act of transcendent courage that will form for many years a kind of ikon of courage. Certainly it still shines like a beacon in the midst of all the gloom that shrouds China at the moment.

Whoever this young man was — young student or older man — there's a high probability he would be familiar with the esoteric yet extremely practical writings of Lao Tsu. So I decided to read through again the Tao Te Ching as a kind of intercession, when I felt most hopeless and helpless at what was happening in China.

What I undertook *for* China, so to speak, was, I found, a huge help to *me*. Let me quote you just a few sentences — I could read you dozens more:-

He who takes upon himself the humiliation of the people
is fit to rule them.
He who takes upon himself the country's disasters deserves
to be king of the universe...
The weak can overcome the strong...
Why are the people rebellious?
Because the rulers interfere too much.

Why do people think so little of death?
Because the rulers demand too much of life.
Therefore the people take death lightly....
If men are not afraid to die
It is of no avail to threaten them with death.

I said that I thought it was appropriate to reflect and meditate in Chapel on this single action of a man. I said so because I think the good that men do — and the evil — pose huge questions about our *origins* which we need to dwell on. No one can say that young man was just a robot. When you reflect on him, you can only say, with Shakespeare: " What a piece of work is a man!"

And reflection on that one man makes you reflect on the very nature of courage.

One of the books I treasure is the war-time book of Churchill's doctor, Lord Moran, *The Anatomy of Courage*. The anatomy of courage brings you back to the very nature of man.

You will have met, as I have met, men and women who seem to have been born devoid of fear. Physical courage seems innate in them. But that kind of courage is the bravery of the tiger, so to speak: not the bravery that knows fear only too well but has overcome it.

At this point in what I have to say — not least because it's also the Bicentennial of the French Revolution — I should like to insert a kind of comparison with the action of that young Chinese man, from the French Revolution.

I don't know whether you know, and love as I do, the story which lies behind Poulenc's opera *The Carmelites,* which was first of all a novel, but based on fact, by the German novelist Gertrud von le Fort, and was then turned into a script for a film, and then made into a stage production by the French writer, George Bernanos, when he had only weeks to live, and was himself a tormented person, terrified of dying. After his death it became the libretto for the Poulenc opera.

The story is of Blanche de la Force — who was born when the coach of her aristocratic parents was overturned by a mob of malcontents and her mother died. Blanche — who, her whole life, in consequence of her birth, was, as it were, the prisoner of fear — joins at fifteen a convent of Carmelites. But there's no escape there. The Prioress is a powerful woman, intent on training her sisters for what most probably lies ahead: the dissolution of the Convent by order of the Revolution.

But when the dreaded hour comes, on the very eve of the arrival of the forces of the Revolution, Blanche deserts her sisters, who are all sentenced to death.

In the last scene, the Carmilites are taken to the scaffolding set up in a crowded square. They mount the scaffold one by one, beginning to sing the *Salve Regina* and the *Veni Creator.* But, from the midst of the crowd, one voice is heard more distinct and resolute than all the others, strengthening their resolve. It is the voice of Blanche de la Force, who eventually comes forward to take her place on the scaffold. It is only at the very last that the fear, born at her birth, has been overcome; and by a miracle of grace, so to speak, she is enabled to conquer her fear at the very hour of her death. Bernanos felt that the story had been written for him at the hour of his death.

The courage of Blanche de la Force is what I mean by courage which knows fear only too well, but overcomes it.

G. K. Chesterton said that "courage is almost a contradiction in terms. It means a strong desire to live taking the form of a readiness to die".

Which brings me back to that young man.

I wonder what he believed about dying: about what followed death. He must surely have realised what danger he was in. *Fear* could, of course, have kept him *out* of it; but *courage* got him *into* it, and kept him *at* it, enabling him to climb onto that tank and talk to its occupants.

That very secular writer, Ernest Hemingway, said that "courage is grace under pressure".

I don't know where it comes from, but I remember someone quoting a proverb that "It is better to live *one day* as a *lion* than a *hundred years* as a *sheep."*

Did that young man believe that? — and know that his day — as a lion — his "hour" — to use Jesus' phrase — had come ?

The Master of Balliol at the turn of the century, Edward Caird, in one of his Lay Sermons entitled "Spiritual Development" has this to say:

"The times when any important decision is made — any decision at least which appears important at the time — are few and far between, and the rest of life seems to be a mixture of routine and accident. And we are apt to despise the day of small things, to attach no weight to the trivial round of actions which make up nine-tenths, or rather ninety-nine hundredths, of our lives. The little exigencies of every day — whether we shall go to see a particular friend, or read a particular book, or devote particular time to this object or that — it seems often almost indifferent whether we decide them in one way or the other; and often it is indifferent. But we are apt to forget that life masks its great issues under the appearance of a series of unimportant circumstances and events, in each of which, however, there is some opportunity for the exercise of courage or cowardice, truthfulness or untruthfulness, magnaminity or meanness, justice or injustice, charity or uncharitableness, love or hate. Steadily, silently, the inevitable process of change goes on, and neither the individual himself nor any of those nearest to him may notice how, in the one case, his character is being strengthened and elevated, and in the other case, is being weakened and lowered. And then, if a great issue does come, and he is put to a decisive trial, neither his friends nor he are able to comprehend how it is that, in the one case he rises to the occasion and shows a strength and resource for which beforehand no one would have given him credit, or in the other case betrays a weakness and poverty of character, which no one, and he himself least of all, had suspected. The truth is that the battle is often won or lost long before it is fought. The man in the one case has become unstrung, relaxed and enfeebled by many trifling acts of self-indulgence, of shrinking from pain or effort, by many neglects of duty in little matters. Or, on the other hand, strengths have been accumulating within him by imperceptible increments, by a self-denial here, a little act of courage or fairness or kindness there, in the long course of unnoticed days, till, when the hour of great decision arrives he finds within him a large reserve of moral energy."

I wonder if that's how it was with that young man?

I don't think I could ever myself be fanatically and exclusively committed to any one religion, because humanity has so *many* religions, and most of them, it seems to me, produce saints — as well as fanatics — and hold insights into the truth. That young man in Peking *might* have been a Christian — it is very unlikely that he was — but he is a witness and a tribute to the God whose Spirit bursts out in the most unlikely places. As John Keble's Whitsuntide hymn to the Spirit proclaims:

It fills the Church of God, it fills
    The sinful world around;
Only in stubborn hearts and wills
    No place for it is found

There are just two other reflections I have on this strange incident in the history of mankind.

It was Berthold Brecht who said that "The defect of a tank is that it needs a *driver*."

At the heart of this incident, there is not just a young man standing alone. There was at some stage what we nowadays are apt to call *eyeball to eyeball confrontation*. There was — in the phrase of Martin Buber — an "I-Thou relationship". The student and the driver — or some other occupant of the tank — were involved in human dialogue, dramatic dialogue. That, too, says something about the central mystery of our human condition. And it is worth simply reflecting on our human capacity for dialogue — for meeting — for meetings that may confront matters of life and death.

I want also to return to the fact of China's one billion and one million population.

When I was last in India I was privileged to have an interview with the then Deputy Health Minister, Professor Kisku, who happened to be a Christian. We talked mostly of the terrifying dimensions of India's population problem — and of the virtual impossibility of reducing the population growth to manageable proportions by voluntary birth control; and the hideous results, in terms of infant mortality, if that were not achieved. China has had a far greater population problem even than India. It has dealt with it by the deprivation of freedom — the strict enforcement of a policy of only one child per family — in the face of the only alternative: huge infant mortality.

What those in command of China have recently done is indefensible. There is little or nothing to be said by way of extenuation. Absolute power seems to have corrupted virtually absolutely. But no one I have read, in the British papers and journals, has set what the Chinese leaders have done against the background of curtailment of freedom centred on population policy which has been their agonized decision in order to preserve the quality of life. Part of our meditation — of our intercession — has surely to be to do what we can to understand those who in the government of such a huge and hugely different country from our own are caught on the horns of a hideous dilemma: the twin horns of freedom and control.

Students who demonstrate for freedom and democracy may either be sensitive antennae of a nation — students often form such a vanguard — or else they may be bourgeois intellectuals — those whose circumstances are not those of the poverty stricken masses — and who as students do not have the full agonising burden of the realities of government.

Finally: just a brief word about Hong Kong. One word — where an hour or so is really required.

I have been astonished that everyone — in these last weeks — almost without exception — has been speaking and writing of *affluent* Hong Kong — which of course it is — to most tourists, and, I imagine, to most barristers and others who visit Hong Kong in the course of their business.

When I last visited Hong Kong it was my privilege to be allowed to visit some of the two million people who were living in government-built tenements four to a room, ten feet by ten feet, with communal wash houses and latrines, and to visit the factories in which the poor rarely looked up from their labour — as though their very life depended on it: which I had no doubt was true. They were not refugees. They were simply the poor to whom Hong Kong's affluence had not trickled down and was unlikely to. Their rates of pay were derisory in such an affluent society.

The poor of Hong Kong — it is safe to say — will never get to Britain, no matter what the emergency. It will only be those who have the means to escape who will succeed in escaping anywhere.

Hong Kong is as hideously divided a society economically as can be imagined. China, its neighbour — its huge and hugely threatening neighbour — has as a society different defects.

R. H. Tawney — economist, historian and Christian — never tired of saying — and this is as relevant to China and the French Revolution as it is to Britain today — that the call for Liberty must always be kept close to the call for Equality, and both need to be held together by the commitment to Fraternity: to fellowship and belonging to one another. Let one of these three terms — all central concerns of Christian people — Liberty, Equality, Fraternity — be detached from the others, and society is in trouble.

Today we pray for that quarter of the world which is China; we pray for France and for Britain; we pray that they and we may be given the gifts of liberty, equality and fraternity; and we give thanks for the shining example of that unknown Chinese student, and for all whose conscience has caused their spirit to rise and revolt against tyranny.

Let Chesterton voice our prayer:

> O God of earth and altar
>   Bow down and hear our cry
> Our earthly leaders falter
>   Our people drift and die.
> The walls of gold entomb us
>   The swords of scorn divide
> Take not thy burden from us
>   But take away our pride
>
> From all that terror teaches
>   From lies of tongue and pen
> From all the easy speeches
>   That comfort cruel men.....
>
> Deliver us, good Lord.

17

WORSHIP AND OTHER FAITHS

Gray's Inn Chapel; July 23rd 1989

I preached a sermon about worship last term: about worship in general and worship here in the Chapel. But there was one aspect of the subject which I feel we still need to think about together, not least because it affects far more than our worship here.

Four hundred years ago, when our Chapel began its life — and even one hundred years ago — it would have been inconceivable that between a quarter and a third of the members of the Inn would come from overseas and that quite a number of those born in England might be Muslims and Hindus; and that our relations with members of other religions — and not least the availability of the Chapel to them would therefore be a question of some importance.

At the beginning of this month, I married here in Chapel Herkishin Jivan Dialdas to Yvonne Capewell. Herky is a Gray's Inn barrister who is Hindu — albeit an Etonian Hindu. Taking the marriage of Herky and Yvonne meant quite a lot of discussion — Yvonne is English and Church of England — to ensure, at the least, there were no hurt feelings; but, even more, that their mixed marriage would be given all the support that was possible. At first Herky's father and mother and family wanted nothing to do with the service here in the Chapel; but I felt quite certain that everything must be done to prevent the marriage service only being for Yvonne's family; everything which did not involve sacrifice of fundamental principle. Of course, parts of the 1662 marriage service were entirely inappropriate and could not be used. It was conceived for a very different situation: of two convinced Christians getting married. I received a letter only this week — on their return from their honeymoon — saying just what it meant to Herky and Yvonne for them and their families to be united here, and how much the service had meant to them.

We are all aware that in earlier times — at the Reformation, for instance — nation states were very clear that there must be no dissent — Catholic dissent in a Protestant state; Protestant dissent in a Catholic state. The later colonial empires generally allowed a considerable variety of religions, but most often when they were confident that political control lay firmly in their own hands.

The Archbishop of Canterbury has recently been publicly extolling the virtue and practice of tolerance, I am glad to say; and I imagine you were as glad as I.

It has to be said that people who are otherwise very tolerant, and who pride themselves on the fact, can sometimes be very intolerant of other forms of worship. It has somewhat dismayed me here how usually tolerant members of the Inn can sometimes become suddenly rather intolerant about, say, using any other form of service here in the Chapel than the Prayer Book of 1662. I detect something of a Professor Higgins — "My Fair Lady" — "Why can't a woman be like a man?" — sort of attitude: "Why can't people be reasonable and sensible and stick to the 1662 Prayer Book, it's so obviously the only rational and beautiful book for us to use."

It helps me to remind myself that although there is quite a history — quite a tragic history — of religious intolerance, the need for Christians to enter into dialogue with other religions has been a fact of Church life right from the beginnings of Christian history. Christianity, early on, came to grips — had come to grips — with, for instance, Greek thought and theology.

Quite often Christianity has entered into dialogue with other faiths in a somewhat condescending and paternalistic way: reflecting the assumption that Christianity represents the fulfilment of the search for truth found in other — ('lesser') — faiths and philosophies.

In the last decades, we have witnessed the triumph of the idea that people have the right to work out their own ideas and make their own mistakes in all spheres of life, including the sphere of religion. Without doubt, this impales many Christians on the horns of a dilemma. Christianity, as most Christians know it here and now, has become almost incurably Western. Once you really start taking seriously what an African Christianity might look like and be like, or an Asian Christianity, the question of whether, say, 1662 is the most appropriate and best vehicle for Christian worship, week in, week out, in England, is given a quite new perspective.

My experience — for what its worth; and I suppose after nearly forty years of ordained mystery, a good many of which have involved ministry to students, I ought not to underrate that experience — is that a fresh beginning for a religious view of life for many young people today has come most often through what I will call confrontation with the elemental experiences of human existence: falling in love; marriage; birth — the birth of a first child, for instance; experience of suffering and bereavement — and of transcendent beauty. And one of those primary obligations of a chaplain and a chapel is to help people to take those events as seriously as possible, and to give the student — of whatever faith, or of none — the opportunity to let his own faith, such as it is, help him or her to explore the heights and depths of their humanity. Many, if not most, students often now come from religion-less backgrounds. The meeting point for those of different faiths and of none is to my mind, as I say, our common human experience: the exploration of the heights and depths of that experience.

It often moves me that falling in love, birth, suffering, death, marriage — whatever our faith, or none — suddenly awakes in people the awareness that "people matter more than things" — or the desperate need to be assured that this is true, and provides a new impetus to wrestle until some answer be found.

The point I am trying to make is that I do not see my job — or the job of this Chapel — as primarily to keep a certain sort of service or set of services going. Neither do I see it as imposing the Christian answer to life's questions — or taking it for granted that the way that the 1662 Prayer Book answers life's questions is the best way. If there is going to be a Chapel, and if there is going to be worship, we have, I believe, a more profound obligation than that: which is to help every member of this Inn, whatever their faith, whatever the state of their belief, to come to as deep an answer to life's questions as we can.

Now I do not pretend this approach presents us with simple questions or obvious answers; and it is of course much easier to duck the big questions and simply "keep to the book".

But there is help to be found in our situation, I believe, in strange and surprising quarters.

Two Roman Catholic Benedictine monks, for instance, have for many years now been living out their Catholic Christian faith in as Indian a form as possible. Dom Bede Griffiths went to India in 1955, and to his contemplative ashram in Tamil Nadu, South India, thousands have journeyed, to find forms of prayer and worship and life which are deeply Christian but which speak to the Indian. Similarly, Henri le Saux, who was born in France in 1910 and went out to India as a Benedictine monk in 1948, founded the ashram to which Bede Griffiths came, but moved north, and now lives permanently beside the Ganges in the Himalayas. His writings, under the name of Abhishiktananda, have gained a world-wide circulation.

Curiously, by seeking to find a Christian faith which is shorn of its Western accoutrements, they have discovered forms of faith which speak to many who have been seeking to find faith itself — or a renewed faith.

Abhishiktananda has underlined in his teaching the obvious point — which nevertheless needed underlining — that when Jesus taught his followers to pray — to pray, for instance, what we call "the Lord's Prayer" — he was not teaching something exclusively Christian: indeed, he was not teaching anything exclusive. They are phrases which, for instance, those of Jewish upbringing can happily voice, indeed, they are phrases which may evoke a response from all but the confirmed atheist. They are not a sort of "irreducible minimum" of religion, but they can be for all of us a starting point from which we may further explore the religious dimension of our humanity. It is to that exploration which I myself believe the Chapel of an Inn of Court should nowadays be dedicated. The Chapel should very clearly provide a welcome and a home to all who are sincerely seeking an answer to life's questions.

Let me end therefore what I have to say this morning by reading to you one or two paragraphs from the writings of Abhishiktananda — written, as I say, in India, for Indians.

He begins his book on Prayer with this paragraph:

"God is always present to us. There is no time and no place in our daily life or occupations in which God is not present to us; there are not even certain times or occupations in which God is more present to us or less present to us. God is always the same, the Almighty, the Infinite, the Eternal. He does not change, neither does he 'come' or 'go' from one place to another. Everywhere and always *he is*, he is himself in his fulness; there is no sense in which he can be more 'here' or less 'there', since he is indivisble.....

Creation is simply the communication of this Presence, this mysterious life of God in himself. Everything that exists, every being that lives and thinks, does so by sharing in his being, his divine life and self-awareness. It is from and through this very Presence of God to himself that all creatures exist, that living creatures are born and grow, that man is aware of himself, and finally becomes an individual being, endowed with a personal call and vocation for time and eternity.

Man, alone among creatures, has the privilege of being aware of this Presence and of being called to reciprocate it; that is, he is called to be present to God as God is present to him...."

Abhishiktananda ends his book with these words:

"Twice in his letters St. Paul reminds us that the Spirit is constantly whispering in the depths of our hearts the sacred invocation 'Abba, Father'. 'Abba, Father' was, to be sure, the ceaseless prayer of Jesus also. It is enough indeed to glance through the Gospels to realize that the remembrance of the Father was always in the heart and mind of Jesus, and his holy Name on his lips. Alike in his times of solitary prayer, and when he was in the midst of the crowds, for example, before performing miracles, he was at all times calling on the Father. 'Abba' was his last prayer in Gesthemane, his last word on the cross. Is not that an invitation.....to make the invocation 'Abba, Father' the centre of our spiritual lives — to make it our most cherished *mantra* on our lips, in our minds, in our hearts? By doing so we will follow and imitate Jesus, not only in the external aspects of his life, but in what was the very core of his whole life....."

It will also be our answer to the call arising from our own hearts, which are made by God and made for God; at the last it will be our answer to the call arising from the whole creation, through all beings, through all events of life and history, through all our encounters with our brother-men, because through and in everything it is always God, the Almighty Father, who comes to us and who calls us to him.

Abba, Father is then the sacred *mantra* which opens the doors of eternity, the doors of the inner sanctuary, the doors of the cave of the heart, and makes the soul share in the most intimate life of God in himself."

It is surely a lovely thing that here in our Chapel we can say together:
"Abba, Father"

18

IN MEMORIAM: DEREK WATTS

St. Michael and All Angels, Highclere, Berkshire;
August 14th 1989

When I first heard from Betty, less than a month ago, that Derek was very ill, and not expected to live, my first reactions were fairly violent: violent anger at God — or whoever is in charge of these things; a kind of violent sympathy for Betty, and the family, and indeed for Derek; and violent dismay that I should see so little of Derek in what remains to me of life. But when I managed to get down to see Derek, a few days later, I felt rather rebuked by his composure and acceptance.

We had a good, brief, chat: as good as I can ever remember in such circumstances.

I asked him — directly — if he was afraid. "No" he said, quietly and confidently — almost as if it was a bit odd that I should think he might be.

He was, of course, tired; but he was also ready to go. And when we said "good-bye", I didn't really expect to see him again, and didn't.

Gwen Rymer, who had lived below Betty and Derek and the family in Wells Way, in Camberwell in the 60's, when she was Parish Worker at St. George's, had driven me down to see Derek, and Betty had suggested we drive back via the Watership Down way to Basingstoke and then to London. From the moment we left here that evening, all that marvellous country was bathed in a golden glow by the setting sun. Gwen and I didn't say much: our hearts were too full. But as I thought of Derek, there came into my mind those words of Kent to King Lear which Laurence Olivier had asked to be read recently at his funeral:

I have a journey, sir, shortly to go
My Master calls me, I must not say No.

When I got home, I put them in a letter to Derek: and, I gather from Betty, Derek indicated that was about how he felt.

Those of us whose privilege it is to have quite a bit to do with the dying, know how very different people are in their last days and hours: how very different one from another.

Some of you may remember how Dylan Thomas implored his father:

Do not go gentle into that good night
Rage, rage against the dying of the light.

But Derek did "go gentle", because he was through and through a gentle man. There won't be anyone here who disagrees with that.

Whenever a friend of mine dies — and although in the last years I had seen much less of Derek than I'd have liked, he was a very dear friend — I always try to set aside some time just to think about that particular person, realistically and thankfully.

As I say, Derek himself helped me to think about him placidly.

Some of you will have known Derek all his life. Our hearts go out particularly to you.

I only got to know Derek closely thirty years ago, when I became Vicar of St. George's, Camberwell, in 1959. He interviewed me, with Cissie Brown, the other churchwarden. That unforgettable interview for me taught me a lot about Derek, which the future would only confirm.

Derek had been a close friend of my predecessor, Fr. Geoffrey Beaumont, who had joined the Community of the Resurrection — two of his hymns we are singing today. Geoffrey Beaumont had qualities which made me a person not worthy to black his boots. But no one in their wildest moments would have called him an administrator. And when Derek came to interview me, it was evident immediately that he had a "crisis" on his mind: a huge parish crisis. It had in fact just become apparent that Geoffrey, before he left the parish, had forgotten to order the Hoop-La stalls for the Garden Fete. And the Garden Fete was tomorrow! Derek had been "coping", and calming people. I shan't forget that moment, because it meant that one of the first questions Derek ever asked me — and it's a question on which the peace of a parish can depend — was "Whose job do *you* think it is to order the Hoop-La stalls?"

He was always quietly efficient and responsible. That, not least, is I imagine, why — in part — those who worked with him so admired him. He was modest; and he often found it difficult to be as confident of his gifts as his gifts should have made him.

But I think I should say just one more thing about that interview.

At the end of it, I asked: "Is there anything more you want to ask me or say to me?". I rather thought there was; but there was quite a silence. And then Derek said hesitantly: "Shall I ask him, Miss Brown?" And she said, "Yes...You ask him". "Do you mind if I ask you" said Derek, gingerly

79

"if you're going to get married?". I remember smiling to myself, and savouring the moment, and purposely being silent for quite a while, and then saying: "It's *possible*". There followed another long silence, during which Derek nodded his head up and down, thoughtfully, and then said: "We'll tell them 'It's *possible*'."

You see why I say: "Derek was a gentle man — and reticent, in a kind and thoughtful way; and wise."

But when I use the term 'gentleman', I must make it abundantly clear that he had no time whatsoever for 'respectability'. Indeed, I think he would have laughed at being called a gentleman at his funeral — and maybe is laughing now.

Derek was as wise a churchwarden as I could have asked for: and I suspect I was quite a bumptious young vicar.

Derek was loyal. He supported, not by agreeing, but by offering friendship.

He was "go ahead"; and while caring for the elderly, had the future of the church particularly at heart, and helped all he could with the youth — as he did, I gather, for a time, in this area.

He never lost his concern for fairness and social justice. To the last he was very concerned at the state of the Health Service in places like Inner London, where his father-in-law had recently been in hospital.

There's one word I've left out, but must bring in — and not as an afterthought. Derek was loving. His love as a friend was great; but as a son and as a husband and as a father, I have reason to know, words fail. In decades when marriage breakdown has been almost the "norm", Derek and Betty's marriage and home, and his gifts as a father to Jonathan and Kate, have been the delight and envy of many.

Derek was a worker, thankful always that he had a job and that he was happy in his work: which he always was.

One of the reasons why I set aside some time to think about friends who die is because nothing makes me believe in God more than when I ask seemingly simple questions like: who thought up, called into existence, created, a person like Derek?

And as I go through that person's gifts, one by one, and mull over who he was, the marvel and mystery of that particular person forces me into believing that only a Person — capital P, only Some One, could have given rise to such a person.

A sort of machine couldn't have given rise to Derek. An abstract idea or philosophy couldn't have given rise to Derek. Only a Person — or even more than a Person — could have given rise to such a person as Derek.

Derek found belief as difficult as I do. He wasn't going to believe for some cheap and slick set of reasons. He was too profound a person for that. He wasn't going to take on what others believed simply because he was told to. He had my respect for that. He was as cynical as I am about some aspects of the church.

Derek and I both delighted in the phrase "Funny old life, isn't it"— and used it a thousand times and more. (And by the way, Derek's humour was one of his greatest gifts.) "Funny old life" wasn't a phrase of disbelief or of unbelief, but a phrase that recognised just how ironic and mysterious life is, and how that mystery keeps on hitting you — in everyday places and things and people. It was a profound belief in the mystery at the heart of things that made Derek fond of that phrase "Funny old life" — and recite it with a smile, almost as though it were the centre of his creed.

I want to end what I have to say — and Patrick Appleford will be saying some more later; and I've left Derek and music to him — I want to end where I began — or near to where I began: with my asking Derek whether he was afraid, and his answering, No.

I don't want to suggest that Derek had suddenly lost the scepticism he had. I do want to suggest that Derek was as conscious then as he always had been that the Mystery of life is essentially the Mystery of Love, and that he was being called further forward, ahead of us, into that Mystery. Quite a lot of people had helped him to experience and come to trust in the Mystery of Love: most of all, of course, Betty.

That surprising lack of fear at the last, in a person who had had his anxieties — God knows! — wasn't, so to speak, gained in a day. There is a whole biography to be written there on just how love casts out fear.

I have thought it best today to be personal; and thus to represent you who in your own way will want to be thankful for Derek.

As I thank God for Derek, I am conscious how much I received from him, depended on him, in his Camberwell days and mine; but I'm also conscious how much I've received from him in this last month.

He who is — our reading said — "the Way, the Truth and the Life", had led Derek further along the Way, into Truth, into Life — we can be confident. But we can also be grateful for all of the Mystery of the Way, the Truth and the Life that has been revealed to us in and through Derek; and it is in that thankfulness that we shall commend him to the King of Love who is still shepherding him and us.

19

SERMON AT A SERVICE FOR THOSE CONCERNED WITH THE ADMINISTRATION OF JUSTICE

Llandaff Cathedral, Cardiff, S. Wales;
October 8th 1989

"Defend the poor and fatherless: See that such as are in need and necessity have right. Deliver the outcast and poor: save them from the hands of the ungodly." Psalm 82.vv 3 and 4.

No one seriously reading the Book of Psalms can ever separate religion and concern for Justice. And my text — those two verses from Psalm 82 — will be particularly familiar to many of you who belong to the legal profession. Quite often you see them, or part of them, over the doorway of a court-house, like the Old Bailey.

Those verses are not, of course, addressed simply to judges and magistrates, but are spoken first to God himself, and then to all who put their trust in Him; and thus to every Christian citizen, and, indeed, to every Jew. They remind us that the administration of Justice needs to be built and based upon, and, indeed, to focus, a society which the whole time is working away at building a fair and just society.

Archbishop William Temple once wrote: "I am convinced that one reason why the church has counted for comparatively little in public affairs of recent times is that its spokesmen have talked a great deal too much about love and not nearly enough about justice. Justice is the first expression of love. It is not something contrary to love, which love mitigates and softens. It is the first expression of it, that must be satisfied before the other and higher expressions can rightly find their place."

For the last seven years, I have spent much of my time preparing for and working alongside the Archbishop of Canterbury's Commission on Urban Priority Areas, and following up its Report, *Faith in the City*. In the course of these years I can claim to have visited, and kept in touch with, most of the main urban priority areas of Great Britain. In preparing what I have to say to you today, I have found it specially helpful to possess the *Atlas of Deprivation in Wales* which is the recent response of the Division for Social Responsibility of the Church in Wales to *Faith in the City*. And it was after I had been poring over that Atlas, which maps, in considerable social detail, the "land of my fathers" as it is today, that I knew I must preach to you this morning on that text:

"Defend the poor and fatherless: See that such as are in need and necessity have right. Deliver the outcast and poor: save them from the hands of the ungodly".

I have felt in these last years that my twin jobs as Preacher to Gray's Inn and Director of the charity Christian Action have been complementary. The first has brought me close to and given me many friends in the legal profession. The second never lets me forget the state of our nation: its justice and injustice.

Day after day, as I have gone round the inner cities of Great Britain, I have seen with my own eyes the widening gulf between the classes and the exclusion of the very poorest from our rapidly rising living standards.

In the last eight years there has been, for instance, a 200 per cent increase in the number of single mothers on welfare, and a huge increase in the single mothers on welfare for very long periods of time.

"Defend the *poor and fatherless*: See that such as are in need and necessity have right..." has seemed to me a very direct and personal command.

In 1970, the number of single-parent families drawing supplementary benefit stood at 191,000. Over the past eight years, that number has tragically risen — by May 1987 — to 644,000, with the number of dependants now standing at over a million. The number dependent on supplementary benefit (called National Assistance until 1966) has risen from 4.4 million in 1979 to 8.2 million in May 1988.

But it must not be simply the increase in the number on low income which must be our concern, but the fact that such incomes are a major determinant of a person's achievement throughout their life: from surviving birth, through and up to, and including, death itself. The number of low birth-weight babies has increased in every year since 1981, so too has the mortality rate of those in the lowest rank of the social scale.The mortality rate of infants in Social Class 5 is now five times that in Class 1.

Since 1979 there has been a measurable widening of the class divide. In 1988-9, the richest one per cent of Britain cornered £4.7 billion pounds in tax cuts. This increase in income is on average greater than the total income of any single person in the bottom 95 per cent of the population. And the simple fact is that in the last decade unemployment has hit the poorest hardest, for they are those without jobs longest.

Three groups are the most easy prey to what has recently been called "the recruiting sergeant of the underclass": those who have been unemployed longest; the single-parent mother on means-tested welfare; and the very elderly on only a state pension. But perhaps the prime reason the recruiting sergeant has been so successful in recruiting an "underclass" has been the conscious and determined redistribution of income towards richer people on a scale unparalleled in this century.

The Church of Wales' *Atlas of Deprivation* pin-points those areas where the major forms of deprivation coincide — that is to say: the places where the injustice of our society is most painfully experienced; the census wards where, for instance, between 28 per cent and 46 per cent of the population between 16 and 24 are unemployed, and where other major indicators of disadvantage coincide, in, for instance, places like the Taff Valley centred on Merthyr Vale.

To be concerned with justice in our courts without being concerned with the injustice of our society at large is a nonsense, for so often the two are intimately interwoven. A respectable and respected senior magistrate in Kirkby, Liverpool, said to me not long ago: "I never thought I should live to be on the side of those who are brought before me charged with shop-lifting — not all of them, of course, but many of them; but that is often where I now find myself when I am acquainted with the reality of their resources and circumstances."

Put it another way: when you visit a place, you so often find the *Atlas of Deprivation* has undeniable implications concerning Order and Law.

"Defend the poor and fatherless: See that such as are in need and necessity have right. Deliver the outcast and poor: save them from the hands of the ungodly."

Quite often these days when you try to defend the outcast and poor, and to bring them justice, you find yourself inescapably involved in the question of Race Relations. After my travels about Britain, I could relate this to many aspects of our British society. Let me be selective this morning, since I am addressing in particular you who are concerned with the Administration of Justice, and say it is a great credit to our Home Office that in 1984 its Research and Planning Unit set in hand a study of Race Relations in our Prisons, which was carried out by the Centre for Criminological Research.

The results of that study are now readily available in a book *Race Relations in Prisons* — published this year by Oxford University Press. It is a book which I believe all those concerned for justice in our land should read. It reveals that though West Indian or African people constitute less than 2 per cent of our population they represented on June 30th 1985 8 per cent of men in prison and 12 per cent of women. But I have to tell you that even since that Report was concluded, in June 1986, the situation has changed very considerably. The percentage of male prisoners from ethnic minorities is now not 8 per cent but 14 per cent, and the percentage of women has doubled from 12 to 24 per cent. In comparison with white prisoners, non-white ethnic minorities are particularly over-represented amongst those remanded in custody and those serving longer sentences. Yet they have had fewer previous convictions and were less likely to serve their sentences in open training establishments.

This major piece of research for the Home Office also very clearly reveals the racism that exists among prison officers. It outlines the precise role in a prison of a race relations officer — which was prescribed for every prison in 1982 — and the training courses set up to equip all staff with the awareness to recognise attitudes or behaviour reflective of ethnic insensitivity. But only a third of prison officers interviewed in the study had even seen the policy statement, and hardly any had ever read it. Over half of the prison officers had wholly negative views about the policy. As many as 40 per cent were unaware that any action had been taken in response to the policy at their prison. The higher the rank of the uniformed officer, the less he was inclined to favour the recruitment of staff from ethnic minorities. The recorded remarks of prison officers — undeniably and explicitly racist — can only be dismaying to those concerned for justice in our prisons as a reflection of concern for justice in our land.

As part of its concern for the mission of the church to the Nation, the Report *Faith in the City* has chapters on Employment, Housing, Health and Education. It is indispensable for those of us who as Christians are concerned for justice in our land to have parallels to these chapters in our concern for justice in our prisons. I shall not forget the man in Liverpool on long-term unemployment who cried out at our meeting in Kirkby, Liverpool "I want my dignity back". Prison rightly takes away a man's liberty. But its point and purpose is surely not to return him to the world having further lost his dignity. If at all possible, that must be given back to him. And that, of course, relates to the conditions inside a cell, and how many hours a prisoner spends outside it, and his or her employment in those hours. At least a third of prisoners at the moment, many of whom are unconvicted, are totally without work, or education, or training, every day. That is a situation which the representatives of Christ and his church dare not tolerate. But, at the level merely of human prudence, it is surely a huge waste of money to coop people up in prisons and not use the opportunity for human healing and growth. To put it that way is immediately to underline the connection between work, education and health. And I should like to emphasize the fact that to take away a person's liberty should not necessarily imply that in prison they should be given no responsibility. Indeed, to return people to the world after prison with diminished experience of responsibility is a recipe for recidivism and for further disaster. The health of a prisoner, and his ill-health, may vary from objective illnesses like AIDS, to depression, to the psychological needs of those who are still discovering who they are: and the age of most of those in prison at the moment is, of course, under thirty.

In December 1984, the Home Office Prison Department issued Circular Instruction No.55. In one of its paragraphs it said that the task of the Prison Service is "to provide for prisoners as full a life as is consistent with the facts of custody — in particular making available the physical necessities of life — care for physical and mental health; advice and help with personal problems: work, education, training, physical exercise and recreation; and opportunity to practice their religion; and to enable prisoners to retain their links with the community, and where possible, assist them to prepare for their return to it." This is a fine definition and a noble ideal. Often I believe it is the mission of the church to help people and institutions to reach their self-confessed and self-defined highest goals.

At the moment, the gap between reality and ideal in most of our prisons is a blot upon our society. Of course, it would be costly to remove that blot, but it would be a cost worth paying; for many return to prison because of our failure with them in their first experience of it.

I can never forget the words of Winston Churchill which he spoke a few months short of eighty years ago when he was a young Home Secretary:

> *"The mood and temper of the public in regard to the treatment of crime and criminals is one of the most unfailing tests of the civilisation of any country. A calm, dispassionate recognition of the rights of the accused and even of the convicted criminal against the State: a constant heart-searching of all charged with the deed of punishment; tireless efforts towards the discovery of regenerative processes; unfailing faith that there is a treasure, if you can find it, in the heart of every man. These are the symbols which in the treatment of crime and criminals make and measure the stored-up strength of a nation and are sign and proof of the living virtue in it."*

Nor can I forget the words of that other great Englishman, William Blake:

"He who would do good to another must do it in minute particulars. General good is the plea of the scoundrel, hypocrite and flatterer."

It is particular places in our land, often particular census wards and groupings of wards, to which those of us who do not live there can so easily turn a blind eye.

It is particular places like prisons to which those of who happen not to be confined in them can close our hearts; but we dare not be just in our courts and unjust in our prisons.

And it is particular people who, in their poverty, we, in our comparative affluence, can exclude from our hearts and minds and imaginations.

But the Psalmist does not let us forget them. He gives us this direct command as we who are concerned with the administration of justice come before the throne of God:

"Defend the poor and fatherless: See that such as are in need and necessity have right. Deliver the outcast and poor: save them from the hands of the ungodly."

20

THE LEGEND OF THE HOLY DRINKER

Sermon for the Annual Vintage Festival Service of the
Vintners' and Distillers' Livery Companies;
St. Olave's Hart Street, E.C.3.
October 3rd 1989

I thought it would be difficult to find a subject more appropriate to this
occasion than *The Legend of the Holy Drinker*. You may know it was the
last brief novel of Joseph Roth, an Austro-Hungarian Jew, who became a
central figure in the intellectual opposition to the Nazis. It was written and
published exactly fifty years ago, in the few months either side of his death,
in May 1939. This year, the publication of Michael Hoffman's translation
of the novel into English has coincided with the release in London of the
film of the book, which won the *Palme d'Or* at the 1988 Venice Film
Festival. I say "It would be difficult to find a subject more appropriate" as
the subject of a sermon before the Master and Wardens of the Vintners'
and Distillers' Livery Companies and representatives of the Wine and
Spirit Trade Benevolent Society, for what is your concern in coming here
to church today if it is not the holiness of drink, and drinking, and drinkers
— like ourselves?

But first, I'd better tell you the story of this remarkable film — briefly:
that's to say, enough to whet your appetite, yet not enough to put you off
reading the book, or seeing the film for yourself.

The hero, Andreas, is a former Silesian miner, now down, and, nearly,
out: an alcoholic, living with fellow clochards under the bridges of the
Seine.

At the beginning of the film he is just a bundle of newspapers; but he
is approached by a rich, elderly businessman, who has been converted to
Christianity by the example of St. Thérèse of Lisieux. He gives Andreas a

couple of hundred francs, stipulating that, should he wish to repay the debt, the money should be paid to one of the priests in a Parisian Church with a chapel dedicated to St. Thérèse.

Andreas promises to settle his obligations at Mass the following Sunday; and his life changes forthwith. He is offered work, and so on. The only difficulty is that whenever he wants to repay the debt, something or someone intervenes — though each distraction he succumbs to is accompanied by a further miracle, so to speak, with new sums of money providentially provided. He finds, for instance, another thousand francs in a second-hand wallet he purchases. He has a romantic encounter with a former girl-friend, whose husband he had killed and therefore spent time in prison. He takes up with a former classmate at school, who has become a rich and generous boxer. Alas, he is still an alcoholic.

At the last, a little girl appears in the bar where he is drinking — clearly meant to be St. Thérèse herself in modern dress. She asks him why he has not visited her. He is in a fairly collapsible state by this time; and he is taken across the road to the church with the statue of St. Thérèse, where he was meant to repay his debt. There he dies, in dignity and peace. I love the last words of the novel: "May God grant us all, all of us drinkers, such a good and easy death!"

Well, what a story! What a story for a Vintage Festival! It's almost a parable.

But why do I think *The Legend of the Holy Drinker* is such an appropriate subject for this occasion?

For a dozen and more reasons.

Let me select just a few.

First, as I've said, there's the title: which is a kind of challenge in itself. Is a Holy Drinker just a legend, or has it, can it have, some substance?

Do you ever see your wine drinking, or spirits, as a challenge: as something to be included in your vocation to holiness? Because, if you don't, it may be for you, as it is for many, something which is really, if only in part, something which you feel slightly guilty about, but must pretend to yourself, and to others, that you don't. And guilt is always unhealthy if it is not recognised and faced. Something which is such a central interest of our life must surely be the raw material of at least some of our holiness.

Secondly: This film is about an alcoholic; and lots of people who have to do with alcoholics have constantly a kind of guilt by association. We all see in the street people like Andreas, and immediately feel guilty. "Have I done something to create that alcoholic?" I often say to myself as I pass by the group of 'winos' who congregate near the office of the charity I work for in Vauxhall.

But I think it is of the utmost importance to remember the Latin phrase:

89

Abusus non tollit usum: "The abuse of something does not destroy its proper use".

I suppose where these days we might justifiably feel somewhat guilty is in the huge power and pressure of advertising which we bring upon people: power and pressure which is simply too much for much human nature to bear. Indeed, the whole point of the advertising is to get us to yield to its pressures.

Advertising doesn't thrive on temperance or on the idea that "enough is enough". Most often it thrives on the overthrow of opposition and control. And someone, not the advertiser, has to come along and warn the Andreas in all of us that alongside every good gift — wine, sex, whatever — lies in wait the destroyer. And the good deed of the holy drinker can soon pass over into the deed that is our destruction and downfall.

The third reason why I think *The Legend of the Holy Drinker* is highly appropriate for today, is because so much in our society is about effort and enterprise, and so little is about what I will call "gift". Now effort and enterprise are marvellous things; but one of my favourite phrases is: "What hast thou which thou hast not received?"

What happens to Andreas is that, to a person who has got used to being down on his luck, a series of gifts come out of the blue.

One of the phrases I most dislike is "the self-made man". Most of us are largely what we are because of, literally, our gifts: the start we had in life, our family, schooling, landing the right job, or a job at all, meeting Mr. or Miss Right. It's tempting to look on other people, like Andreas, wrapped in newspaper, and say: "He's a self-made alcoholic, whereas I'm a self-made success." But life isn't really like that. Coming to Church ought to renew in us compassion for those who haven't landed on their feet but on the pavements — in newspapers.

There's a fourth reason why I'm attracted to *The Legend of the Holy Drinker*.

As a priest, I meet a good many people who are compulsive gamblers: on the Stock Exchange or on fruit machines, or who can't keep away from betting shops. There are about 15,000 youngsters who are arcade addicts at the moment. Then there are compulsive people sexually, who can't keep away from the secretary or the typist, or who have some homosexual compulsion; and there are others who have some alcoholic or narcotic compulsion. The varieties of our human compulsions are so many and so various — and so strong, so compelling — that we must count ourselves very lucky — or blessed — if we manage not to be a compulsive this or that.

Now at no point is the book or the film of the Holy Drinker judgmental about Andreas. It never for one moment underrates the destructive power of our compulsions. How could Joseph Roth, who himself died of drink around the age of forty, do that? But the film is deeply understanding and compassionate towards Andreas.

Most compulsive people I know, hate themselves, or part of themselves; indeed, if the truth were known, the drink (or whatever it is), is probably one way of their dealing with their self-hate. But this book, this film, is a loving portrait of Andreas without being at all indulgent.

You come away from the film, and from reading the book, with affection for Andreas. His alcoholism has not wholly destroyed his holiness, you feel; indeed it may have opened him up to receive gifts and grace, whereas many holy people believe that you can only be holy if you're under tight control.

Which brings me to my last point. Most creative people that I know are neurotic. The artists I have known have also often been near to breakdown. It's almost the price of their work — like Joseph Roth's as a writer. In the church I come across a good many virtuous and controlled people, lay and ordained; and I do not want to denigrate their control or their virtue; and I've seen too much of the damage and destruction caused by being out of control to wish that upon them and their families. And yet, I have to say, my heart went out to Andreas, and even a good deal of my admiration.

The reviewer of the film in the Catholic weekly *The Tablet* wrote: "This is an extraordinary film: peaceful and illuminating and full of windows on lives of which we shall never know more. It is holy, humane...one to be remembered and savoured."

Do go and see it. It will help you in your vocation to be a *Holy* Drinker. It will help you to celebrate well and wisely and with true thanksgiving this year's Vintage, and not only this year's.

21

THE DYER AND DON GIOVANNI

To the Worshipful Company of Dyers;
St. James Garlickhythe,
October 11th 1989

I was greatly delighted and honoured by the invitation I received from the Prime Warden to preach to this *Worshipful* Company — a term which seems eminently appropriate here and now; but, to be honest, I was also at first greatly embarrassed; for my ignorance of the work of the Dyer, I soon realised, is all but entire.

But your kind invitation has stimulated and provoked me in various ways. I have found myself studying, for instance, in a way I would never otherwise have dreamt of doing, the whole scientific mechanism of how we perceive colour at all — and, indeed, what colour is.

And, since I received your invitation, I have found myself observing the work of the Dyer, and pondering it, on all sorts of surprising occasions, rather like a new recruit to the pursuit of *Lepidoptera* might observe the butterfly in quite a new way.

At, for instance, a recent performance of Mozart's *Don Giovanni* at the London Coliseum, I suddenly found myself, while everyone else was rapt in attending to Mozart, looking at what was before my eyes on the stage, and all the ravishing colours of the costumes, and the curtains, and some of the furnishings of the set, and at least some of the wigs, and, indeed, some of the appurtenances of the audience, as witness to the work of the Dyer. And something said to me: "Stay there! See what this performance of *Don Giovanni* has to say to you about the work of the Dyer!"

So I'm going to ask you now to stay with me as we reflect together on the Dyer and *Don Giovanni*. And I warn you that, perforce, at times, you may feel we have strayed quite a way from the Dyer. I will only assure you we will join up with him again in the end.

In fact, I have yet to meet anyone who doesn't enjoy a night out at — or, rather, with — Don Giovanni. And that somewhat surprises me, in view of the nature of the story. It surprises me, for instance, that the clergy of the Church of England should enjoy such a story.

And although I've met some who say: "Of course, the story is just nonsense, and is to be ignored", I've never taken that remark very seriously, for it has always been clear to me that my companions who made such a remark were not entirely there for the music, marvellous as it is, and were enjoying the story in spite of it, and themselves.

Of course, the story has fascinated writers from Molière to Shaw; but I doubt whether it would stand up in the theatre, simply on the grounds of probability; and in an opera, doesn't really need to. Which makes one ask: "What was it in the story which so fascinated Mozart? And what is it in it that so clearly fascinates most of us?"

It's not, of course, obvious material for a sermon, except as a cautionary tale. Giovanni is a libertine, a sexual predator and a blasphemer. How successful he is in seduction is not altogether clear, in spite of his claims. And you will not expect me to evince great experience in these matters. But:

> Ah, la mia lista!
> Doman mattina
> D'una decima
> Devi aumentar

("Ah, my list! Tomorrow you must increase it by ten!" strikes me as either arrogant exaggeration or pathological hyperbole — two thousand sexual conquests!)

Clearly "the Don" is an egoist: a man who embodies the self-confidence of his class, with not a trace of *noblesse oblige*. He is a ruthless, and, in some respects, vulgar character. He exploits his servant, but not only his servant. There's no denying he's a sensualist. Food, wine and music arouse him as much as a pretty woman. His blasphemy is no surprise, for it's clear he has no regard for the spiritual. In the graveyard he insults the dead and takes no heed of the Talking Statue.

If there's a moral to the story, (and perhaps too many look for a sermon there), it is portrayed in the appearance of the Stone Guest at Supper. There, suddenly, is a power even greater than the power Giovanni has wielded over the characters in the story.

How does Mozart handle that story? Above all: how does he manage to transform a story about a seducer and a betrayer into one of the most sublime operatic experiences?

Well: perhaps I should remind you that the title of the opera was originally *Il Dissoluto Punito* — The Libertine Punished — ossia *Don Giovanni*.

And the Overture, from its first towering chords — so significantly of D Minor, followed by awesome silence — confronts us with, not a Stone Guest, but with a force to be reckoned with: certainly a terrifying power from another world.

Trombones were instruments used mainly for church music and for divine utterance in opera. Mozart's use of trombones in this first section of the Overture expresses the inescapable reality of the spiritual, of another world than this, and of the inexorable reality of judgment, realised or ignored. In the allegro of the Overture, which follows, we hear not a portrait of Giovanni, but the sudden breaking forth of a life force, so to speak, which simply cannot be contained. The Overture does not introduce the characters of the opera, as one might have expected; they will be introduced as the story unfolds. What we are confronted with is two conflicting powers of terrifying force and energy, preparing for a dramatic confrontation, which only one can win.

Of course, Mozart was always looking for musical opportunities which he could exploit; but, let it be clear, he always sought to express a view of life in his music.

In a letter to his father in October 1777, ten years before *Don Giovanni*, he wrote:

"God is ever before my eyes. I realise his
omnipotence and I fear his anger; but I also
recognise his love, his compassion and his
tenderness towards his creatures. He will
never forsake his own. If it is according
to His will, so let it be according to mine.
Thus all will be well, and I must needs be
happy and contented."

Mozart's sense of Providence here should not be construed as fatalism. He fought, for instance, the servants of the church in a manner which is far from fatalistic. He had a strong sense of Providence and a highly developed sense of vocation, and in that vocation, through his music, he portrays God's power, judgment, love, mercy, tenderness — and, dare one say it, humour.

Incidentally, *Don Giovanni* is entitled a drama "giocoso": playful, comic. And sometimes I would like to argue that humour is one of our human attributes which most reveals our divine creation. Where else could such a gift spring from?

Well: now I have said all of that, I want to return to my original question: What is it in the story which so attracted Mozart? And what is it that so fascinates most of us, whether we're clergy, or Dyers, or whatever?

I do not myself think that most of us, when we listen to *Giovanni*, are most pleased with the moral sentiments which are expressed, and with the fact that Don Giovanni gets his "come-uppance". We do not come away from *Giovanni* feeling primarily we have been present at a Morality Play.

Certainly we know we have been confronted with the verity of beauty, through music; but a symphony or a sonata might have achieved that.

I want to suggest to you we sympathise with *Don Giovanni* as an opera, as distinct from Giovanni as a person, because it pays such tribute, in unsurpassable music, to what I can only call the life force: to the *élan vital*. It is the sheer vitality of life, which embraces a whole range of skills, which is set before us; and what is faced and acknowledged is that our sexuality lies very close to the heart of this; and we all know this to be true. Paradoxically, it is in this portrayal of a libertine of whom everyone disapproves, if somewhat amusedly, and even a little enviously, that we recognise something of ourselves, which otherwise we most often fail to acknowledge, and, indeed, are discouraged from acknowledging. And whatever is true, but lies hidden and unacknowledged, is better faced and brought out into the open.

Lust is a word which in Church circles is most often used only negatively. In scientific circles we recognise it is lust which makes the world go round: without sexual desire the species would not continue to be propagated: the birds and the bees, not least with their colours, and no less the human species, thanks to the Dyer. It is this rich power of vital life, in all its variety and vitality, which Mozart manages to celebrate in exquisite music. *Don Giovanni* focusses on the exploits not only of the Don but of Leporello and all those lively characters who seem at one in their lust for life and their capacity to enjoy, experience and celebrate it. And that lust for life has to be revealed not least in all the costumes and design of the opera.

Of course, that power and capacity needs control and direction. But such power — God knows! — cannot always be neatly controlled and nicely directed. Such power, like a river in torrent, in spate, will sometimes overflow its banks, however cared for in construction and preservation those banks may be. True, there is little in *Giovanni* which even suggests that dykes against sin may sometimes be necessary if we are not to be cruel to others as well as to ourselves.

But *Giovanni*, I am suggesting, is an opera which opens and ends with judgment, yet nevertheless celebrates something even greater than divine judgment, and that is creation itself: life itself: the flow, full tide and colour of creative life; and does it in such a way as to make the remark of that usually dour and astringent theologian Karl Barth more than possible: "Mozart may well provide the music that angels play and sing to each other while God the father eavesdrops."

95

St. Paul had a remarkable phrase in his First Epistle to the Corinthians which could well serve as my text for today: "That was not first which is spiritual but that which is natural". In *Don Giovanni* Mozart celebrates the spiritual in and through the natural. On other occasions in his music he will proclaim our need of redemption — notably in his *Requiem*, which alas he left unfinished. But in *Giovanni* Mozart reveals the spiritual through the natural, and divinity through humanity. And when all is said and done, isn't that near to the very heart of the Christian Gospel?

And you, the Dyers of this world, surely play your part when the art and skill of your Company aids and abets an opera like *Don Giovanni* to be all Mozart meant it to be. You, too, are then doing what you can to reveal the spiritual through the natural: the divine through your own humanity and the humanity of others.

22

OUR GOD IS A
CONSUMING FIRE

The Epistle to the Hebrews 12 v.29.
Guy Fawkes Day;
Gray's Inn Chapel, November 5th 1989

Alas for the Preacher on the 5th November: there's not a single reference in the whole of the Bible to fireworks. Firebrands: Yes! Fireworks: No! But there are many references to fire — which is, of course, a very important Biblical word, as the text I have taken makes abundantly clear: "Our God is a consuming fire": The Epistle to the Hebrews Chapter 12 verse 29.

Some of you will already have detected that image and that theme behind, or, rather, within, the hymns and the psalm and the readings for this morning; and at the end of the service we shall be treated to Handel's *Musick for the Royal Fireworks*.

Fire is, of course, a deeply natural and elemental theme; yet it's hardly less ecclesiastical. Many churches at Easter, for instance, as it begins to dawn, ignite the Paschal Fire.

Fire rituals are found in religions the world over. The symbols of darkness and light are closely allied to the symbol of fire. And, no doubt, the volcanic mountain top that blazed with fire spoke to primitive peoples of the God whose glory is above all the earth.

Carl Jung discusses the significance of fire in his *Psychology of the Unconscious*. There can be little doubt that the sexual and the sacral are brought close together in fire.

As I've suggested, there's much about sacred fire in the Old Testament. There's the Burning Bush — the bush that burnt but was not consumed — which revealed the presence of God. There's the Pillar of Fire — which led the Children of Israel by night. There's the fire that descended from heaven in response to the prayer of Elijah. There's the chariot of fire and the horses of fire that carried Elijah to heaven. In the Book of Daniel, Nebuchadnezzar consigned three men to the Burning Fiery Furnace, but saw four walking in the midst of the fire; and the form of the fourth, he said, was "like the Son of God." Ezekiel had a vision of wheels with fire between them — perhaps by association and assimilation, the origin of our Catherine Wheel; for the symbol of St. Catherine of Alexandria is usually a wheel — on which she is said to have been tortured and martyred; and the wheel of torture became a wheel of fire. The prophet Malachi thinks of God as a refiner's fire.

In the New Testament, Jesus Himself says that He is "come to cast fire on the earth". And at Pentecost, Whitsuntide, the Spirit of God descends upon the apostles as tongues of fire. The Book of the Revelation of St. John the Divine contains a score of references to fire. "And there were seven lamps of fire burning before the Throne..."

Dante saw Deity as a "river of fire" that filled the universe.

For St. John of the Cross, the Holy Spirit is the "Living Flame of Love". So we could go on.

In 1942, as a seventeen year old, on my way to work, I bought a first edition of "Little Gidding", the last of T.S. Eliot's *Four Quartets* — which I still possess. Eliot was, of course, drawing on the Biblical resources and resonances when he wrote "Little Gidding":

The dove descending breaks the air
With flame of incandescent terror
Of which the tongues declare
The one discharge from sin and error.
The only hope, or else despair
   Lies in the choice of pyre or pyre —
   To be redeemed from fire by fire.
Who then devised the torment? Love.
Love is the unfamiliar Name
Behind the hands that wove
The intolerable shirt of flame
Which human power cannot remove.
   We only live, only suspire
   Consumed by either fire or fire.

"Our God is a consuming fire", Eliot was saying; "but we may experience that fire either as the warm, attracting, drawing, redeeming fire of Love, something that enables us to live — or we shall experience it as something utterly destructive." The "consuming fire" of God can either be our Heaven or our Hell.

And Newman, in *The Dream of Gerontius*, has the monitory phrase: "Learn that the flame of everlasting Love doth burn ere it transform."

What I have said so far may have spoken primarily to our heads rather than our hearts; so I must press the question: Does it matter how we worship God? Does it matter whether we think of Him and worship Him as "consuming fire"?

I think it does; for we so often, too often, make God in our own image.

I sometimes think we are inclined to worship God here in Gray's Inn, for instance, as the God of Law and Order. We tend to make Him in our own image and our worship reflects that image. Here we fall down and worship an image of God which is anything but fire. Here is a place for conservators and stabilisers of society. We come with our offering of God given virtues; but they are the virtues of the careful, the controlled, the cautious, the conscientious, the thorough, the accurate, the industrious, the judicious: all such good and laudable virtues in themselves. But what has happened to the fire and the passion?

Our chapel altar has upon it two pure white candles, so beautifully balanced, with two such gentle flames; but where, we may ask, is the blaze of the consuming fire?

I have been trying to answer lately, concerning the Church of England, and, in particular, concerning my own profession, why we have found it so difficult to face the whole question of the nature of sexuality? And I'm beginning to conclude that my own profession and the Law may have much in common in this respect. Of course we can discuss sexuality as an intellectual subject, unrelated to the realities of who we are. Our God is, so to speak, a damped down fire. True, a damped down fire may be hotter within than an open fire; but we ought to be aware, and able to face, what there is below the surface.

I spend a lot of my time trying to get people to be honest with themselves and about themselves in order to be Honest to God: facing who they are; for I'm convinced that there's no true spirituality, and no spiritual growth, except by way of such honesty. We dare not simply worship a "pale Galilean" — a God who is the God of fear-full control: fear-full because we fear the fire of God once it's out of control; so we worship the God of balance and order; and the consuming fire of God is pent up, until it suddenly bursts and blazes into flame; and we wonder what on earth has happened. We do not own and recognise the God of fire as our God.

I have said: "I spend a lot of my time trying to help people to be honest with and about themselves and thus Honest to God". In the pastoral context I meet people with, say, AIDS, or people who are suddenly confronted by the breakdown of their marriage, and who are often dismayed and surprised and sometimes shocked at what has happened to them. Of course, they have their own responsibility to bear; but I also think the Church, and maybe the Law, has some responsibility for playing a game of "let's pretend": "Let's pretend that 'consuming fire' is not at the heart of the God who has made us — and has made us in his image." We rarely talk about

99

that kind of God. We rarely face that part of ourselves — and our worship is careful to exclude it too — and, preferably, the sermons that are preached to us. The Law's answer — and religion's is often like unto it — is to batten down the hatches: to suppress and repress and control by fear, and to confine God to the intellect.

So many people I know have come to the conclusion that they must leave the church if they are to be real about themselves; and I am myself very sad about that. They have been instructed and nurtured — it seems to me — in belief in a God who is anything but a "consuming fire": who has shared that fire with his creatures.

Of course, I'm aware that for the church to face afresh the nature of sexuality is to allow the potential for disorder, disunity, conflict, chaos, and increased anxiety, to surface, at a time when much in society appears already "out of order". And quite a lot of people want to use the church to get things back into order.

Likewise, I'm aware that for the church to allow the God who is a consuming fire into its worship would tax and disturb those who want to keep God under their control.

Gerard Manley Hopkins, commending his poems to Robert Bridges, wrote a verse radiant with pulsing beauty:

> Sweet fire the sire of muse, my soul needs this;
> I want the one rapture of an inspiration.
> O then if in my lagging line you miss
> The roll, the rise, the carol, the creation,
> My winter world, that scarcely breathes that bliss
> Now yields you, with some sighs, our explanation.

On November 5th, the night sky of our winter world is suddenly lit up and alive with showers of stars and the explosion of light in darkness in which the child in us all delights.

Is it too fanciful and far-fetched for the adult in us to respond in the winter world of our imaginations and see the sparklers, Roman Candles, Catherine Wheels, Chrysanthemum Fountains, and the rest, as but the signs and symbols of Him who "calls us out of darkness into his own marvellous light" and who is the consuming fire both within and beyond us all?

23

I WILL MAKE YOU A NAME

Gray's Inn Chapel;
Remembrance Day November 12th 1989

In preparing my sermon for this year's Remembrance Day it was not easy to resist the temptation to look East: to the Berlin Wall and to other events in Eastern Europe. But it was a temptation I felt that had to be resisted. It was the more difficult to resist because it is only those of us who are older than fifty who can now have any personal remembrance of the two World Wars, and that inevitably begins to change Remembrance Day from what it once was.

For many it is not and cannot now be remembrance, strictly speaking: recalling an event within the memory.

And I have a duty to preach today to the young, or the relatively young, as well as to the relatively old.

Yet I suspect the point I have just made can be exaggerated; for, being born in 1925, I knew nothing at all of the First World War by direct experience, yet my home life and childhood, I would say, were deeply coloured by that War: dyed red, indelibly stained, with the blood of men I'd never known. And the fear of war — fifty years ago, in 1939 — my fear of war — was the terror of something I'd never myself experienced but had certainly caught from those around me.

This year, now fifty years have passed since the Second World War began, I feel a stronger obligation to say something to those who have no direct memory of either of the two World Wars; and yet I'm reluctant to preach simply another "peace" sermon, so to speak. So what shall I say?

Several things. But I'm aware they'll be rather a "rag-bag", and will not form a unity.

First: A few weeks ago I was privileged to see the video which has been made by the Commonwealth War Graves Commission. My text today is, in fact, its title: "I will make you a name".

I would be astonished if that video left any unmoved except the very very youngest. It's simply a film of war grave cemeteries. The camera often moves silently from grave to grave, sometimes slowly, fastening upon a single name, sometimes quickly, covering, as it were, a field of graves, and, sometimes, a vast prairie of graves, which extends to and beyond the horizon. Not all who have been buried have been given Christian burial, for there are Jews, Buddhists, Hindus, Sikhs, buried amongst the one and three quarter million graves. There is a Commonwealth War Cemetery now by the River Kwai. Usually, on the tombstone, there's a regimental crest and a name; but some there are with no name. If those buried were all in procession, marching four abreast, the column would stretch from London to Edinburgh.

I must confess the film had me in tears several times; and it needed to make no great attempt to do so.

When I'd sent the video back to where it belonged, I thought I would just sit down with pen and paper and try to analyse just why I was so moved.

In fact, whenever I see a cemetery of war graves, I find I'm deeply moved; and I don't think I'm alone in that. It speaks to one, of course, of mortality: of other's mortality, but also of one's own. Any cemetery might of course do that, but doesn't. And I doubt whether that was the primary reason why I was so moved.

Probably it was because so many of those who died in the two World Wars were so young. But I found myself wondering whether I would have cried if the graves were all German, or all Russian, or even all French or American. Was it anyone's and everyone's young mortality that moved me? I wondered. Nationalism is so strong a force in all of us, for better and for worse.

And then I remembered how moved I had been by the Viet Nam memorial in Washington. But on that memorial the name of one young friend of mine was engraved: a young lad, Bruce Nickerson, who had worked with me in my South London parish. Do you have to know someone in one of those cemeteries for them to come alive? I doubt it.

I think I wept, in part, because of the waste, the woeful waste of young lives those endless gravestones represented.

And yet it was not all waste.

The First World War — the "war to end war" — we know did not achieve that; and I've never been wholly convinced that the 14-18 War was necessary in the way that the crushing of Nazism was necessary. No cause still seems to me more worth fighting for than to crush that degraded creed.

And yet the aftermath of victory, in both World Wars, has had so much waste about it — and not just the aftermath.

There was the irony — if that's the right word — of relying for the crushing of Nazism so largely on the strength of atheistic Communism — which of course so soon became our so-called "peace-time" enemy; so that after only a few years, Germany — our old arch enemy, whose moral and political reconstruction and education were expected to take a generation — was quickly re-armed as the corner-stone of our defensive alliance.

I wondered whether I had cried in part for, so-to-speak, a wasted cause: for the way a clear cause had been deposed and replaced by confusion. But once you look at it with detachment — if ever that is possible — war can only appear as an extraordinarily messy and unreliable way of achieving anything that can be described, however loosely, as consistent with God's purpose. Dresden and Nagasaki make that abundantly clear. They say something about the barely controllable — never-know-where-it-will-lead-to — aspects of war.

Some months ago, the Archbishop of Canterbury spoke most movingly at the Kristallnacht Memorial Meeting. He said: "The remembrance of Kristallnacht is primarily a Jewish event. That is why I am so deeply moved by the invitation to be with you this evening, and to share in the memory of Jewish suffering. Perhaps you know that in the final days of the last war, I was a soldier. I was among the first troops to enter the Belsen concentration camp. When people ask me whether I regret my part in fighting, I have often replied — The war closed down Belsen and Auschwitz!"

There was clarity of intention and purpose; and I remember being thankful for the Archbishop there and then.

But the Archbishop went on to say with painful honesty: "But I recognise that we did not go to war to close down the concentration camps. Indeed, we, and most other nations, had closed our frontiers to all but a small number of those seeking asylum. The desperate search of many for visas led, literally, to a dead end. We went to war to prevent Germany dominating the whole of Europe."

For years we had known what was happening in Germany and did hardly more than stand by. There is of course the excuse (but hardly more than excuse) that we feared to plunge Europe yet again into war.

But the church was so silent — even the church.

The travesty of Kristallnacht, and all that followed, is, not least, that so much was perpetrated by Christians, and even in Christ's name. Neither inside nor outside Germany did the churches speak — until too late. One or two Dietrich Bonhoeffers do not make a summer. Many Jews knew that it was people who called themselves Christians who pushed them into the gas chambers — or refused all but a few of them visas into England.

103

And one form of racism has now been followed in the aftermath of war by others.

As I watched that War Graves video, I found myself reflecting that some of those whose names appeared on gravestones were black. The recruiting sergeant of the allies was colour-blind, however much racial prejudice there has been in Britain and the USA since the War.

And some of those gravestones were not the graves of those who had fallen in the two World Wars but of those who had fallen in Korea, Palestine, Malaya, Cyprus, Aden and the Falklands. They seemed somehow again to alter and confuse the purpose of Remembrance Day. There were those two marvellous lines on the Second British Division's monument at Kohima:

> When you go home, tell them of us and say
> For your tomorrow we gave our today.

Could we really relate those lines to the victims of the Falklands War?

On Sunday evenings this month, I'm preaching at Westminster Abbey. Last Sunday I went there early to listen to the organ recital before the service, but my eyes wandered to the memorials; and it suddenly hit me that so many of the regimental flags and martial monuments there bear ingenuous testimony to the belief, common to all the so-called "Christian and civilised countries" before 1914, to the gut belief that the nationally organised assertion of superior force, however unpleasant in some of its effects, was *ipso facto* righteous. 1914 began to alter all that — but only began.

It is often, I find, the task of the great poets, to frame with brevity and clarity the thoughts which, in the rest of us, are only confused and inarticulate. W.H. Auden, after the Second World War, wrote two lines which he called Epitaph for the Unknown Soldier. That two lined epitaph says, sharply and succinctly, what I've been struggling to say so far today:

> To save your world, you asked this man to die:
> Would this man, could he see you now, ask why?

It's a question worth asking again today: after the Berlin Wall has gone up, and now that it's coming down.

A question — although it was often used to great effect by Our Lord Himself — can never be all that a sermon is meant to be; and I'm left now with the question of how to end an — I think — inevitably somewhat confused and maybe somewhat confusing sermon.

I have decided to end in what to some may seem a disjointed and even surprising way.

This week, I have twice had to visit The London Lighthouse — the new hospital hospice in Notting Hill for those with AIDS. It has a couple of dozen patients there. Nine have died in the last month.

I always regard it as a great privilege to be allowed into a hospital late at night when the place is quiet and almost in darkness, and when only those who can't sleep and those who are looking after them are awake.

At the Lighthouse, appropriately, they light a candle at the reception desk when a patient dies, and they light another in the lovely small quiet room or chapel. One had just been lit last Monday.

The patients are, of course, of different races, colours and creeds. Yet no one objects to — indeed everyone welcomes — the idea of lighting a candle, and putting on the altar a photograph of the person who has died, and a card with a few brief words.

When I went up to the altar — the simple table — in the chapel, there was the candle alight, and a photograph, with a card which said:

> I want to give thanks for Eric
> Above all for his gifts as a friend
> I want to be thankful for all he was to me
> but not only to me
> I want to give thanks for the way he has died
> as well as the way he has lived.

Of course, when I saw the name "Eric", something gave a kind of involuntary jerk within me. He could so easily have been me, and I him. But my text for today came into my mind:

> I will make you a name.

Whoever it is who creates us, gives us an unique identity and unique gifts; and our faith is that He who has brought us to birth and given us a name, signifying our unique nature, will have unique ways of looking after us. He it is who gives meaning to our individual, national, and international existence, and gives meaning to history. He will gather up the fragments of our lives, and of our world, so that nothing will be lost.

Each of those gravestones in that video represented and represents an unique person. He has made each of us a name — you and me, and each person we want to remember today, and each of those one and three quarter million people commemorated in those War Graves Cemetery gravestones — named or not named on the gravestone. And He will call his sheep by name.

"I will make you a name"

24

KING'S — TO THE
BRIGHTNESS OF THY
RISING

Opening of Epiphany Term Service; King's College,
London,
January 10th 1990

The Sixtieth Chapter of the Book of the Prophet Isaiah, and the Third
Verse: "Kings: to the brightness of thy rising."

The Christmas cards that I sent out this year were all in fact given me
by a friend who's recently returned from three years as Curator of
Decorative Arts at the Los Angeles County Museum of Art. He's come
back to enter the Fine Arts world on his own account; and it was one of
his first purchases, which, when photographed in colour, formed the subject
of my card.

It's a remarkable piece of silver-gilt, technically called a "plaquette": a
small plate; about five and a quarter inches in diameter; 16th century;
probably Flemish in origin. It's subject is the Epiphany — in relief:
hammered out and chased with great skill and artistry. The Wise Men offer
their gifts to the Christ Child, whom Mary is helping to stand on her lap.
The Infant Jesus stretches out his hands, acceptingly.

My friend, who's an expert on these things, assures me that this plaquette
was probably fixed within a drinking cup, so that whoever put the cup to
their lips would be confronted by the Epiphany, and could hardly escape
drinking in the scene, so to speak.

We meet here, in this Chapel today, at the beginning of the Epiphany
Term, to drink in afresh the mystery of the Epiphany; and, as we gather
here, I thought that text from Isaiah might, as it were, whimsically sum
up what we're on about: "*King's* — to the brightness of thy rising."

The plaquette of the Epiphany I've described, was fashioned at a particular point in what I might call the long history of Christian imagination. It's one of the many products of meditation upon the Mystery of the Epiphany. Indeed, even the Gospel record of the Epiphany — which you will know occurs only in Matthew's Gospel — is itself to some extent a product of Christian reflection and imagination.

At first, the Wise Men were thought of as astrologers — hence their concern with the stars — and were said to have come in droves, not just three; but, in time, they stabilised (or should I say "stable-ised"?) at three — no doubt because of the three gifts (though it would be disastrous if at the check-out at Tesco's one person could only carry one purchase!).

No one before Tertullian, in the 2nd. Century, ever thought of the Wise Men as kings; and probably they were only called kings because of that reference in Isaiah to kings coming to "the brightness of thy rising", and another in the Psalms to the kings of Arabia bringing gifts. In the wall paintings of the catacombs and in some Byzantine mosaics the magi wore Mithraic robes. No one actually named them until the 9th Century. Their names — Baltazar, Melchior and Caspar — first appear in an episcopal prayer book, a pontifical, at Ravenna. If you go to the Cathedral at Autun, you'll see, in stone, the three kings tucked up in bed under a large blanket: all wearing their crowns like nightcaps. An angel wakes them, to point out the star. One of the kings has his eyes wide open, in wonder; another is bleary-eyed and half-asleep — or, maybe, half-awake. The third remains sound asleep.

It was Prudentius, in the 4th Century, who began the business of giving different mystic meanings to the different gifts:

Incense doth their God disclose;
    Gold the King of Kings proclaimeth,
Myrrh his sepulchre foreshows.

And so on — until my plaquette, in, as I've said, the 16th Century — and beyond even that, till today. Because we ourselves are part of that history of the Christian imagination.

And I wonder what should be our contribution to the long history of the imaginative interpretation of the Mystery of the Epiphany. Eliot and Auden have made theirs in our generation, in poetry. What about ours? What about King's today — not just "theologs", but each faculty, bringing such different gifts.

As I pondered that question over Christmas, a present arrived in the form of a book by Bede Griffiths. It's called *A New Vision of Reality: Western Science, Eastern Mysticism and Christian Faith*. Bede Griffiths, some of you will know, was formerly a Benedictine monk, Prior of Farnborough Abbey, until he left England over thirty years ago, for India. The Ashram he lives in, in Tamil Nadu, is a pioneer attempt to found a Christian community which incorporates the customs of a Hindu Ashram and the traditional forms of Indian life and thought. It's a centre where people of different religious traditions meet together in an atmosphere of prayer.

Fr. Bede's last book, *The Marriage of East and West*, spoke, I know, to a good many young students. His latest book is a far more substantial work.

Bede Griffiths' years, his experience, his spiritual integrity, his study of theology, philosophy and science, combine to give him a prophet's perception.

His vision, like the vision of so many of the prophets, is, in the end, apocalyptic. He believes that the Western world, and all that it has touched, is breaking down. Materialist exploitation, which considers human beings only as producers and consumers, has the mark of death upon it, he maintains. The collapse of what he calls the "mechanistic society" is to him inevitable.

Bede Griffiths has steeped himself in the new physics and the new biology of Fritjof Capra and David Bohm — to whom Bishop John Robinson introduced me ten years ago. Fr. Bede avers that both science and religion now speak of a "complicated web of interdependent relationships."

It's difficult to summarize such a profound and complex book; but, fortunately, the eminent Roman Catholic lay theologian and publisher, John Todd, reviewed it recently in *The Tablet*; and I make no apology for quoting at length from that review.

John Todd wrote:

> We have become used, in the last two or three decades, to holistic ideas and hypotheses, issuing now in the Green movement. Bede Griffiths manages to bring them into coherence with an empirically and intellectually genuine spirituality. Underlying everything, implicated in everything, and driving everything on, is the divine, the Spirit. All human societies have experienced an intuition of this, and recognised themselves as part of this natural world, and part also of another world, one which Bede variously calls "the trans-mental world", "the psychic world", and "the subtle world".
>
> Here we have a major theme of the book, and an important distinction. "We must distinguish between the subtle or psychic — and the spiritual. The subtle level of consciousness is the basis for, and is followed by, the spiritual level." It's part of the success of this book to have spoken with such convincing assurance of this 'subtle' level of consciousness. The assurance comes from combining the certainties of the Christian faith with the ordinary assumption of Indian culture, that we all live in this 'subtle' world, which is more real than the discerned world. Christian mystics have witnessed to it. Indian, and mostly Tibetan, spiritual masters have delved deeply into its resources and applications.
>
> Bede Griffiths takes us through the history of the growing consciousness of humanity, as the revelation of the divine emerged in the major religions....

Finally, we reach the Cosmic Person — in the New Testament and in Hinduism, Buddhism and Islam. In the case of Christianity, Bede takes us back behind the intellectual working of the first three centuries that led to the doctrines of the Incarnation and the Trinity, to the crucial New Testament revelations of "the Son of Man", the representative man, crucified and raised up by God. Without denying the Incarnational implications, he wants us to see the Judaic New Testament text in its original freshness, and in the light of the idea of the Cosmic Person....

Towards the end, Bede outlines the way ahead for Christianity and the Church, as he sees it. The Gospel must surrender its exclusive claims, as must Islam and Judaism. There is no possibility of fruitful advance for humankind without that surrender. He sees no contradiction between such surrender and the vision of the Christian Gospel as unique....The Gospel is indeed unique; but the Church does not have to be structured in the future in the institutionally exclusive style which the interplay of Greek thought, Roman law and barbarian tribalism have inevitably given it for its first two millenia.

Bede Griffiths makes a comparison of our times with the end of the Roman Empire. But that civilisation collapsed under the impact of attack from outside, whilst ours, if he is right, is collapsing under its own failure.

John Todd concludes his review:

I believe many theologians would accept the theological dimension of the thesis expounded in the book. Perhaps the second Anglican/Roman Catholic International Commission should be asked to be attentive to it. Probably the future holds a twist no one can foresee, but much of Bede's vision seems true.

I've made that long quotation from John Todd's review not because I believe that everything in Bede Griffiths' book is right — on the contrary, I think that some things in it are almost dotty! (All the best prophets are a bit dotty!) But I believe it is a very important book, and that is underlined not least by the number of different disciplines of this College and University to which it is relevant — Physics, Biology, Mathematics, Medicine, Psychology, History, English, Classics, Geography, Theology — to name but a few.

It is, of course, possible to read a book like Bede Griffiths' — or a review of it like John Todd's — and to be intellectually excited and imaginatively stimulated. "Good stuff" we may say to ourselves, as we turn to the next book — or review — or 'phone a friend to see whether they're free for a film in the evening.

But I think that Bede Griffiths' book is too magisterial a volume to be dealt with quite so trivially.

A New Vision of Reality: Western Science, Eastern Mysticism and Christian Faith holds within it a challenge and a vision which could greatly affect and shape our lives — unless we have already some better, clearer vision of reality. But it also reveals how a man who began with the kind of Catholic certainty, which alone can carry you to the heights of a Prior

109

of a Benedictine Abbey, by being open to his uncertainties — and to the Spirit — can discover the prophetic vocation within him.

As I've suggested, I chose my text for today — *"King's*, to the brightness of thy rising" — with a smile, even a smirk. I saw myself sitting in this Chapel, over forty years ago, with my life and ministry before me; and now, as in three months time I draw my pension, I found myself grateful for the new vision of reality that I received in my years here from people like the then Dean of King's, Eric Abbott, but recognising, frankly, that it wasn't a large enough vision for the world I have come to know as I have been privileged to travel in it in Africa, India and the Pacific, as well as in the USA, and in the universities and inner cities of our land.

It is time — when materialist communism in Eastern Europe is so clearly failing — and Western capitalism is also failing, but not so clearly and dramatically: it is time — high time — to drink in afresh the Mystery of the Epiphany: to let it stir our imaginations, and minds, and hearts, and wills — to a new vision of Reality.

So, to conclude what I have to say, let me just read you the last paragraph of Fr. Bede Griffiths' book.

He writes:

> Western Europe rejected the perennial philosophy at the Renaissance and has been led step by step to the materialistic philosophy which rejects fundamental human values and exposes humankind to the contrary forces at work in the universe. The only way of recovery is to rediscover the perennial philosophy, the traditional wisdom, which is found in all ancient religions and especially in the great religions of the world. But those religions have in turn become fossilised and have each to be renewed not only in themselves but also in relation to one another, so that a cosmic, universal religion can emerge, in which the essential values of Christian religion will be preserved in living relationship with the other religious traditions of the world. This is a task for the coming centuries as the present world order breaks down and a new world order emerges from the ashes of the old.

25

LANGUAGE AND WORSHIP

Gray's Inn Chapel; January 28th 1990

1 Corinthians 14 v.19. "In the church I had rather speak five words with understanding, that by my voice I might teach others also, than ten thousand words in an unknown tongue."

Recently, the Prince of Wales has "spoken out", concerning the decline and decay of English, and the use of the Authorised Version of the Bible and the Book of Common Prayer.

With much of what the Prince had to say I was in very considerable agreement, for I regard the English of both the Authorised Version of the Bible and the Book of Common Prayer — as I'm sure you do — as two of the most beautiful examples of English prose that we possess; and would no more want to lose them than the buildings and music of their times.

Yet although language and worship is a hugely important subject, just because that is true, it cannot and must not be related only to one particular sort of language and one particular style of prose; and it seemed to me that it was in the appreciation of this point that the Prince's words could be thought somewhat lacking.

I cannot forget a staff meeting at Trinity College, Cambridge — where the Prince received a not insignificant part of his education. The Chapel Staff consisted then of the retiring Dean of Chapel, Professor Burnaby, who was also Regius Professor of Divinity; Harry Williams, the newly appointed Dean of Chapel — now a monk at Mirfield; an aged historian, F.A. Simpson, who was also a cleric and a noted eccentric; and the two chaplains — Simon Phipps and myself.

The meeting began with a request from Harry Williams, the new Dean of Chapel. "I wonder whether in future we might have the Epistle at Communion read from a modern translation?" he asked gently. "Why?" rasped out the former Dean, Professor Burnaby, rather irascibly. "Well" said Harry, "I do think St. Paul would be less difficult to understand in a modern translation." "You think the difficulty of St. Paul is one of

111

translation?" Burnaby responded. But before Harry Williams had a chance to reply, the aged Simpson, suddenly surfacing from behind us all — who had looked for all the world as though he was asleep, awoke, and wailed: "Oh, *do* let us leave St. Paul in a decent obscurity" — which was the end of Harry Williams' attempt to have the Bible read from an alternative to the Authorised Version.

Harry was nevertheless making the valid point that truth must be a primary consideration, if not *the* primary consideration, of what is read in church and chapel; and not just truth in the abstract, but what best leads that particular congregation to come to grips with the truth. On many occasions there will be no need to regard a beautiful version as an alternative to a version where the text is accurate and translated with power. I should certainly myself like those who read our lessons here in Chapel to avail themselves always of that translation — ancient or modern — they judge best to convey the truth to us; so that the words we hear we receive "with understanding" and not in an "unknown tongue".

It is, of course, by no means certain that will mean using the most modern translation. I confess, for instance, I had never so much as heard of the word "darnel" until I encountered it in the New English Bible version of the "Parable of the Wheat and the Tares" — which it calls the "Parable of the Wheat and the *Darnel*". ("The Wheat and the Weeds" would surely have been more lovely!) "Darnel" is something I am prepared to leave to the botanical scholar — and the Scrabble player.

I suspect that most of those who come here to Chapel would welcome at least the occasional reading from a modern translation — for the truth and understanding's sake. But, to my mind, the Prayer Book presents a much greater problem than the Bible; for, marvellous as the Prayer Book is for the beauty of its prose, it is, of course, shaped not only by the Gospel, but by the thought forms of the age — and not only the thought forms, but the patterns of society in the Age of the Prayer Book.

Donald Nicholls, who studied politics at the London School of Economics, and history at Cambridge, and theology at Yale, and who has taught theology and politics at Oxford, has recently produced a book, based on his 1985 Hulsean Lectures, called *Deity and Domination*, which examines the social context of common ideas and images of God: king, lord, judge, ruler; might, majesty, dominion, power, sovereignty. He traces how language used about God has reflected the passage of time and history. He brings to those ideas and images his knowledge not only of theology, but of sociology, history, political science, anthropology and literary criticism.

Take, for instance, the opening of one of the most beautiful prayers in the Prayer Book: the Prayer for the King's Majesty: "O Lord our heavenly Father, high and mighty, King of kings, Lord of lords, the only Ruler of

princes, who dost from thy throne behold all the dwellers upon earth..."
Hearing that, you can tell, almost to the century, when it was written.

It is to me unthinkable that the 1662 Prayer Book should by itself be to the people of our land today the primary vehicle of its worship. Here — well, we are, of course, an untypical grouping; and if that be recognised, no great harm will be done. But even here I believe it is important for our spiritual well-being that we should feed on more than the images and ideas of the Book of Common Prayer.

The poet, Janet Morley, who is also a theologian, has recently tried to confront the problem I have outlined with a book of prayers which, significantly, she has entitled *All Desires Known* — a phrase from, of course, the prayer at the very beginning of the Holy Communion in the 1662 Prayer Book: "Almighty God, unto whom all hearts be open, all desires known...."

Let me read you a prayer of hers I particularly like, the beginning of which could not be more different from what I will call the "Almighty God" approach of the Prayer Book.

> Vulnerable God,
> you challenge the powers that rule this world
> through the needy, the compassionate,
> and those who are filled with longing.
> Make us hunger and thirst to see right prevail,
> and single-minded in seeking peace;
> that we may see your face
> and be satisfied in you,
> through Jesus Christ, Amen.

That prayer sensitively sets within it resonances of the Beatitudes and of passages from St. Paul, but addresses an important aspect of God — his vulnerability — which the Prayer Book never acknowledges, let alone addresses.

Other prayers of Janet Morley address other aspects of God neglected by the Prayer Book. For instance:

> God our lover,
> in whose arms we are held,
> and by whose passion we are known;
> require of us also that love
> which is filled with longing,
> delights in the truth,
> and costs not less than everything,
> through Jesus Christ, Amen.

It is not, of course, only the ideas and images of domination — related to God — that reveal the historical conditioning of the Book of Common Prayer.

113

It was Harry Williams, whom I have already mentioned this morning, who, in the now despised Sixties, attacked the Book of Common Prayer for Cranmer's obsession with guilt which it revealed — which Harry Williams believed could be psychologically damaging to those who use only the Book of Common Prayer regularly for their devotions. I have never seen the contentions of Harry Williams' Essay on Theology and Self-Awareness, in the volume *Soundings*, successfully rebutted. He wrote — in 1962 —

"The God, for instance, of the Book of Common Prayer seems sometimes to be a merciless egocentric tyrant, incapable of love, and thus having to be manipulated or cajoled into receiving his children. It is one thing to make a straightforward confession of sin, as is done in the Confiteor at the beginning of the Roman Mass. It is another thing altogether to harp continuously and at length upon our utter unworthiness to approach God, as is done in Cranmer's Communion Service. The General Confession, with its repeated and elaborate protestations of guilt, looks like a desperate attempt to persuade God to accept us, on the score of our eating the maximum dust possible. Even after the Absolution we are uncertain whether we have succeeded in our project. We must be reassured by four quotations from Scripture. One would not, for instance, in an airliner, feel very comfortable if an announcement that all was well was made twice by the pilot, then by the wireless operator, then by the stewardess. One might be excused for fearing that something was seriously wrong. It is inevitable that what looks like Cranmer's deep lack of faith in God's mercy should communicate itself to many who use his liturgy, and should produce in them that spirit of bondage again unto fear from which Christ came to deliver us.... It is not being in any way denied that, on one level, Cranmer was an orthodox believing Christian. What is being suggested is that there lurked within him, along with his belief in the Christian Gospel, belief in a celestial Mr. Pontifex, unloving and incapable of being loved, who must thus be manoeuvred into giving his children what they need. This will not disturb those strong in faith. But it was for the little ones who believe in him that Christ was concerned. And who knows how many of them have been caused to stumble by our incomparably unchristian liturgy? If they were aware of the harm done then, it would matter less. But they are not. They cannot diagnose their servile attitude, their inability ever to presume anything good about themselves, as that which prevents them having life, and having it more abundantly."

Again, let me contrast the confession in Janet Morley's book of prayers:

O God, you have searched us out and known us, and all that we are is open to you. We confess that we have sinned: we have used our power to dominate and our weakness to manipulate; we have evaded responsibility and failed to confront evil; we have denied dignity to ourselves and to each other, and fallen into despair.

Of course, that is not the General, all purpose, Confession of the Prayer Book.

What I have said so far this morning is not meant to be a plea never to use the Prayer Book again. I began, you'll remember, with a tribute to the beauty of its prose. What I have been trying to do is to share my conviction that the Prayer Book provides an insufficient diet for Christian worship today. It needs to be carefully and sensitively supplemented and complemented.

One of my clerical friends, an erstwhile Sheffield vicar, Alan Billings, was deeply involved in giving help to the shocked families and friends of those crushed and killed in the Hillsborough disaster.

He sent me, this week, some of his reflections, after a year. He wrote:

If chaos is to be kept at bay, people have to be able to give expression to their sense of bewilderment as well as their feelings of deep sadness and sorrow. We live in a society which seeks to push away the reality of death on the one hand and which has progressively done away with ritual on the other. We have frowned upon too much overt expression of grief: "Don't upset yourself"; "don't become morbid"; "don't let yourself go". We have shortened the time of mourning to twenty minutes at a crematorium. We have forgotten how to pray. We have locked up our churches. After Hillsborough, there was no ritual to hand. But these emotions need ritual expression; mere words would seem inadequate and superficial. So the people of Liverpool and Sheffield, especially the young, had to devise their own way of praying, their own ritual for expressing disorientation and bewilderment as well as grief, largely without benefit of clergy: the tying of the scarves on the railings in Leppings Lane and on the barriers in the terraces at Anfield, the lighting of candles, the placing of bunches of flowers. Perhaps some of this was sheer sentimentalism or people being caught up in mass emotion; but one could not help but be moved that night by the genuineness of the prayer which was offered, and the quiet and dignified way people created holy places in the following week. These ritual acts were the prayers of the inarticulate, and the prayers for those for whom any words that might be said would not be good enough. Those of us who set great store by words and live so much of our lives in heads full of them can sometimes be very dismissive of the ritual of folk or common religion. After Hillsborough, that which is usually well hidden stood revealed: people need appropriate ritual to put them in touch with their deepest emotions and so with God.

Fortunately, the cathedral churches of Liverpool and Sheffield recognised the religious needs of people, and the services they held were not only dignified and appropriate but also played an invaluable part in helping people come to terms with what had happened: they triggered that emotional release with which the parish clergy are familiar, as the funeral address is given, or the coffin is lowered into the grave, or passes from sight at the crematorium.

The 1662 Prayer Book Burial Service would have been quite inappropriate for and incapable of meeting the needs of those bereaved at Hillsborough. And I have found that to be more and more true of the needs of the bereaved to whom I have to try and minister.

Let me therefore end what I have to say with a third prayer of Janet Morley:-

O God our disturber, whose speech is pregnant with power and whose word will be fulfilled; may we know ourselves unsatisfied with all that distorts your truth, and make our hearts attentive to your liberating voice. In Jesus Christ, Amen.

26

FAUST

Gray's Inn Chapel; February 4th 1990

Most opera goers are more than a little snooty about *Faust* — Gounod's *Faust*. If you have been — or are, I'm going to suggest you give it another chance. I've recently been to the English National Opera's production at the Coliseum, and can highly recommend it.

To tell you the truth: I only went because of the Providence of Almighty God. That's to say: because my secretary had a spare ticket the evening that I had a cancelled engagement.

But there was another aspect of Providence to it. My mother and father used to reminisce interminably about the Carl Rosa Opera Company's visits to the Bedford Music Hall in Camden Town at the turn of the century, and taught all their offspring that *Faust* was the very quintessence of culture. And the influence of family is undoubtedly another of the most powerful gifts of Providence.

There's a third reason why I went to *Faust* the other night. Gounod knew more than most musicians that melody is almost all-important in music. He didn't see why the Devil — that's to say Mephistopheles — should have all the best tunes. And if tunes are one of God's best gifts to mankind, Gounod was one of God's best ministers.

But why should I want to preach to you about *Faust*? Gounod's, not Goethe's — or Berlioz's.

Well, first of all, I should at least give you a synopsis, as they say in the best opera houses: a brief reminder of the story; because God manifests himself not only in tunes but in stories: from Adam and Eve, to the Good Samaritan, to Grimm, to Graham Greene.

Faust has reached old age when the opera opens. He's given his life to science and philosophy. Disillusioned and despairing, he decides to destroy himself, and calls the Devil to his aid.

Enter Mephistopheles!

Mephistopheles offers Faust his youth again — and sexual pleasure: that's to say Marguerite.

Act Two finds us with Marguerite. Valentin, her brother, is off to the wars — but worried — and not without reason — about the girl he's leaving behind him, unattended: Marguerite.

Seducing Marguerite — with, of course, the able assistance of Mephistopheles — is for Faust what we nowadays call "a doddle".

Valentin returns from the wars, to the sound of the Soldiers' Chorus, to discover Marguerite pregnant. He and Faust fight it out; and (again with the aid of Mephistopheles) it's a "push-over" for Faust.

Valentin, with his dying breath, curses his sister. Marguerite loses her child and goes berserk, and is put in the local lock-up — which is also the local asylum.

Faust, a bit late in the day, turns penitent, and implores her to escape with him; but she refuses. Angels proclaim Marguerite saved, but Faust damned.

Well, there's a cautionary tale! The perfect subject for a sermon — in Paris in 1859; and even in the Haymarket, four years later. But in Gray's Inn, 1990? Perhaps!

I think that what makes *Faust* not only a popular but a powerful opera now is that it still touches several nerves.

The instrumental Introduction, which passes for an Overture, is quite a profound piece of music: which makes it clear that if Gounod was good at tunes he could sometimes be expert at harmony; and that if *Faust* began as Opéra Comique it didn't end there.

In fact, I know few middle-aged to elderly people (I will not define that phrase) who have been to *Faust* and have remained unmoved by the very first scene. An old man sits alone, at a table piled high with books; and the first word he sings is: "Rien!" "Nothing!" "In vain!".

If we have any wistfulness in us, any regret, any longing, that scene, when the curtain goes up, will touch it. And I've forgotten to mention — that from without comes the sound of young girls, singing.

Perhaps the legal profession is different; perhaps its members never have a second's thought on retirement that it's all been in vain. Every minute, every hour, has so obviously been worthwhile. I can only say that most human beings I know — from other professions — immediately recognise something of themselves in Faust, when the curtain goes up.

So far, there's been nothing that's not right on the human nerve.

I suppose it's when Mephistopheles appears that we tend to be amused and entertained rather than moved. Few really believe in the Devil these days — not in a personal, personalised Devil. So it's here that we turn off. Now it's just the music that speaks to us.

I think that at this point I ought to remind you that Mephistopheles stands in a great tradition. In Christian history, the Devil is Satan, Lucifer, less frequently Beelzebub; but certainly he's personified. Most Christians, I think it's true to say, have cleaved to the idea that the Devil is a creature: not simply a kind of independent, abstract power or principle.

The New Testament powerfully portrays the personal reality of the Devil. Though vaguely defined, he is Christ's tempter and the Prince of this world. The Early Fathers offered further definitions. Satan was created by God with a good nature. He was a "top angel" who fell of his own free will, seducing many another angel *en route*.

The history of the Devil through the Middle Ages is fascinating. It fuelled the Great Witch Craze, the excesses of which provoked a reaction that was reinforced by Rationalism, the Enlightenment and Liberal Protestantism.

The Death of the Devil — or at least his nadir — occurred, to my mind, in about 1920 or 1930.

And then came Auschwitz and Buchenwald — and Hiroshima, and a recourse to the sense that we ignore the destructive impulses of our humanity, the dark side of our nature, to use the Jungian jargon — the dark side of each one of us — at our peril.

We may have difficulty with the mythology of evil — especially the Mephistophelian mythology; but again: the reality of evil is very near to the nerve of each one of us.

Faust, in fact, makes me "switch off", not so much when Mephistopheles appears, as when the Devil seems to have only one subject of conversation. That's surely another aspect of the mythology of evil. But evil is far too profound a subject: too powerful a force: too pervasive an influence, to be limited to, let alone centred upon, sexual sin. The Problem of Evil is ultimately the problem of our very existence. It's an integral part of who we are, and what the world is, and even who God is: the Dark Side of God — as Arthur Koestler called it. If Mephistopheles can only persuade us that getting unmarried girls into trouble is what evil is all about, he will have succeeded in seducing us away from confronting the real reality of evil: that evil which is to be found in good people; and not just in individuals but in societies; and not just in our enemies but our friends; and, of course, in ourselves.

Sometimes, the Devil is represented as a little imp. It's a representation which has some cogency and power. Imps are exterior to ourselves, and small, even trivial. And the Devil always succeeds in his work when he can make us believe the Mystery of Evil is all about an imp; rather a joke, and trivial.

So Mephistopheles, to me, never really succeeds in portraying the profundity, the immensity, of the Mystery of Evil. To do that in music, you have, probably, to possess the gifts of a Bach or a Beethoven.

But let me revert to the production of *Faust* at the Coliseum. That's to say: let me return from the general to the particular.

119

There are two moments in the Coliseum production which are different from any other production of *Faust* I've ever seen; and both of them are moments of genius.

In the fourth Act, the soldiers return from the War. You hear the Soldiers' Chorus before they enter. The whole town has turned out to greet them. With such music, you expect — as clearly the town's people expect — a joyous return and reunion. But, as the soldiers enter, they look like soldiers straight from the Somme. The producer has contrasted a kind of "Land of Hope and Glory" tune with the reality of War: soldiers stumbling along blind, blindfolded with bloody bandage, limping, being carried by their comrades. Gounod, of course, never intended such a scene; but the producer, Ian Judge, has delivered a master-stroke. It is the difference between Rupert Brooke and Wilfred Owen.

Similarly, in the final Act, when Marguerite is in prison — that's to say, in the asylum — each occupant of that madhouse seems at first to be mad in their own individual way. It's a remarkable study of the way madness may afflict different people so very differently. And then you notice, to your astonishment, that the inmates, the prisoners, the patients, are in fact each caring the one for the other. It isn't just a wild manic scene, but one, strangely, of care and compassion. Again: a great producer can convey remarkable and humane insight through the medium of an opera.

The end of *Faust* is what Eliot would call "unsatisfactory". The walls of the prison open. The soul of Marguerite is borne aloft to Heaven. Faust falls to his knees and prays. Mephistopheles is struck down by the Archangel's shining sword.

We are reduced to such imagery — literally reduced — for "eye hath not seen nor ear heard" how the reality of individual responsibility will ultimately be dealt with; or the final form the reality of judgment will take; or, indeed, the form, the ultimate form, of the reality of salvation. We are left with our trivial images. Words fail. But not only words. All operatic productions finally fail when we come to talk of the Last Things. Music by itself succeeds better than word-paintings of angels, and the powers of heaven and hell. For, as the words of St. Paul, inscribed on the mirror of our Chapel, so eloquently say:

> Now I know in part; but then shall I know
> even as I am known. Now abideth faith, hope,
> love: these three, but the greatest of these
> is love.

It's qualities which abide: qualities which cannot easily be staged.

Well, if you go to *Faust*, you'll get the Calf of Gold, the Jewel Song, the Flower Song and "Even bravest heart may swell. At the moment of farewell..." as well as a madhouse and a church scene; but I think you will get even more than you bargain for. You will get what each one of us has great need of: profound insight into

Man, Sin and Grace;
Death, Judgment, Heaven and Hell;
Beauty and Truth.

And such insight we all greatly need, whether we are near the beginning or the end of our life's journey.

27

SEXUALITY AND COMMUNION

Trinity College, Cambridge;
February 11th 1990

When I came to consider the very daunting subject you have asked me to address, two previous Deans of Chapel here sprang immediately to my mind.

The first, Harry Williams, whom many of you will know is now a monk at Mirfield, I heard preach a sermon in this Chapel, more than thirty years ago, which had an electrifying beginning: "I have been asked to preach this evening on 'God and Sex'" he said. "My first proposition is that God is sex."

Now, of course, Harry Williams did not mean that sex is God, but that, as the hymn ascribed to St. Ambrose states most marvellously: *Rerum Deus tenax vigor*: "God is creation's secret force".

We are created in the image of a powerful loving creator God. And our sexuality involves far more than its genital aspects. It is the well-spring of that passionate drive which is the source of art, of creativity, of work well done, of making music, and making dinner as well as making love.

The second of the Deans of Chapel who was brought to my mind by our subject is the last Dean of Chapel: Bishop John Robinson.

And my mind went back — again nearly thirty years — to the morning of October 27th 1960, when every eye in Court No.1. in the Old Bailey was fixed on the forty-one year-old Bishop of Woolwich, as he then was, as he entered the witness-box in the case of Regina v. Penguin Books Ltd., commonly known as The Trial of Lady Chatterley.

Mr. Gerald Gardiner QC, the Counsel for the Defence — later Lord Chancellor — who died only a few weeks ago — first asked John: "What do you say are the ethical merits of the book?" and he replied: "What I think is clear is that what Lawrence is trying to do is to portray the sex relationship as something essentially sacred."

This was too much for Mr. Justice Byrne, who interrupted incredulously: "He was trying to portray *what*?" "The sex relationship as something essentially sacred" insisted John; and went on "I was quoting Archbishop William Temple. He once said that Christians do not make jokes about sex for the same reason that they do not make jokes about Holy Communion, not because it is sordid, but because it is sacred, and I think Lawrence" he continued "tried to portray this relation as in a real sense something sacred, as in a real sense an act of holy communion. For him flesh was completely sacramental of spirit."

"Sexuality and Communion"

May I remind you that it was as a research student of this College that John Robinson had done what might be called "remote preparation" for those days at the Old Bailey. Elected in 1943 to the Stanton Studentship, he had taken for the subject of his dissertation: "The notion of personality and its relation to Christian theology, with particular reference to the contemporary I-Thou philosophy, and the doctrine of the Trinity and the Person of Christ." Ten years later he was to write another piece of "remote preparation" for the Old Bailey — his second book *The Body: A Study in Pauline Theology.* Although only a small book, it was recognised by scholars all over the world as a little masterpiece.

You may say: well you have related your subject to Harry Williams and John Robinson, but we have come here this evening to hear what *you* have to say on "Sexuality and Communion".

Well, yes, I accept that; but I must underline that what I have quoted already is what I, too, believe, and must discharge my debt to those two former Deans of Chapel.

Archbishop Michael Ramsey, in a recently published portrait of him, is quoted as saying "Sex is the bond of a union between two persons in their totality as persons." That powerfully resonates with our subject "Sexuality and Communion". But I have become very conscious over the years of what I will call the "journey" — the long journey — that many of us have to undertake in order to discover who we are, to discover our identity as persons, and not least our sexual identity — which identity is of course inseparably related to the question of communion between persons.

The first awareness of our sexual identity is for most of us fraught with a good deal of uncertainty and unease. The advertisements presume it always occurs in the days of our youth — which it doesn't; and is simply a natural and joyous affair — which it is, of course, for many; but the presumption can be dangerous; for we can be literally desperate with anxiety to be "normal", that is to say, heterosexual. And even within heterosexuality there are varieties of normality and abnormality.

The first awareness of our sexual identity is for some too painful for them to bear. This is specially true, of course, for many who are homosexual. At first, they keep the knowledge to themselves, and may remain "in hiding", so to speak, for years, even for a lifetime: not daring to face the implications of who they are, or to face others with them.

For most homosexuals there is, nevertheless, early on, as for others, a strong desire to come out of hiding; for their sexuality to lead to communion; but there's also often a continuing fear. It's not "the love that dare not speak its name" — to which Oscar Wilde's friend 'Bosie', Lord Alfred Douglas, referred; that may come later. It's the identity that dares not speak its name. This forces a good many to play fairly desperate games of "let's pretend", consciously or unconsciously.

There are, of course, various reasons for who we are and what we are. No one reason for any particular person's sexual identity is a certainty. Some may be who and what they are sexually for psychological reasons: different reasons for different people. For others, there may be more biological and genetic reasons. Whatever the cause and origin, the fact of our identity is eventually experienced as real, incontrovertible, and "natural", for both heterosexual and homosexual. But for the homosexual there is a particularly painful question of hiding and coming out of hiding in order to establish communion with others.

The question of the identity of the lesbian is, of course, as important as the question of the identity of the heterosexual and the homosexual; but although masculine and feminine homosexuality have much in common, they are not necessarily the same.

At this point, if time allowed, I would have liked to have inserted a long section on Friendship. Because, really, friendship is another word for Communion, and, as the American Catholic Andrew Greeley, wrote in his book *The Friendship Game* "All intimate friendships are sexual". And friendship is the school both of sexuality and communion.

How I would love to delay and dally now with the subject of, say, Shakespeare and Friendship, and Aelred of Rievaulx and Friendship, and C.S. Lewis and Friendship, and Forbes Robinson (John Robinson's uncle) and Friendship.

The subject could not be more important in itself, or more relevant to our subject of Sexuality and Communion. Let me just read you a few paragraphs from Andrew Greeley which will focus what I have in mind:

> It is frequently assumed that love is what man feels for his mate or for the person who is substituting for his mate, and that friendship is an emotion that he feels for someone with whom he is not sleeping. But such an assumption is based on pre-Freudian notions of sexuality, since it supposes that love is sexual and friendship is not. But all human friendship has profoundly sexual overtones, and marriage just happens to be that sexual relationship which provides a context for sexual intercourse. There are a number of conclusions that follow. Marriage

is a friendship. If it is not a friendship, then it is not a satisfactory human relationship. And if it is not a satisfactory human relationship, the pay-off in sexual intercourse between husband and wife is bound to be considerably less than satisfactory. Or, to put the matter more dramatically, sleeping with a member of the opposite sex is fully pleasurable only when one is sleeping with a friend. If the powerful physical urges of courtship and early marriage are not sustained by a developing friendship between husband and wife, then they rapidly decline both in power and pay-off.

The marriage relationship is therefore the primordial human friendship. The surrender of man and woman to each other in intercourse is a symbol of their friendship and a powerful reinforcement of that friendship. It is possible to look at the marriage relationship as a laboratory for a study of the dynamics of friendship. It's not the only kind of friendship nor the only kind of sexual relationship (since all intimate friendships are sexual), but it is that sexual relationship where both the terror and the ecstasy are most obvious and most explicit. The only vocabulary that we have that enables us to discuss friendship adequately is the vocabulary that was developed to describe romantic love, a love that we are arguing can only survive in marriage if we happen to be married to a friend.

Sex without friendship is at best unsatisfactory, and at worst, inhuman. Intercourse between two people who are not friends is a sham, since they are making love where in fact there is no love.

Let me say at this point that I am aware that my sermon is only one of a course on "Life in the Body". And I cannot say too strongly that the Body is the very means of Communion. It is, so to speak, the matter of the Sacrament.

Our sexuality is an important means, perhaps the most important means, though not the only means, by which, in the body, we learn to be lovers and transcend our separateness. Our awareness of each other as men and women, women and men, our acceptance of our affection for each other as God's creations, our delight in the special gifts that each of us brings to a relationship, because of our sexuality, our reverence for, and tenderness towards, the embodied persons we are — all these are evidence for, and ways of responding to, the blessings that God has given to us through our being sexual beings, yet not simply separate sexual beings. Most profoundly, when sexual intercourse is recognised as a Christian sacrament, our bodies become the means by which God teaches us what it means to be ourselves without holding back, to love another with generosity and enthusiasm.

Our sexual relationships, whoever we are, are meant to be occasions of joy: moments when we discover the richness of the life-giving and life-enhancing meeting with the person we love: with, indeed, communion. More: our sexual encounters can be moments when our physical and emotional connecting with a beloved human being can open our ears and hearts to the expression and the promise of our loving relationship with

God Himself: with a Communion greater even than human communion; and all this in and through embodied relationships.

But I must also say that many of us, in and through our upbringing, have developed a kind of split between body and mind, body and soul, body and spirit, which is deeply unchristian in the theological sense, and is often therefore, and thereby, destructive of communion. So the healing of that split is one of the most important undertakings many of us have to embark upon, and that healing may take many years and need a good deal of skilled help and much patience with ourselves.

Our sexuality is a gift that calls us to an intimacy, which, in the centre of our being, affirms and confirms that our bodies are not to be down-graded or ignored. Our bodies are good, a fact that has been reinforced for us in and through the Incarnation, by which, as an ancient theological formula states, our humanity in its wholeness has been "taken into the Godhead."

Yet I dare not conclude without saying that the great power of our sexuality can be used as an instrument of our destruction as well as the source of our joy. Our sexuality apart from God can give rise to jealousy and strife, to manipulation and exploitation, dividing and alienating us just as surely as it can bring us together in communion.

As I've already hinted, it's over thirty years now since I was a Chaplain here. In the intervening years, I have seen something of a good many of the well over a thousand undergraduates I got to know when I was here. I have taken a good many of their marriages, and talked with some of them when their marriages were breaking down. I have talked with some when they discovered they were "gay" — maybe after they had got married — and felt it my privilege to help them towards embodied sacramental love: using their sexuality as the very means of communion.

Looking back, I am clear on one point: that whatever subject one reads at university, one of the primary purposes of being here is to take a few steps forward along the way of discovering one's own identity, and of healing such splits as there are within the psycho-physical unity — in the profoundest sense of that term — that each one of us is. So that however helpful or unhelpful my words to you may be this evening, I am clear that you have chosen as important a subject as you could possibly have addressed. But do not regard this course of sermons as the end: think of it simply as steps on the journey to who you are, and who you are becoming: to the glory of Him who gave us each our unique identity, who will be with us all our steps upon our Journey, and who is Himself our Journey's End.

And did not that wisest of men, William Shakespeare, say that Journey's End would be "Lover's Meeting"? Our sexuality, that is to say — in more technical language — leading to Communion.

28

HE WAS TAKEN FROM PRISON AND JUDGMENT

Westminster Abbey; Easter Day 1990

Psalm 142 v.9: "Bring my soul out of prison: that I may
give thanks unto thy name".

and

The Book of the Prophet Isaiah 53 v.8:

"He was taken from prison and judgment".

I've never noticed till this Easter, how often Christ's Resurrection is referred to as a prison break-out.

Because half of my mind this last week, like everyone else's here in Britain, has been on Strangeways gaol and other prisons — and, of course, with Nelson Mandela's arrival here today, after all those years in prison — every Easter reference to escape from prison seems this year to stand out a mile.

How marvellous it was to begin this service with that most lovely Easter carol, "This joyful Eastertide", which states so simply yet so boldly:

Had Christ, that once was slain,
Ne'er burst his three-day prison,
Our faith would be in vain.

And we have also been singing:

Come, ye faithful, raise the strain
    Of triumphant gladness:
God hath brought his Israel
    Into joy from sadness.
'Tis the Spring of souls today:
    Christ has burst his prison....

In my cynical way, I'd thought at first it's because "prison" and "risen" rhyme so obviously that you find them so often together in the Easter hymns. And then I noticed: "Come ye faithful" was written first in Greek, by St. John Damascene — no less, and in the 8th Century. The metaphor of prison — of Christ breaking out of prison — clearly goes back to the very earliest years of the Christian Church.

And no wonder.

For the imprisonment of the tomb, and of the grave, and of death itself, as we all experience it, first with those we love, and then for ourselves, could hardly be more complete and final. Death is so often like the slamming of a prison door. And the overthrow of death itself is literally like escape from prison. Where I was preaching this morning — on a working class housing estate just across the Thames, a woman was in the congregation whose son had been murdered earlier this year. She had not been to church for years until her son was killed: but this Easter, with its message of release from the prison of death, clearly meant much to her.

And yet: marvellous as is the truth of Christ's own "bursting from the spiced tomb", as the great hymn of St. Patrick describes it, there is more to the Resurrection even than that. It is more even than a Gospel about the overcoming of death.

Resurrection Life is something for the Christian which begins now. Easter is not only the destruction of death. It's the celebration of the life — the Resurrection Life — which is available to us now: to inspire and empower us.

John Bunyan, even when he was in prison, wrote to a friend:

> For though men keep my outward man
>   Within their bolts and bars,
> Yet, by the faith of Christ, I can
>   Mount higher than the stars.

There's a superb anthology by Lady Elizabeth Bassett, called *Each in his Prison*. In it she has gathered together the writings of people in very different kinds of captivity. She has culled them from novels, biographies, memoirs, poems, newspaper articles. They describe the experience of political prisoners, prisoners of war, prisoners of conscience, the kidnapped and the hi-jacked, and those simply serving sentences in gaol. There is much in that anthology which is harrowing, but much also to inspire those who may otherwise be crushed by the daily evidence of man's inhumanity to man. It's clear that those who have suffered most are often most able to forgive and to understand. Strength to face intolerable conditions clearly comes to those who believe in a God of love; and, indeed, such faith may be born through suffering. *Each in his Prison* is a celebration of the human spirit's capacity to transcend suffering, to rise above it, and make of it a creative, rather than a destructive experience.

One of the persons whose books are quoted, Julia de Beausobre, I was privileged to meet when I was a curate, not far from here, forty years ago. I was leading a lunch time discussion group in the Colonial Office, then on Millbank; and Eric Abbott, later the much-loved Dean of this Abbey, suggested I should invite Julia to address the group. I had read her story: how her husband had been imprisoned in Russia and then shot, in 1933; how she was herself appallingly tortured in the same concentration camp. When I first met her — as she got out of a taxi, at the bottom of Great Peter Street — I expected her to be emaciated and crushed. But when I first set eyes on her, it was her radiance which astounded me.

When I asked her how she survived in the concentration camp, she said quietly four unforgettable words: "It was simple really", and then went on: "I tried to love my torturers; because if I loved them, I would not be adding to the evil in the world by hating them. And if I loved them, it just could be that it might have some effect on them, reducing the evil they did and reducing the amount of evil in the world." "So" she said "at the simplest level of prudence, Christ's way of love and trust and forgiveness seemed to be the only way."

It's people like Julia de Beausobre who have helped me to understand the meaning of Resurrection Life as something to be experienced now: not only by people in prisons or concentration camps, but imprisoned perhaps by circumstances, or by some disability that might otherwise imprison and embitter them totally.

Resurrection Life is something which is to be experienced and shared personally; but it should also inspire and sustain us in social action: in action for justice and peace.

With the image of prison and the reality of prison so inescapably in our hearts and minds this Easter, let me just read you some sentences spoken in Parliament eighty years ago by Winston Churchill when he was Home Secretary. He said: "The mood and temper of the public in regard to the treatment of crime and criminals is one of the most unfailing tests of the civilisation of any country. A calm and dispassionate recognition of the rights of the accused — and even of convicted criminals — against the State; tireless efforts towards the discovery of curative and regenerative processes; and an unfaltering faith that there is a treasure, if you can only find it, in the heart of every man — these are the symbols which in the treatment of crime and criminals mark and measure the stored-up strength of a nation, and are the sign and proof of the living virtue in it."

This particular Easter, we must pray that our nation will be renewed and inspired with the power of the Resurrection in its concern for those in our prisons.

Today, Nelson Mandela has arrived in our land after nearly thirty years of imprisonment. A few days ago I had been talking about him with Bishop Trevor Huddleston, who had been with him for several days in Sweden

129

— they had last met in Johannesburg, more than thirty years ago, just before Mandela was imprisoned. Trevor Huddleston said that he was astounded at the entire absence of bitterness in Mandela; who had said to him that he had lived on Hope in prison. Those who visited him in prison knew he had burst his prison before he was released — through Hope.

"Bring my soul out of prison": something like that prayer of the Psalmist must often have been in Nelson Mandela's heart and mind.

Today we make that prayer for all who are unjustly imprisoned: for all oppressed minorities and races. And we make it in the power of that Resurrection which is a blazing beacon to us even now in this world.

> Had Christ, that once was slain,
> Ne'er burst his three-day prison,
> Our faith would be in vain.
> But now hath Christ arisen.
> Alleluia!

29

VAN GOGH

Gray's Inn Chapel; April 29th 1990

Luke 24 v.26: "Ought not Christ to have suffered these things,
and to enter his glory?"

Van Gogh first fell in love in Brixton. That you may not know — though you will probably know this year is the centenary of his death.

He was born in Holland, in 1853, in his father's parsonage at Groot Zundert, near the Belgian frontier. He was the eldest son. His favourite brother, Theo, who would be his moral and material stand-by to the end of his days, was born four years later.

When Vincent was sixteen, he began work at the Groupil Art Gallery at the Hague, and then moved to their branch in Brussels. When he was twenty he was transferred to London, to their Southampton Street premises off the Strand.

Vincent found lodgings in Brixton, at a house in Hackford Road, of which he made an interesting drawing. It was the landlady's daughter there who cast her spell on Vincent. Alas, she spurned his advances, and drove him to the depths of despair.

You can find all this — and more — in a fascinating book which has recently been published: *Young Vincent: The Story of Van Gogh's Years in England*. It's by Martin Bailey, who tells how, only nineteen years ago, a Camberwell postman, Paul Chalcraft, an amateur artist, who paints when he's finished his delivery rounds, discovered the precise address where Van Gogh had lived in London, in Brixton and Kennington, round the corner from where I live.

Most people I know delight in Van Gogh's work: his flowering cherries, his unstable chairs, his self-portraits, and so on.

This year, is, of course, a good time to learn a little more about his life, since, as I say, it's the centenary of his death: on July 29th 1890.

In fact, Vincent's life went from bad to worse. He was sent to Paris after only a year at Groupil's London branch, but, after hardly more than a year in Paris, he was given the sack. It was about then that his obsession with the Bible began. He returned to England, and was, very briefly, a schoolmaster at Ramsgate, and then at Isleworth; but he became more and more obsessed with his religious vocation: he preached his first sermon at Kew Road Methodist Church in November 1876; but in May 1877, aged twenty-four, he went to Amsterdam, with a view to studying theology. Surprise, surprise: he failed to pass the entrance exam. This did not stop him becoming a lay evangelist to the miners of a small Flemish town: a place of terrible social conditions. He himself lived in abject poverty.

He showed immense zeal; nursed the sick; and slept on bare boards; but it wasn't long before he was relieved of even this job. In a way, this was a blessing; because it was at this time that he announced his decision to become an artist.

He picked up with prostitutes, whom he used as models, especially one, Christine, who lasted as a companion for twenty months, though she had a five-year-old daughter, and was pregnant again, and survived on alcohol. It was more loneliness than love that drew them together; and they never married.

It's difficult to exaggerate, even now that Vincent was living back across the Channel, the importance of his years in England. It was the English illustrators of the day who dominated his work as artist. His mind was often also shaped by English writers, like Dickens, and by the paintings he had studied in places like the National Gallery and the Dulwich Art Gallery, while he continued to be wistful for London, and for the Thames itself and its dockyards. The grief-stricken old man sitting in a chair, which Vincent painted only three months before he died, was based on Arthur Houghton's illustration for Dickens' *Hard Times*.

But Vincent was already now mingling with many of the great artists, and learning from them: Toulouse-Lautrec, Gauguin, Seurat and Pissaro. Everyone knows about his cutting off his ear after a row with Gauguin, in which, in fact, Vincent tried to kill him.

In 1889, when he was thirty-six, he was admitted, at his own request, to the asylum at Saint-Remy, near Arles. There were intervals of sanity, it should be said, between Vincent's spells of madness. But in 1890, he shot himself. He was only thirty-seven when he died.

It's as tragic a life as you can imagine.

And yet, a dozen years earlier, in November 1878, Vincent had written to his brother Theo:

> "As you know, one of the deep-rooted, fundamental
> truths, not only of the Gospel but of the Bible

as a whole, is 'the light that shines in the
darkness'. Through darkness to light."

And, only eight months before, he had written to Theo:

"By loving steadfastly what is really worthy
of love, and not wasting it on the insignificant,
the empty, the insipid, we gradually acquire more
light, and consequently, greater strength."

You might say that Van Gogh's life as an artist became a kind of search
for light. Gradually, his paintings emerge from a fitful light that scarcely
penetrates the darkness, into a light that you can hardly bear.

There's the light above the potato-eaters: just a single light in the centre
of a very dark room over the table. Then there's the lights above the
billiard-table in a night café. And then the lights grow into great stars in
the night sky. Later, the light bursts forth and brims over, unimpeded, on
cornfields, and sunflowers, until everything's ablaze with light and glory.
The strong sun of the south eventually won, and enabled Vincent to paint
his greatest works.

And yet, Vincent's last words were: "There'll never be an end to human
misery."

When he managed to see the whole earth full of glory, he was probably
out of his mind.

Whatever do we make of that literally ghastly and glorious story? As
an artist, journeying from Darkness to Light, while as a human being,
journeying in the very opposite direction.

I'm sure we mustn't attempt some simplistic reconciliation of those
opposites and contradictions.

I went last week to the Tate Gallery to look once again at one of the last
of Van Gogh's paintings, and, therefore, one of those most full of light:
"The Wheatfield with Cypresses". And, as I stood there, I found myself
asking: "Was Vincent's suffering, in some inscrutable way, essential? Had
he not suffered, would his paintings have been what they were? Would
this painting have been what it is?"

I could not really answer my own question.

Clearly we should be thankful for the glory that artists — like Van
Gogh, but of one sort and another — reveal. Maybe we need to be more
aware of the huge price many of them have to pay. Often they seem to
have to undergo their own crucifixion if Light is to shine in — and out of
— their darkness.

And, of course, there's something of the artist in all of us: so what was
true for Van Gogh is true to some extent of us all.

Does the text I have chosen today — not to expound in any traditional
and conventional way, but to set as a kind of banner above all I have had
to say — does it say something about the rudiments and elements of our

133

very existence: "Ought not Christ to have suffered these things — and to enter his glory?" — in order to enter his glory.

Is there any way to enter Light — glory — without suffering — except by suffering? Not only for Christ in his humanity but for us who share his humanity as he shares ours, and thus share his divinity and his glory. Is there some sort of necessity in the suffering?

I must leave you with that question. Or, rather, I must let Van Gogh's life leave you with an unanswered question. We raise ourselves to God, I believe, as much by asking the right questions as by giving the right answers.

"Ought not Christ to have suffered these things — and to enter his glory?"

30

THE DOORS WERE SHUT ....FOR FEAR

Gray's Inn Chapel; May 6th 1990

The Gospel according to John 20. v.19: "....the doors were shut where the disciples were assembled for fear of the Jews..."

Fear of the Jews was for the disciples more religious than racial; though, in the end, it was like most fear, fear for their very existence and identity. It may have involved fear of the future; fear of the unknown; fear of failure, and, maybe, other fears besides; but in the end, it was, as I say, fear for their life, their existence, their identity. And there is only one basic answer to that fear, and that is something which assures you that your identity will never be taken away. And that is what Easter is about.

Now, in a sense, that concludes my sermon; and the rest is illustration: a story, a piece of history, to illustrate and drive home the point I've already made.

So here's the illustration: the story.

My dining-room table in my home in Kennington is something I particularly treasure. It was given me by an old lady, not long before she died. She was a very unusual old lady, who, in her late seventies, had persuaded me, rather against my better judgment, to let her what she called "help" me, in the South London parish where I was then vicar. Sometimes her "help" would consist of re-arranging to her liking the flowers my parishioners had already arranged to theirs.

I had met her when I was taking her grand-daughter's wedding to a Trinity Cambridge undergraduate when I was chaplain there. She was a remarkable and redoubtable old lady. She had, for instance, sat cross-legged on Northolt Aerodrome during the Second World War until "Cousin Oliver" — as she called him — Oliver Lyttelton, then a Cabinet Minister — eventually caved in, and gave her permission to visit the people she called "my gels": YWCA workers in places like New Guinea. Hilda, Hilda

Grenfell, had for years bicycled around London in trousers, with her dress pinned up with safety pins, ready to be lowered when she took off her trousers on reaching her destination.

She would happily sit for hours under the mulberry tree in my vicarage garden in Camberwell, translating from the French, into impeccable English, the then untranslated works of Teilhard de Chardin. "I won't disturb you for more than a moment" she would say, as she "just popped in" from the garden to share with me the nugget she had just unearthed from de Chardin; but of course, that "moment" was always of somewhat uncertain duration.

One day she said to me: "Dear Eric..." — and I always got a little apprehensive when she addressed me thus, for I knew it usually signalled another "little" request. But on this occasion my apprehension was misplaced. "Dear Eric" she said: "I want you to have a rather special table of mine..." She was at the time preparing to make one of her last moves to where, at least in theory, she could be more looked after.

So, later that morning, we went off to her flat in Cadogan Square, and she showed me the table. It was a small Victorian, three-legged, rosewood, round table, about four feet in diameter. Hilda called it her "peace-making" table, because, she said, "Daddy" — General Sir Neville Lyttelton — when he succeeded Kitchener in the South African Command in October 1900, had had it shipped out to South Africa; and she remembered how much he had striven to get people who once had been enemies to sit round it, having to face each other in close proximity.

Hilda could clearly remember John Buchan sitting at that table. Not long after, he would marry her cousin, Susan Grosvenor. His first job, as a member of Milner's "Kindergarten", as it was somewhat unkindly called, concerned the refugee camps at Bloemfontein that were known to the world as Concentration Camps; and Hilda and her sister had been taken as girls of sixteen and seventeen to see the camps. Their father had gone with them, and had told them it was part of their education to see them. Over a hundred thousand white, and forty thousand coloured people, were herded together, with terrifying mortality, because of disease. Hilda Grenfell never forgot visiting those camps.

Neither did she forget the erstwhile Boer generals — Botha, de Wet and Smuts — coming to sit round that little table with her father. He was of the opinion that a home was a far better place really to meet people than any H.Q.

It's significant that long after their South African service had ended, the coterie who continued the association of Milner's "Kindergarten" back in England, concerning themselves with international affairs from the perspective of the Commonwealth, called itself *The Round Table*, and, indeed, gave that title to a quarterly journal they founded, in 1910, which continues to this day.

136

When Hilda Grenfell that morning — sixty years on — showed me that round table, I gladly and gratefully accepted it; but I immediately asked the question which seemed obvious to me: "Did you ever see a black South African sitting at that table?" Hilda was silent. She could see that to one of my generation the question was obvious; but she also knew that at the turn of the century, in South Africa, what I implied by my question was ludicrously out of the question. She ended her silence by going to her shelves and picking out a book of Winston Churchill's — to whom her sister's husband Charles Masterman became private secretary when Winston was Home Secretary. It was a beautifully bound edition of a book of Churchill's I did not then know. It was about his South African adventures, and called *London to Ladysmith*.

I read again this week the passage she had read to me that morning, and I read it sitting at what I will call Hilda's round table. Winston Churchill wrote:

"The true and original root of Dutch aversion to British rule is not Majuba Hill nor the Jameson raid but the abiding fear and hatred of the movement that seeks to place the native on a level with the white man... The servant is to be raised against the master; the Kaffir is to be declared the brother of the European, to be constituted his legal equal, to be armed with political rights. The dominant race is to be deprived of their superiority... 'Educate a Kaffir?' said the Boer. 'Ah, that's you English all over...They were put here by God Almighty to work for us...Insist on their proper treatment, will you? Ah, that's what we're going to see about now. We'll settle whether you English are to interfere with us before this war is over.'"

Thus Winston Churchill: 1900.

But although the Boers did not settle that question then, and, of course, lost the war, the doors of apartheid remained shut for fear; and the curious fact is that the attitudes of those who had lost the war conquered many of those who had conquered them; so that until now — ninety years on — the doors of apartheid have been shut upon the "Kaffirs", not only by the Boers but by many English and others who settled in South Africa, and became so to speak, Boer-ish — until these last memorable weeks.

Let me now repeat my first paragraph.

"Fear of the Jews was for the disciples more religious than racial; though, in the end, it was like most fear, fear for their very existence and identity. It may have involved fear of the future; fear of the unknown; fear of failure, and, maybe, other fears besides; but in the end, it was, as I say, fear for their life, their existence, their identity. And there is only one basic answer to that fear, and that is something which assures you that your identity will never be taken away. And that is what Easter is about."

My Easter this year could hardly have been more memorable.

After the service on Maundy Thursday evening, in Kennington, at which I had preached, I was asked to meet four young men who were members of the ANC. They had just arrived in England to study at Lancaster. They were all, of course, black: all under twenty-four. One of them had been in prison for two years for his ANC activities. Another had had his lower arm blown off by a grenade. All of them were impoverished to a degree, possessing little more than the clothes they stood up in.

I asked them to accompany me to Westminster Abbey on Easter Sunday, where I was preaching in the afternoon. The Dean kindly placed them in his own stall. They had never heard music like the Abbey's or seen a building like it. Immediately after the service, I took them to Livingstone's tomb, in the centre aisle, where he had been buried in 1874.

I pointed out to them the words that Livingstone himself had written which were cut into the stone that marks his grave: "May heaven's rich blessing come down on every one — American, English, Turk — who will help to heal this open sore of the world."

As we walked out of the Abbey, the young men who had been imprisoned began to discuss my sermon.

I had said in the pulpit that I had never noticed till this Easter how often Christ's Resurrection is referred to as a "prison break-out". But this year, the events at Strangeways Gaol, and Nelson Mandela's arrival in England that very day, had made all the Easter references to "escape from prison" stand out a mile. The Abbey choir had begun the service with that most lovely Easter carol "This Joyful Eastertide", which states so simply yet so boldly:

Had Christ that once was slain
Ne'er burst his three-day prison
Our faith would be in vain.

My young ANC friend used a word to me which astonished me. He said "I liked your sermon very much. I particularly liked the way you 'contextualised' it and related Easter to Mandela's release from prison..."

I had to remind myself where that young man had come from — not least from prison — and how far he had come from that derisory, scornful phrase with which Churchill had sought to epitomise the Boer: "Educate a Kaffir? That's you English all over...They were put here by Almighty God to work for us."

On Easter Sunday evening I was privileged to represent Christian Action at a supper party at the home of one of our honorary Benchers, the Commonwealth Secretary-General, Sir Shridath Ramphal, to welcome Nelson Mandela. My predecessor as Director of Christian Action, Canon John Collins, had promised Mandela, on his last visit to England before he was arrested, to do all he could to see that black South Africans, arrested and taken to court, had British barristers to defend them; and that, if they were sentenced, their dependants would be looked after. In order to keep his promise, Canon Collins caused Christian Action to found International Defence and Aid, and thus, for thirty years, the promise made to Mandela has been kept. So Easter Sunday night, I stood in, so to speak, for Canon Collins, who, alas, died in 1981.

It meant I was privileged to talk with Nelson Mandela, and able to assess for myself his remarkable bearing and presence, his stillness and inner security, his freedom from bitterness and fear. I have rarely met anyone who more exemplified what Easter is about: the conquering of fear of the future, of the unknown, fear for identity and existence. It wasn't only the intellectual, but the spiritual stature of this "Kaffir" which was so remarkable.

Of course, the way ahead is still fraught with danger. The fears of the white South African minority will not disappear overnight, nor the fear of the oppressed black majority. President De Klerk said, after the three days of talks this week: "Those who are terribly afraid will, I think, be against us." But there are at least some real signs of Resurrection in South Africa, and of the healing of this "open sore of the world".

Before I finish what I have to say this morning, I should like to read you a poem. It is one with a significant title: and has significance, I believe, for the church and the world, and not least for the church which is gathered here this morning in this Chapel. It's entitled "In Search of a Round Table" and it's by Chuck Lathrop.

Concerning the why and how and what and who
of ministry,
One image keeps surfacing:

A table that is round.

It will take some sawing
to be roundtabled,
some redefining
and redesigning.
Some redoing and rebirthing
of narrowlong Churching
can painful be —
for people and tables.
It would mean no daising
and throning,
for but one king is there,
and he was a footwasher, —
at table, no less.
And what of narrowlong ministers —
when they confront
a roundtable people,
after years of working up the table

to finally sit at its head,
only to discover
that the table has been turned round?

They must be loved into roundness,
for God has called a People;
not 'them and us'.
'Them and us'
are unable
to gather round —
for at a roundtable,
there are no sides
and All are invited
to wholeness and to food.

At one time

our narrowlong Churches
were built to resemble the cross
but it does no good
for buildings to do so,
if lives do not.
Roundtabling means
no preferred seating,
no first and last,
no betters and no corners
for the 'least of these'.
Roundtabling means
being with,
a part of,
together, and one.
It means room for the Spirit
and gifts
and disturbing profound peace for all.

We can no longer prepare for the past.

We will and must and are called
to be Church,
and if He calls for other than roundtable
we are bound to follow.

Leaving the sawdust
and chips, designs and redesigns
behind,
in search of and in the presence of
the Kingdom
that is His and not ours.

31

THE BAPTISM OF FRANCES UNDERHILL

Gray's Inn Chapel; May 13th 1990

This afternoon, I shall be baptising, here in Chapel, the infant Frances Underhill. Her grandfather, Michael Underhill, a much loved former Bencher, many of you will have known. He is commemorated in David Peace's engraving on glass which so beautifully adorns our Chapel.

Baptism should be separated as little as possible from the normal life of the church itself, so I like to take any opportunity I can to join the afternoon Baptism with this service by preaching on Baptism — as I note I did last in a sermon I preached here two years ago, on *Baptism and Piero della Francesca.**

Perhaps I might begin today by saying that I've never regretted, as a curate in Westminster or as a vicar south of the river, having to face, time and time again, the challenge of having to put in simple, direct words just what Baptism means, when confronted by, let us say, Rose and Joe Warner; he, a lorry driver, and she, the woman who does the school meals, and who live on the ninth floor of a tower block.

When I'd got inside their flat, and finished admiring the baby, and sat myself down amongst the drying nappies — in those days — and got them to turn off the T.V., because what we were going to discuss was even more important than *Coronation Street*, I'd be well aware I'd got quite a tough task ahead; because the likelihood of their being regular church-goers was small, and yet they "wanted it done". And it seemed to me that if this was still something which, out of inarticulate faith — which often could barely be called faith at all — they were still willing to come and ask the church to do, it ill behoved us to refuse to serve them, in the way that they asked. (It's odd how the church loves to be called the 'servant' church, but

---

*Judge Not   p.181

seems not to realise that servants just get on and do what they're asked to do!) Yet I had to use the occasion as profitably as possible.

I think it's still worth asking: Whatever is it that makes anyone ask for Baptism? — particularly in secular, non-church-going, urban, working class areas.

Let me hazard some kind of an answer.

It always interested me that quite often when I was a vicar, if the man opened the door, he'd quickly say: "Ah, vicar, I'll get the wife". And often, eventually, the man would say: "To be quite honest, it was her, really, who wanted it done". But the mother would say, often quite anxiously: "Well, I know it sounds odd — 'cos I know I don't come to church often — but I'd still like it done."

Why? Why is it that so often — in my experience — there's a considerable difference between the response of the man and the woman to baptism? Is it that women are more religious than men? I doubt it. But I certainly suspect that the psychological difference — the deeply psychological, even psycho-physical, difference — between a man and a woman has a good deal to do with it.

Perhaps we could put it this way: that it's not easy for everyone to have children; and miscarriages are still not infrequent; and even these days, when often the man may be present at the birth of the child, the child is nevertheless in a sense more part of the mother; and even now there's still some danger in childbirth, and you never quite know what may go wrong. The actual birth of a baby, a bouncing baby, is a very natural and elemental reason most often for thanksgiving. There is an inarticulate need to say thank you to someone — someone who in the case of many people must still be given a capital S; and they look to the church for a language, indeed for a liturgy, of thanksgiving and celebration, which takes their thanksgiving further than, say, just a "knees-up". They need a Christening "robe" of language, and a celebratory and special building, too, to "robe" the occasion.

And when the baby is born, it is evidently something wonderful — something literally that: wonder-full; and something of a mystery. There can be very few parents who, looking at their baby, and what they have brought into the world, do not feel something of a sense of awe, and wonder, and mystery.

But there can be few parents who are not also at least a shade anxious. A baby is so evidently helpless and damageable. At this time of all times parents feel in need: in need of more than they, and the combined forces of mothers-in-law, can provide.

I am not suggesting that anyone would say all this. Simple people think inarticulately, and most of us are, where and when the birth of a baby is concerned, very inarticulate and simple. I do not myself doubt that something of this is there; and it is in this kind of need that people respond to those lovely phrases in the Baptism service like: "Doubt not therefore, but earnestly believe, that he loveth this child..." and rejoice to hear that Jesus himself said: "Suffer the little children to come unto me, and forbid them not; for of such is the Kingdom of Heaven."

But I have to tell you that what I have said so far would satisfy few theologians. They would say that, so far, I have given an entirely inadequate theology of Baptism. And I would agree. But I am speaking, in this instance, as a pastoral theologian, and describing merely one baptism visit; and I would maintain any first visit to a home which expects to get across a great deal of dogma and doctrine is bound to fail. No marriage guidance counsellor worth their salt would attempt on a first visit to do much more than establish a relationship — or would expect to do most of the talking themselves.You have in all pastoral work to start where people are, and go only very slowly towards where you think they should be.

But let us go a little further into the doctrine of Baptism.

Sometimes you hear people say that an infant is "made a child of God" by baptism. It says so in the Catechism. I, personally, prefer the very simple statement of F.D. Maurice, Professor at King's College London and Chaplain of Guy's hospital, in the mid-19th Century — whose thoughts were usually very complex. He said that "Baptism is the proclamation by God that this child is a child of mine."

It's, if you like, a proclamation of who and what a human being is. That phrase puts theology at the very heart of our anthropology.

When I was Vicar of St. George's, Camberwell, I used to enjoy baptisms as much as any other service — not least because, with several baptisms together, there was often a larger congregation than usual; and everyone imagined the others were "regulars"! And I would particularly enjoy taking hold of one of the babies and saying to the mother,and to the other mothers, fathers, relatives and members of the congregation: "Is this a piglet?" "No" the mother would invariably exclaim, sometimes frantically — "It's my Georgie". But I asked the question intentionally, so that, gradually, I could work out with her and the congregation what is the difference between a piglet and a human being. What would Joe Warner — as well as Rose — think it takes to become a human being: a truly human being? And how might the church help them to help their baby become a truly human being? Animal feeding stuffs for piglets; Kellogg's Cornflakes for kids — muesli, of course, in Hampstead. But what does it take to *feed* a child of God? to enable that child to become what it is? I was always aware that I was asking one of the most profound theological questions that could ever be asked.

Two more illustrations from my experience as a parish priest.

At the first baptism I ever took in St. George's Camberwell, the child was named Olayemi Olushola Odanye. The child was Nigerian, and the family was living in, literally, two rooms in Boundary Lane, Camberwell. I learnt the baby's name off by heart because I could not have pronounced it had I not learnt it; and it has stuck in my memory for thirty years. But I could not simply proclaim "this child is a child of God" and not help them with their housing problem, and with the problem with their neighbours — who thought that the smell from the cooking of Nigerian food betokened the presence of the devil. Baptism and belonging were inseparable. It could not be an isolated, separated affair; a hole-and-corner affair; something for that family alone. Proclaiming someone to be a child of God means always proclaiming their membership of the whole family of mankind: the family that can say together *"Our* Father".

My second illustration is similar to the first.

Again, when I was in Camberwell, a woman called at the vicarage and asked for her baby to be baptised. She was from the hostel for the homeless on the borders of the parish, though I did not realize that at first. I asked her about godparents. "I haven't got any friends" she said. "Well" said I, swallowing hard at the remark, "you and your husband can be godparents." "My husband's left me" she said. Now it would have been technically possible to refuse baptism for that child — though it would have been for her one more rejection. The woman was a 'bird of passage'. The likelihood of the child receiving a Christian upbringing was small. But in fact that baptism enabled us to do two things. First: to get some of the congregation to think of, and try to treat, that woman, and her child, as theirs to care for and love. Baptism proclaimed that they belonged to each other. It was the sign and seal of that proclamation in the name of God. Secondly, we were able to proclaim to that woman that her homeless, fatherless child was as valuable to God as any child in the world, and that "of such is the kingdom of heaven." We had a party in the vicarage to proclaim that fact.

There is to me a direct connection between baptism and housing, health, education and social care. To put it another way: pastoral care and politics are rarely far from one another.

But there is one other aspect of baptism — some would even say the most important — which I must proclaim before I end.

We baptise in the name of Jesus Christ and with the sign of the Cross. It would take at least another sermon — and another half dozen visits to the house — to spell that out in detail. But I can put it in its briefest, starkest form in this way. Alas, not all the babies I have to baptise are bouncing babies. I think of a young priest friend of mine and his wife — she, a physical training teacher. They were both the very picture of physical health; but I remember his coming to me straight from the hospital on a Sunday evening to tell me that their child had been born, but was "Down's syndrome", and would be severely disabled. He sat there sobbing. How that phrase "Baptism is the proclamation by God that this child is a child of mine" resonated that evening. But it was not just in the name of a kind of Adonis Christ that we baptised that child, but in the name of someone who, as Isaiah said, "in all our afflictions He was afflicted." The signing with the cross is no empty ritual. It says that at some stage in that infant's life — bouncing baby that it may now be — it will be confronted by the problem of suffering, evil, and, indeed, mortality. We sign the child with the sign of the cross "in token that thou too shall tread the path He travelled by."

Baptism is, in the end, not only a celebration, not only a sacrament, but confronts the very depths and heights of the reality of our human existence, our adult experience, in this world, and confronts it with all the resources of another world than this which surrounds and interpenetrates this world of time and space.

32

IN MEMORIAM: BISHOP GEORGE EDMUND REINDORP

St. Stephen's, Rochester Row; June 24th 1990

Most of you will understand the complex emotions that are mine today as I stand where I first stood thirty-nine years ago: to preach now as one of the many curates under whom George used never to tire of averring that he served; to preach in memory of him who, when I was ordained to serve here under him, I was twenty-six years of age, and he not yet forty years old.

It has been suggested to me that, since this is the third of the three sermons that George characteristically commanded should be preached in his memory, mine should not attempt to memorialise him, as others have done — that's to say: go through the various periods of his life and ministry — which it was appropriate that Bishop John Neale should do at Salisbury and Bishop David Say at Guildford; but that my sermon this morning should rather be in memory of George, and be on a subject dear to George's heart: "the Mission of the Church" — which was to have been the particular subject of concern of the St. Stephen's of today on this particular Sunday.

Well, if that be so, I have *No Common Task* — to coin a phrase. And where shall we begin?

"For anything to be real it must be local" wrote G.K. Chesterton. Mission and Ministry must be local — George knew that. And this Church became the place that it did because he knew it. He took the local seriously — the different local estates: Ashley Gardens, Page Street, Millbank, Regency Street, Queen Mary's Buildings, and so on. He took the local hospitals seriously, and the local hostels — G.F.S. and Church Army; and the local offices, like the Colonial Office, the Board of Trade and ICI; and, certainly, the local schools: Burdett Coutts, Greycoat and Millbank. And the local

146

people. Oh yes — and "the local"— though George was never really happy leaning up against the counter of the public bar of this "local" and that.

Though there was one curate — who'd better remain anonymous — into whom the devil entered, who got to know the publican's wife of the *Duchess of Clarence*, opposite the corner of Vauxhall Bridge Road and Rochester Row. And, alive with the sense of the Mission of the Church with which his vicar had imbued him, he evoked from the "Duchess" herself — as the publican's wife was known to her intimates — a desire to come to Evensong at St. Stephen's. "What about next Sunday?" asked the curate; and he was delighted when she accepted and came — "with a glory of golden hair" (that's to say, hennaed). After Evensong, the curate told the Vicar: "The Duchess of Clarence is in the congregation, Vicar, and would like a personal word with you about a problem." "Take her round to the Hall" said the Vicar: "Look after her till I come. Introduce me, and then leave me." In due course, the curate was able to introduce "The Duchess of Clarence". "'Allo dearie" said "The Duchess" to the Vicar — in tones which instantly revealed all. The subject was never mentioned again, not even at Staff Meeting.

I tell that story, not least because I must also tell you that in the first week that I was here, George took me aside, and told me, as gently as possible, and as professionally (he was very professional) that my Cockney Dagenham voice, in his judgment, was in urgent need of radical care and attention, and that the Cockney had to go; and that the parish would pay for me to go to the Abbey School of Speakers to learn to speak the King's English.

I mention this, because it says something complex and very important about the Mission of the Church of England as well as about Mission locally here — and George. Tomorrow morning I shall be speaking BBC English on "Thought For The Day" to eight million people — thanks almost certainly to my training by George: who found me my "Professor Higgins", who, I have to say, was a marvellous teacher, (though I'm no Liza Dolittle!) and ensured that I now speak "proper".

Jesus, had he been one of George's curates, would undoubtedly have been sent to the Temple School of Speakers. Does it not say in St. Matthew: "Thou also wast with Jesus of Galilee: for thy speech bewrayeth thee."?

The subject is of some importance in relation to Mission — and, as I say, of some complexity — because there will probably be several people here whose gifts came to fruition under George's pastoral leadership, and who were able themselves to take up jobs, as a result, in a different walk of life. They will have got on — and, probably, got out — maybe even to Guildford, or even Salisbury. But, by and large, the problem of Page Street — as we called it then — remains, though Page Street, Westminster, itself is being 'privatised'.

I would maintain that it is always wrong to speak of the problem of this parish as the 'problem of Page Street'. The problem is never the problem of Page Street alone. It's the problem of our socially stratified and divided society, which we encourage in various ways. And even to refer to 'the Page Street problem' is woefully inaccurate; for it is just as much the Ashley Gardens — and Guildford and Salisbury — problem: which is content with and encourages such different ways of life and standards of existence in terms of housing, income, health, education, space and power. It is fundamental to the question of Mission to see the parts of a parish as "members one of another" in more than mere words — liturgical words.

Indeed, I think there is a special problem of Mission to the high-powered people who now live in, say, Carlisle Mansions during the week but leave London on Friday afternoon for another part of the country, and who have little loyalty to the locality where they live during the week, or, indeed, often, to the locality where they live during the week-ends.

In order to tackle 'the problem of Page Street' — and Millbank — George caused St. John's, Causton Street to be built. It was one of his main responses to the question of Mission here. It was opened in 1958 and closed in 1976, surviving only eighteen years. George needed no more justification for the building of St. John's than the argument of a book that was published six years after St. John's was opened — *The Church in the Back Streets* by Canon Stanley Evans. It brilliantly analysed the problems of the Back Streets and then had three more chapters on: the Church as Servant; the Church as Centre; and the Back Streets Parson. There's not one word of that book with which I would disagree. And I commend it even now to St. Stephen's — and to others — for further study.

Most parishes in London are now far too large. We need to take Mission to the *estates* seriously. For anything to be real it must be as local as that — and sometimes one tower block is a vertical receptacle as large as an estate. But you can't solve the problem of Mission to each estate simply by building. You need premises that are local to the estate. You need people trained and skilled in community work: which takes seriously the gifts of the people, and takes tenants' associations seriously. You need worship centres — plural. You need varieties of ministry: a ministry which can serve and penetrate each estate. St. John's, Causton Street, was built at the beginning of a decade in the Church of England which saw the clergy of the Church of England decline by 10,000: that meant the staff of St. Stephen's was bound to be cut. Maybe St. Stephen's had banked and depended too much on its full-time staff.

It is an irony that I have heard what was St. John's, Causton Street — now the H.Q. of the Diocese of London — referred to in that building, by people who haven't as much pastoral skill as George had in his little finger, as 'Reindorp's Folly'.

But the problem of the Mission of the Church — as it is experienced in a parish such as this, and as it is to some extent spelt out in *Faith in the City* — is one which has beset the Church of England for more than a century. It was Disraeli who said "The Church of England has not lost the great cities, it has never had them." It's important to see what an intractable problem this parish presents, and to set it in its historical context.

People here at St. Stephen's have seemed to me sometimes to be saying: "We have formed our seventy Lay Visitors and visited you. We have built a church for you. We have run clubs for you — old people's and youth clubs. But still you don't come to church. We have piped and you have not danced."

The great German theologian Adolf Deissmann — whom David Loake would certainly have studied at Tübingen before he came here as a curate under George — said: "Religion resides in prepositions". And I suspect that the preposition "for" and the preposition "with" have much to say about the failure of the Mission of the Church of England, not least in Westminster.

"For" is a word dear to the heart of colonisers, civilisers and paternalists. "With", alongside, is nearer to the heart of the Gospel. It's easier to do things *for* people than to live alongside them — *with* them:

With the poor and mean and lowly
Lived on earth our saviour holy

There is a second aspect of the Mission of the Church which I must try and address — in memory of George.

George was undoubtedly a man with a Mission, and he spoke with authority, as did Another before him.

George never ceased to be proud — even cocky! — that he had reminded Field Marshal Montgomery at Mürren that Jesus gave a Direct Order. "Do this — in remembrance of Me." I've no doubt the success of George's ministry here was due not least to his authority. He lifted burdens from people by authoritative actions. "Don't worry, my dear," he'd say: "Leave it to me. I'll get on to the Local Authority in the morning." After the War, people who had no power of themselves to help themselves against tyrannical local authorities needed someone like George to care for them and contend for them. "What you must do...." George would say with great authority — not least in the confessional. Non-directive counselling was simply not his scene. And many people respond to directive counselling, and at various stages of their life, may well need it — for, as I say, at that time, they may have no power of themselves to help themselves.

Shakespeare in *King Lear* makes Lear ask the disguised Kent:

"What wouldst thou?"
Kent replies: "Service".

Lear asks: "Whom wouldst thou serve?"
"You" Kent replies.
"Dost thou follow me fellow?" asks Lear.
"No sir" answers Kent "but you have that in your countenance which I would fain call master."
"What's that?" Lear asks.
"Authority" Kent replies.

But Lear gained his authority by unburdening himself of his possessions and embarking on what can only be called a way of suffering which gave him an authority he never had when he was seemingly 'every inch a king':
— clad in all the regalia and vestments of royalty.

"Take thou authority" said the Bishop of London to George when he gave him charge of St. Stephen's.

"Take thou authority" the Archbishop of Canterbury said to him at his consecration as a bishop.

But authority has to be won, Lear teaches us, even though it has been given and bestowed. If it is not won, what has been given will shrivel and be empty.

The authority of Jesus was never greater than when he was enthroned on the Cross. It was the authority of triumphant suffering.

Sometimes you can simply "take" authority — speak as though you had it — because you're uncertain.

George had a marvellous and undeniable authority, which comes over in each of his books: *Putting it Across: Ten Points for Preachers* (which, of course, I rapidly read again last night). *What about You? No Common Task*. And so on. But he was always uncertain, for instance, in the presence of Eric Abbott, Dean of King's, and in the presence of almost all theologians. He could behave over-certainly in relation to the local Cardinal because inside he was threatened. He could be dismissive of a Muslim, I remember, locally, because his security was so bound up with the Church of England.

I don't think George ever acted more certainly than when he was uncertain. And within him there was — as there is certainly in me, and I imagine in most of us — a person with great reasons for uncertainty.

He would speak out dogmatically on sexuality because he couldn't face and cope with its complexity.

He said to me once as a curate: "If you can't say it simply, don't say it." But there are many things you can't possibly say simply.

George had a huge gift of simplicity, and something of a curse of over-simplification. I wanted to quote to him Tertullian: "All things go out into mystery". But George often found mystery threatening. It had too much of the Unknown and Uncertain about it. He preferred to reduce the

Mystery to a size he thought that he and many of his congregation could "manage". But the great mysteries refuse to be thus reduced.

No one should deny that at its best — at *his* best — George could speak with profound and enviable simplicity about great matters.

He could speak with marvellous simplicity at Baptisms — to simple people — but not only to simple people. And that was important for the Mission of the Church. He could speak with equal simplicity at Marriages and Marriage Reunions; and at the hospital bedside to those who were sick and dying, and to those who were nursing them; and, out of his own experience, at funerals of infants and of the aged.

I shall never forget Richard Dimbleby's funeral at Westminster Abbey. George, as the preacher, was speaking that day, on radio and television, to the whole nation; for everyone watched or listened to George: speaking with great authority and simplicity. It was one of the best examples of a man fulfilling most wonderfully the Mission of the Church on a crucial occasion.

George said:

"Now he has left us. Sometimes as we stand on the shore waving goodbye to a ship as she fades hull down on the horizon, lost to our sight, we say 'There she goes', and turn away heavy-hearted. But we forget that on the further shore, eager eyes are watching for her, and eager hands stretch out in welcome. So too with us today."

What a gift with words! What simplicity! What God-given gifts out of God-given experience! For there spoke the sensitive naval chaplain who knew so well the bereavement of setting sail and the joy of being "safe home, safe in port" — as we believe he now is.

And there, my Vicar would say, "Eric, you should stop". And the tenth of his *Ten Points for Preachers* is on "Ending". George gives five instructions on how to end. But I shall ignore all of them today. I shall ask you simply to sit where you are while I read the Prayer Book Collect for All Souls' Day, of which George was so fond:

> O Eternal Lord God, who holdest all souls in life: We beseech thee to shed forth upon thy whole Church in Paradise and on earth the bright beams of thy light and heavenly comfort; and grant that we, following the good example of those who have loved and served thee here and are now at rest, may at the last enter with them into the fulness of thine unending joy; through Jesus Christ our Lord. Amen.

33

THE POWER AND THE GLORY

Gray's Inn Chapel; July 8th 1990

I have been learning in the past three months some of the benefits of being an old-age pensioner. I'm finding it easier to recall events of fifty years ago than the names of those I was introduced to fifty minutes ago. For instance: I can vividly remember, fifty years ago this year, reading a novel which, when I put it down, I knew was one of the greatest I would ever read. 1940 was, as some of you will remember, a curious year, which heightened all our sensitivities — with the Fall of France, and the invasion of Norway and Denmark, and the beginning of the Blitz. In fact, I remember reading two new novels that year: the one about the Spanish Civil War, Ernest Hemingway's great novel *For Whom the Bell Tolls* had a powerful message for those dark days; but I found an even stronger message in the second: Graham Greene's *The Power and the Glory*.

I could not then begin to imagine that in fifty years time I would go to a place, then unbuilt, called the Chichester Festival Theatre, in as peaceful surroundings as anyone could then conceive, and see *The Power and the Glory*, adapted as a play as powerful as the novel.

And little did I know, when I first met the actor Edward Petherbridge, at Michaelmas 1969, when he read a passage from Kahlil Gibran at Bishop John Robinson's farewell to the Diocese of Southwark, it would be he who would play the central part of the priest in the play. Yet I knew how much John Robinson's *Honest to God* had meant to him on his spiritual journey. Indeed, I next met Edward Petherbridge in this Chapel, one Sunday afternoon, when he came, not so long ago, to be a god-father at a baptism, and we were able to talk over those Woolwich days again, and the spiritual journey which was preparing him to give a performance in *The Power and the Glory* at Chichester now which one reviewer has described simply as "a miracle".

To go back to 1940. The thirty-six year-old Graham Greene was then literary editor of *The Spectator*. In 1926, he'd been received into the Roman Catholic Church, and had visited Mexico in 1938 to report on religious persecution there. *The Power and the Glory* was his second great novel. The first was, of course, *Brighton Rock*, published in 1938.

What was it about *The Power and the Glory* which so gripped me?

Well, the story is set in the Mexico of the 30's Graham Greene had so recently visited. The experience was clearly vivid for him. A left wing revolution had suppressed the Church, destroyed many of its most beautiful buildings, and made it illegal to say Mass.

The central character in the novel is simply described as "the priest": a man who takes great risks to say Mass for the peasants in secret. Even to buy wine for a celebration is dangerous, for the Government has introduced prohibition. The priest disclaims any pretence to be a hero — he is one of Greene's many *anti*-heroes — and does not object to being called a "whisky priest". He is also, as a celibate priest, the father of a child. But, he claims, a bad priest is better than no priest, because the Lord, in his inscrutable wisdom, can still use him — even him — to give to the peasants the greatest gift they could receive: the Body and Blood of our Lord Jesus Christ in the Sacrament.

When I first read *The Power and the Glory* I was fifteen, and out at work, and still had eleven years to go before I was myself ordained priest. But I knew that if ever, and whenever, I was ordained, I would always understand within myself what Graham Greene was writing about: the contrast between one's calling and who one actually is; and I understood this as a layman of fifteen because I have never believed the priesthood is something confined to ordained priests: it's something about the nature of the humanity of us all — men and women — which is focussed in the role of the priest. To my mind, one of the main tasks of a priest is to remind others of their priesthood: the priesthood of their humanity. And there's never a time for any of us when the gap — the chasm — between who we are and who we are called to be, is not part of our daily experience. We all have this treasure in earthen vessels. So *The Power and the Glory* is not simply about a "Whisky Priest", in the Mexico of the 30's: like all great literature and great drama it's a profound exploration of our human nature, and of the ambiguity of good and evil.

If I have any criticisms of the Chichester Production it is that although Edward Petherbridge has the grey hair and furrowed face of a man who has suffered, and seen others suffer, he looks much more the kind of overworked Anglican priest I see week by week, in, say, South London, than the shambling, whisky-sodden, tramp-like figure whom Graham Greene clearly had in mind.

But, in a sense, it doesn't matter; because, in the last fifty years, the scene in Mexico and South America has so radically changed, and yet you know, whatever the politics, Fascist or Communist; whatever the top surface of the church — "the heart of the matter"(to use another great Graham Greene title) will always be the same.

Corrupt police don't only exist in Greene-land. Nor does the unbeliever who is more Christlike than the passionate believer — seedy dentist though he be — and out of England and in Another Country, and at home nowhere.

It always interests me how people respond to *The Power and the Glory*, both as a book and as a play. When you ask them what they think it's about, they quite often say: "Well, it's about a failed priest, isn't it?" And I say "Yes; but everyone's a failed priest." And the story of a failure by itself doesn't make a great play. A great tragedy is never simply about a great failure.

But *The Power and the Glory* is not only about a failure. It's about God's use of failures — for he has no other material.

Graham Greene is always at his best when he describes how God uses failures; and you always feel that, great writer that he is, he must himself also be conscious of great failure in his own life: many passages have the unmistakable power of autobiography. Let me read you just one such passage:-

"The years behind him were littered with surrenders — feast days and fast days and days of abstinence had been the first to go; then he had ceased to trouble more than occasionally about his breviary — and, finally, he had left it behind altogether at the port, in one of his periodic attempts to escape. Then the altar stone went — too dangerous to carry with him. He had no business to say Mass without it: he was probably liable to suspension — but penalties of the ecclesiastical kind began to seem unreal in a state where the only penalty was the civil one of death. The routine of his life, like a dam, was cracked — and forgetfulness came dribbling in, wiping out this and that. Five years ago he had given way to despair — the unforgivable sin — and he was going back now to the scene of his despair with a curious lightening of the heart. For he had got over despair too. He was a bad priest, he knew it: they had a word for his kind — a whisky-priest, but every failure dropped out of sight and mind: somewhere they accumulated in secret — the rubble of his failures. One day they would choke up, he supposed, altogether the source of grace. Until then he carried on, with spells of fear, weariness, with a shamefaced lightness of heart."

Can anyone say that passage is simply about priests — or about other people?

This week I have been to the ordination of a young friend of mine who is not only a priest but a social worker who specialises in cases of child abuse — in Tower Hamlets. I preached on Friday evening at his first Mass in Stoke Newington.

As he said for the first time in his life those extraordinary words: *"The same night that He was betrayed*, Jesus took bread, and, when he had given thanks, he brake it, and gave it to his disciples, saying, Take, eat, this is my body which is given for you: Do this in remembrance of me: Likewise after supper he took the Cup; and, when he had given thanks, he gave it to them..." — When I heard that young priest say those words for the first time I knew that God's use of him would be great — but that he would also feel a failure at what he was called to be; and *be* a failure — because we — we *all* — have this treasure in earthen vessels.

That's the end of what I have to *say* today: but instead of proceeding immediately to our next hymn, as we usually do, I'm going to ask the choir to sing again that very brief Elgar anthem we heard earlier — *Ave verum corpus natum* — while we sit and give thanks for the God who uses us, with all our failures, and in spite of our failures: uses us all in and through the priesthood of our God-given humanity.

34

THAT WAS NOT FIRST
WHICH IS SPIRITUAL

Festival Eucharist of the Three Choirs' Festival,
Worcester Cathedral; August 19th 1990

St. Paul's First Epistle to the Corinthians, the 15th Chapter and the 46th
Verse: "That was not first which is spiritual but that which is natural".

The Three Choirs Festival, everyone knows, is related to three particular
places: Gloucester, Hereford, and — "'Tis good, Lord, to be here" — this
year — in this particular place: Worcester. And the first point I want to
make this morning, therefore, is simply to state, and underline, and reflect
upon, the significance of place.

Some may perhaps think that has very little to do with religion; but hear
again my text: "That was not first which is spiritual but that which is
natural"; and think of Bethlehem, and Nazareth, and Jerusalem; and think
of G.K. Chesterton's great phrase: "for anything to be real it must be local";
and think of those places which have been most real to you — and think,
thankfully, of Worcester.

I start with the significance of place: as one of the most important aspects
of the natural which are the very vehicle of the spiritual. But let me remind
you that place is often as significant for us when we are absent as when
we are present. I do not doubt that Worcester meant much to Elgar when
he was away from it: when he was wistful for it, and for all that surrounds
it. Much music has been written away from particular places but with those
places in mind. The Bromsgrove-born Housman was a long way from
Bredon — and so was Butterworth — when they wrote of their "land of
lost content":

Here of a Sunday morning
    My love and I would lie,
And see the coloured counties,
    And hear the larks so high
    About us in the sky.

156

So here, this Sunday morning, I speak first of the significance of place.
And there's a second aspect of the natural which, for me, the Three
Choirs underlines: the aspect of time.

The first festival in the early 18th century.

Worcester, only every third year. And — once upon a time — Elgar and
Ivor Atkins walked here; but not now.

What music on earth can ever ignore Time? In heaven, perhaps, we shall
say, with Gerontius:

> I hear no more the busy beat of time
> No, nor my fluttering breath, nor struggling pulse;
> Nor does one moment differ from the next.

But here, and now, time is, as we say, "of the essence" — even the
duration of a sermon!

At such a Festival as this we can appropriately recall old times. And,
no doubt, some will think so-and-so took such-and-such a piece too fast
— or too slow. But I cannot believe anybody here will deny that time is
one of the most important aspects of the natural, and that it, too, is the
vehicle of the spiritual.

Time is so natural that we take it for granted. It's a kind of invisible
skein, unwound by we know not who. But it's the natural, indispensable
raw material of our existence.

Auden wrote: "Music is the best means we have of digesting time".

Shakespeare, whose marriage bond is to be seen in the Diocesan
Registrar's Office here in Worcester, wrote:

> Ruin hath taught me thus to ruminate —
> That Time will come and take my love away.
> This thought is as a death, which cannot choose
> But weep to have that which it fears to lose.

Which leads me to the third natural ingredient of such a Festival as this:
Place; time; people — *persons*.

I was taught the organ fifty years ago, when I was a boy, out at work
on Shakespeare's Bankside at Southwark. I was taught at Southwark
Cathedral by Edgar Tom Cook, who had been educated here at the Royal
Worcester Grammar School, and in the organ loft of this Cathedral. E.T.
Cook was assistant here to Hugh Blair, and then to Sir Ivor Atkins, and
taught me the Elgar Organ Sonata, and introduced me to W.H. Reed —
"Billy" Reed, the biographer of Elgar, who helped him with the bowing
of his Violin Concerto. He was the leader of our orchestra at Southwark;
and I shall never forget, in those dark wartime days, his playing the violin
obligato for "Have Mercy, Lord, on me", in the *St. Matthew Passion*,
accompanying the young Kathleen Ferrier.

157

How much those who people the world of music mean to those of us who come to a Festival like this!

I imagine many of you will have come to Worcester this week to hear a particular soloist, or the work of a particular composer, or to meet again and be with a particular person, or, this year of the Newman Centenary, maybe specially to hear *Gerontius*.

"That was not first which is spiritual but that which is natural". People are part of the natural world in a very particular way. The whole dimension of our sexuality, for instance, by which we come to exist at all, firmly fixes us in the natural world. Yet what is abundantly clear is that none of us is *merely* natural.

Newman put on his cardinal's coat of arms — and thus on the pall at his funeral — the four marvellous Latin words: *Cor ad cor loquitur*: "Heart speaks to heart."

It's always dangerous to think of individuals existing in isolation. They just don't. People — persons — exist in relationship. "First, that which is natural": families and friends. A Festival such as this is always a Feast of Friendship. But the way friends relate and communicate, and the language of our communication, is of huge importance.

There's a sense in which language is yet another natural ingredient of our existence. *Cor ad cor loquitur*. Sometimes we speak by silences; sometimes with words. And here, in this Festival, music itself is our means of communication. Sounds, semibreves, intervals, accidentals, keys and clefs, strings, wind, and brass, are the natural vehicle of the spiritual.

I've said that it's dangerous to think of individuals in isolation. Those of you who're in the Festival Choir will say "Amen" to that. I shall look forward to meeting some of you this week as individuals. I've heard of doctors, nurses and probation officers singing in the Festival choir — all of them individuals. But a choir that sings together — in harmony — is itself a sort of a natural symbol of the spiritual — and more than symbol: it's a natural vehicle of the spiritual: And so, too, of course, is an orchestra.

But there's one other subject which I must mention — albeit reluctantly, at a Festival.

Perhaps the most moving of all Newman's sermons he called "The Parting of Friends". He preached it in Littlemore Church, Oxford, just a few days after his resignation of the incumbency of St. Mary's, Oxford, on September 18th 1843; and, two years later, he was received into the Roman Catholic Church.

Some of the ruptures of our relationships are undoubtedly due to natural causes. We have to move away from one place to another. Sometimes there's a transcendent obligation which causes the parting: as Newman's embracing the truth as he saw it led to his parting with his friends. Then the parting is not natural but spiritual. Sometimes we speak of death as due to natural causes; but not always. When, on the small scale, the rows, which I'm told even musicians sometimes have — and choirs — and clergy — and even Cathedral chapters! — when such rows sunder and separate us; and when, on the large scale, nation wars against nation, as in the Middle East today, do we relate such events to the natural or to the spiritual? Is man's fallen nature natural and its redemption spiritual?

King Lear asks concerning those ghastly daughters of his, Goneril and Regan: "Is there any cause in *nature* that makes these hard hearts?"

It would be romantic, escapist and deeply unchristian to evade and omit all reference to our ruptured relationships, and their redemption, at such a Festival as this.

Here in this Eucharist, we shall soon, of course, recall that it was "the same night that Jesus was betrayed that He took bread, and gave thanks, and broke it, and gave it to his disciples, saying: Take, eat; This is my Body which is given for you." At the worst time, he did the best deed. "First, that which is natural". He took the bread and wine — *and* the raw material of his betrayal — and made of it something profoundly spiritual and endlessly redemptive. So that some of the greatest music ever written wrestles, through the music of the Mass, with evil and its redemption. Such music — Bach, Beethoven, Mozart, Britten, Howells — often transcends our divided dogmas. We are greatly indebted today to Jonathan Willcocks for the Mass he has provided as the vehicle of our worship.

I do not intend to wrestle further this morning with this great theme and subject. Let me simply remind you of the words of St. Thomas Aquinas: "God does not destroy nature, he takes it and perfects it". And let me suggest you regard this Festival as — not least — an invitation to you to fashion again your understanding of the spiritual, through the vehicle of the natural. So that when you come to hear, or to sing, those so familiar words of Newman:

> Praise to the Holiest in the height
> And in the *depth* be praise

It will be from your own heights and depths that you respond — and: *cor ad cor* loquitur: your heart will respond to the heart of that Love which has so wonderfully created, given us our nature, and has yet more wonderfully redeemed us.

35

I JOURNEYED TO LONDON

Christ's Hospital: The St. Matthew's Day Service;
St. Paul's Cathedral, September 21st 1990

"I journeyed to London".

Those four words you will find near the beginning of T.S. Eliot's pageant in dramatic verse, which he called *The Rock*. At the centre of that pageant — the first of all his plays in verse — he placed a nameless individual with a sensitive, enquiring mind and heart. It's that individual who journeys to London, with his eyes open, and looks around.

Eliot was writing nearly sixty years ago.

I wonder if, at the end of today, you were to begin a poem — or, if that's not your line, an essay — or simply an entry in your diary — with those words: "I journeyed to London" — I wonder what you'd want to include in it.

Eliot, who worked in a bank in the City for a few years, in Cornhill, observed not only the bankers and stockbrokers. It was 1934, so he observed the unemployed. As a commuter, he even observed the people next to him in the tube-train.

Of course, just a few hours in London, and much of that spent here in St. Paul's, and in the Guildhall, may not give you opportunity to observe a great deal of London; but I suspect already you have seen some things to make you want to say with Dunbar, the 16th Century poet: "London, thou art the flower of cities all". But to balance that I think you would need to go into say St. Bartholomew's Hospital round the corner, to realise the full extent of the crisis in the Health Service in London at the moment, with, for instance, one in five beds in London Hospitals closed since 1982.

You'd probably need to go beyond the Tower of London, to the Borough of Tower Hamlets, to experience to the full the crisis in education in London. That Borough alone will need 500 to 600 new teachers every year for the next few years.

160

If you were able to go just south of Waterloo Bridge, you would see for yourself something of the crisis in homelessness — with over 3000, mainly young people, sleeping rough in the streets of London.

If you were to go to, say, Islington, you could learn of the crisis of Law and Order in London, for in recent years about one in four cars in that Borough have been either stolen or broken into.

You'd need to talk with a Borough Engineer before you could literally get to the bottom of the crisis in sewers, which is quite serious. But you'll only need to walk along, say, Piccadilly, and look at the state of the pavements, to realize that there's recently been a very serious decline in the quality of life of our metropolis.

And there's, of course, the all-but-insoluble problem of the traffic: which has things to say not only about the traffic itself but the environmental crisis which is now upon us.

Thankfully, that's only part of the picture. London is in many ways a very prosperous city. Its economy generates about 17% of the gross domestic product and accounts for 16% of national employment — though that arithmetic on the wall may be the writing on the wall.

I doubt whether there's a city which at the moment has more to offer: by its museums and galleries, its theatres and concert halls; its parks, its cathedrals and churches. The tourist industry, understandably, is flourishing, so that a place like this Cathedral is in constant demand.

You've probably already been struck by the cranes that are to be seen on every skyline, betokening the huge amount of office building that is going on just now. Canary Wharf, on the Isle of Dogs, with its million square feet of office floor space, pushes towards the heavens at nearly a floor a week.

But what is above all dismaying to my mind is the lack of deep feeling — except in pockets — that we are all now in it together. Economic inequality is growing apace, and black people are far worse off, on average, than white people. Pensioners, and people with disabilities, are undoubtedly having a particularly tough time. The weakest are going to the wall.

And now we are simply a series of separate boroughs, with very little cohesion, or common awareness, of each other's problems, or of the possibilities of helping one another.

I so wish that you were not simply journeying to London for this day alone, but staying here for at least a few days. And I want to urge all of you who are not familiar with London to resolve that somehow you will journey to London and stay here for quite a while to familiarise yourself with this great city: not simply with its cinemas and concert halls but with the realities of ordinary people.

There are in fact quite a number of initiatives going on at the moment

161

to counter the distress that now afflicts so much of London. Let me mention one.

I'm rather privileged to be one of the trustees of a project called *The Inner Cities Young People's Project.*

It's a fairly new initiative: started only last year. It was set up just because we live in such an increasingly divided society; because these divisions have reached crisis point in our inner city areas; because the lack of genuine contact between people breeds misunderstanding and ignorance; and because, in the end, anyone who does not know intimately the problems that beset such a city as London is — let's face it — fundamentally uneducated.

The Project has been set up to give young people the opportunity of short residential courses, living with other young people of different background: learning about and experiencing their environment with the people who live there: not simply as, so-to-speak, spectators.

We've felt that these courses should be for only a few people at a time — twelve at the most — so that there's a real opportunity to get to know one another. The groups, we think, need to be together not only in the inner city. The idea is that they should meet together several times for several days.

The results of our pilot project have been hugely encouraging. In just these last few weeks the project has thrived in several parts of London: Lambeth, Battersea, Camberwell, and elsewhere.

Now I'm aware that you pride yourselves at Christ's Hospital that it's not simply another Public School or Private School; and why I've always loved coming to Christ's Hospital is, not least, because of the varied backgrounds you come from — unlike people from what I will call "the average public school".

But I'd be surprised if all of you feel you know all you need to know about the inner city areas of this great city. I'd imagine that quite a number have, understandably, at least a degree of fear of the inner city, and are not yet certain that you're as "streetwise" as you might be where the inner city's concerned. The motivation of social action by public schools in former times has often been a kind of do-gooding, and has not lacked an element of condescension. The motivation *now* is much more of education of oneself, and what good is achieved is a by-product. Schools' social action today needs to be with and alongside people rather than simply for them.

One person on the project wrote:

"Overall, I feel that despite the sometimes very heated disagreements among us as a group, in which I've been involved, I've enjoyed the experience of meeting the same people three times already. It has brought together a group of people who would otherwise have no idea of each other's existence."

162

Another wrote:

"The London experience was excellent. It was extremely interesting — but scary — to meet with homeless people. It made me realise that the problem of homelessness is not simply a financial one. The problem runs so much deeper than that, and is deeply rooted in the fabric of our society".

You may say: "What a peculiar sermon! No text — no mention of God or Christ — just T.S. Eliot's words 'I journeyed to London'". Well, I'll give you a text. It's St. Paul's words: "We are members one of another". All I've been saying is in those six words.

So: enjoy your visit to London. Keep your eyes open. Keep your hearts open. And, this evening, write something beginning "I journeyed to London..." and resolve that your journey to London — to its heart — to understand what makes its people tick — will not end with today.

36

CHRIST AND CONFLICT

Gray's Inn Chapel; January 20th 1991

Since we last met here in Chapel, much has happened in the world at large; but the God of unchangeable power and eternal light, remains the same; and so does the task of a Preacher. As always, I have to try and interpret, be a servant of, the word of God, in the situation: the new and changed situation.

Most of you know that I have felt it a particular privilege to do that not only here, in the pulpit, but in the three minutes of *Thought For The Day* on BBC's Radio 4 and on the World Service of the BBC. But I can honestly say that I have never felt both more privileged and more tested than I was earlier this week. On Tuesday, I was 'phoned by those in authority in the BBC World Service and asked to prepare immediately a four minute broadcast that would go out round the world *if* and *when* war broke out. I spent the evening of Tuesday agonising over what I should say, recorded it in Bush House early on Wednesday, and — alas — within twenty-four hours it was beginning to be broadcast around the world.

I should like to share with you what I said.

"I'm speaking to you at one of the darkest hours in the world's history: at a time when — you will well know — a terrible war has now begun.

It's a war which will mean very different things to different people.

Maybe you're an army officer in the Gulf listening to London. Maybe you're the mother of a soldier, or a soldier's wife, who can't sleep for anxiety. Maybe you're on the staff of a hospital which you know has been preparing to receive casualties. Maybe you're a diplomat who has been very busy in these last weeks and months. Maybe you're a young student who passionately believes this could all have been, and should all have been, avoided, and that it wouldn't be happening at all if it wasn't for oil. Maybe you're someone who has helped to build the planes, the tanks, or the ships, which may soon be embattled. Or maybe you're one of the great multitude who did not want war, but it came to you, not a few hours ago but last August, where you live, in Kuwait; and your world was shattered then. Maybe there are even some listening at this hour, inside Iraq.

War has come to us all — we have that in common; but we are all different people in different situations.

When, in 1981, the Pope went to Hiroshima, he used a prayer which I believe has become not simply one of the great Christian prayers but one of the great prayers of humanity. Let me read it to you:

'To you, Creator of nature and humanity, of truth and beauty, I pray:

Hear my voice, for it is the voice of the victims of all wars and violence among individuals and nations.

Hear my voice, for it is the voice of all children who suffer and will suffer when people put their faith in weapons and war.

Hear my voice, when I beg you to instil into the hearts of all human beings the wisdom of peace, the strength of justice, and the joy of fellowship.

Hear my voice, for I speak for the multitudes in every country and in every period of history who do not want war and are ready to walk the way of peace.

Hear my voice, and grant insight and strength, so that we may always respond to hatred with love, to injustice with total dedication to justice, to need with the sharing of self, to war with peace.

O God, hear my voice, and grant unto the world your everlasting peace.'

You may say: 'Yes; that's a good prayer — or was — for surely it's a prayer that has failed.'

No; there is never a time when we should stop praying for peace, or for the victims of violence, or for love to be the response to hatred, or for total dedication to justice, wherever that may lead us.

There can only be one reason for most of us being willing to be involved in this war: that it is, in this complex and compromising world, what people believe, rightly or wrongly, is most likely to bring justice. And, of course, all human beings can be mistaken.

So perhaps there is another prayer which we might all use at this dark hour — a prayer for all who are in any ways involved in the war: a prayer of only three words: *Lord, have mercy.*"

As I've said: I felt privileged to be asked to do that broadcast; but, of course, I also felt a considerable responsibility; and I was glad to do it particularly for one reason: I could no longer halt between opinions or stand on the sidelines. I had to put myself with and alongside all sorts of people who, however reluctantly, had been caught up in the war.

I've said that I agonised over the script that evening; but I was aware that really I had begun to think out what I wanted to say — without knowing I was doing it — at the beginning of last December. I had been asked to give three sermons on consecutive Sunday evenings in Westminster Abbey, for the Sunday evenings before Christmas. With the anxiety of the War in the Gulf hanging over us, I became clear that I must take for my subject on those evenings: *Christmas and Conflict.*

At the beginning of December we were all still thinking, hoping, and praying, that mediation might still be possible; and at the time I was reading a very relevant book, by Andrew Acland, called *A Sudden Outbreak of*

Common Sense, subtitled *Managing Conflict Through Mediation*. Andrew I had known when he was on the staff of the Archbishop of Canterbury: indeed, he was Terry Waite's assistant when he successfully managed to get hostages released from Libya. He has since been involved in mediation in industry, in inner city situations, and in South Africa, and is now what's called a professional mediator.

In early December, mediation seemed to be the priority, and highly relevant to Christmas; for one of the great Christian books of our time, by the Swiss theologian Emil Brunner, was simply called *The Mediator*. You could say that one of the best alternative title to "The Prince of Peace" is simply "The Mediator".

But, as the weeks of December went by, it became clear that mediation in the Gulf was less and less likely to succeed. And I found myself, as I meditated on Christmas and Conflict, having to face up to confrontation as part of the work of mediation.

The power to confront evil is one of the most important gifts that is given to us at our birth, as it was to Jesus Himself, and lies at the heart of much of the conflict in which we are inescapably involved in the course of our later life.

A baby in a cradle can't, of course, do much mediating. And even the Christ child — if He's portrayed as a sort of "Peter Pan" figure: a child who never grew up — can do little for our sort of world: ravaged with conflict.

But many of the Christmas carols, I noticed, made it clear that the Baby Jesus was born in order to come to grips with the down-to-earth realities of this world, and that He could not escape conflict, suffering and death. One of my favourite carols — "Sing Lullaby" — says:

"Soon comes the cross,
the nails, the piercing..."

The French novelist, Francois Mauriac, in his *Life of Christ* has a marvellous description of Christ cleansing the Temple. He describes Him with a whip in His hands, the sweat pouring off His face, as He drives the money-changers from the Temple. And then he says: "Nobody that day could tell He was love". But Mauriac's whole point is that He *was* Love. He was the *Prince of Peace* that day — in spite of appearances: in spite of the conflict in which he was embroiled.

It's important that we never cocoon Christ in His cradle, or put Him into snow-like cotton wool. He can only speak to our conflict-ridden world if we face the realities of His adult life in the world — like the realities of His Cleansing the Temple.

It's always odd to me that people never quote the Jesus who, for instance, said to one group of people "O generation of vipers!" The words are too confrontational for our image of "gentle" Jesus. I've never heard anyone preach on the words which Jesus used of Herod: "Go tell that fox..." Again: the words are most often too confrontational for our liking.

And I believe it greatly helps to look at the political realities in which Jesus' life was inescapably set: the details of the political set-up at the time of his birth and his upbringing.

One of my very favourite verses in all the Gospels is Luke Chapter 3: "In the fifteenth year of the reign of Tiberius Caesar, Pontius Pilate being governor of Judea, and Herod tetrarch of Galilee, and his brother Philip tetrarch of Iturea and of the region of Trachonitis, and Lysanias the tetrarch of Abilene, Annas and Caiaphas being the high priests, the word of God came unto John".

I like that text because it is difficult to gather together in one verse a bigger gang of rogues; but it was under the rule of those rogues, and amid the realities of that political situation that Jesus had to work out his vocation.

This morning we had read to us the story of the wise men and of the slaughter of the innocents. Most Biblical scholars I know believe both those events to be more myth than history. Yet it is not without significance that Matthew's readers did not find anything at all surprising about the fact that Jesus was born into the midst of such slaughter.

Jesus was in fact born towards the end of the reign of King Herod — who died in 4 BC. *That* Herod is often referred to as Herod the Great. It was the historian Lord Acton who said that "great men are almost always bad men". Herod was well qualified for the distinction. His father, Antipater, was an Idumean — Greek for Edomite — a member of a Southern non-Jewish tribe which had been forcibly converted to Judaism a century earlier. Antipater had been appointed by Julius Caesar as administrator of Judea in 47 BC when the high priestly rulers were proving incompetent. The politics of the area at the time were as messy as one can imagine. The Romans were not yet ready to take direct responsibility for the administration of Judea, although they knew it to be a vital link in their imperial communications, not least to the Tigris and Euphrates and what we now call the Gulf. A friendly client-king was just what they needed. They conferred upon Herod the title King of Judea — which meant nothing more than permission to conquer a kingdom, if he could. With a small company of personal followers, but without Roman military assistance, he landed on the shores of Palestine, and by 37 BC he had set up his kingdom in Jerusalem.

Herod at once devoted his energies to the task of ruthlessly eliminating every possible rival upon whom his paranoiac suspicions fell. His reign, though undisturbed by foreign war, was stained with — no: soaked in — cruelties and atrocities. The high priestly family was almost wiped out. It was said he made life and property in Judea safe from every tyranny but his own.

167

But the Jews were never reconciled to him. They knew he wore his Judaism like a cloak: to be thrown off when he attended Greek festivals and games in honour of pagan Gods. He erected costly buildings with other people's money. His rebuilding of the Temple — intended to please his subjects — caused great offence. By what right, they asked, did this Idumean lay hands upon their holy place. When Herod was growing old, his sons, by different wives, vied with each other for the succession. Fearing that one of them might assassinate him, Herod disposed of them as he had earlier disposed of his rivals. Augustus in Rome said: "I would rather be Herod's sow than his son". And this is the background to the birth of Jesus.

I've retold this bit of history because I've wanted you to say to yourself "If there is conflict now in *our* world — well that was the sort of world in which Jesus was born and grew up: He faced political conflict and faced it with courage, dedication, and undaunted faith in his Father.

These are undoubtedly dark days, tragic days: but they are days recognisably like the days of Our Lord's birth, childhood, triumphant suffering and death. We are right to be dismayed by what has happened in the last days. We are right to be made anxious by them. But they that wait upon the Lord — upon Our Father — shall renew their strength and vision — and courage — for all that lies ahead.

37

A MATTER OF IDENTITY

Gray's Inn Chapel; April 21st 1991

I have subjected you to some strange sermons in these last thirteen years, but I suspect today's is the strangest. It may seem a little less strange if I tack on a text at the beginning of it.

Psalm 17 v. 16:

"When I awake up after thy likeness, I shall be satisfied with it".

This time last year, the idea of having my portrait painted — and paying for it myself — would have been unthinkable to me. Two quite different events made the idea not only thinkable but realizable.

Last August, while I was away in Worcester, preaching at the Three Choirs' Festival, my house was burgled; and it did not seem right either to replace all that was stolen or simply to give to charity all I received from insurance. About the same time, the photograph of the portrait of F.A. Simpson arrived which I was to use for the cover of my book about him called *A Last Eccentric*. Simpson had several portraits drawn or painted during his lifetime, but this particular portrait was a revelation to me. It spoke of him in a way that others did not, though the artist remained unknown. I could not stop looking at it. I had been collecting people's memories of Simpson, but I had not anticipated that a portrait would tell me so much, and go on speaking to me.

A friend of mine, who is knowledgeable in the world of Fine Arts, suggested I should consider having my portrait painted: that it might be useful some time for a book, just as Simpson's portrait had been. He mentioned the name of Diccon Swan, who had painted his portrait several years ago and with whom he had read Theology at Oxford. My first reaction was an emotional negative. He was not put off; indeed, he hinted that my reaction might say more about me than about the idea of having my portrait painted, and volunteered to have a preliminary talk with Diccon Swan and raise the question of the kind of money, after the burglary, that I was able to afford. The result was that I agreed to meet and talk with Diccon.

Our first meeting, at my home, took a different form from what I had anticipated. To my surprise, Diccon arrived with easel, canvas and paints, and immediately started looking around to see where the light was best for painting. "But weren't we going to discuss terms?" I asked. "Oh no" he said, "I'm very happy to go ahead with what I gather you can manage"; and immediately we began moving the table and chairs away from the window of my dining room, to make room for Diccon's easel where the light was best.

The decision had been taken almost without my knowing it. I felt like someone in the dentist's chair who, still bracing himself for what lies ahead, is suddenly told "It's out".

But there remained one unavoidable question: "*How* shall I be painted?". Diccon said: "Only you can decide that: whether you should be painted in scarlet cassock, in 'dog-collar', or in suit, shirt and tie". It was my first realization that a portrait is so inescapably involved with identity.

It was not an easy decision, not least because identity concerns not only how you see yourself but how others see you. Painted in robes, as, say "the Preacher to Gray's Inn" — I know of no previous portrait of such a Preacher, though the office dates back over four hundred years — Gray's Inn might just conceivably want eventually, when I'm dead, to have the portrait. Painted in suit, shirt and tie, that possibility, I imagined, would be, very considerably reduced. Glad as I am to be a Chaplain to H.M. The Queen, I have never considered that role relates closely to my identity, so that although a portrait of me in scarlet cassock might be more colourful, dignified and distinguished, it was not difficult to decide that was *not* how I should be painted. But the question of a 'dog-collar' was more difficult. I wear one these days mainly on Sundays, for services and for official functions. It certainly isn't essential to my identity, any more than it was to the identity of Jesus! I don't think most of my friends think of me in 'dog-collar', neither do I think the absence of a 'dog-collar' in any way diminishes their thought of me, or my thought of myself, as a priest. If a portrait is about identity, I did not immediately want to be classified as a 'cleric' — in 'clericals'. A portrait, it seemed to me, should first say "Behold the man", and in beholding the man you should — or you might, or might not — behold the priest.

Portraits tell people of one age about people of another. The portraits here at Gray's Inn, ancient and modern, have a peculiar and particular fascination. There's an exhibition of portraits on at the moment in Norwich entitled *History and Identity*. Should that have any bearing on my decision? Yes, I concluded. Perhaps at some future time people should learn that in the 1990's some Anglican clergy were less concerned about what they wore than they once were.

I had a week to decide precisely how I should be painted, for Diccon and I had decided to meet each week for a two-hour sitting; and, with few reservations, I took the decision to be painted just as I am most days: suit, shirt and tie.

Answering just this preliminary question had involved a surprising amount of theology, but what surprised me more was that the theological questions kept on coming.

Diccon asked me if I would mind coming to his Brixton studio for sittings. My small house in Kennington is overlooked at the back by a block of flats and in the front overshadowed by a crescent of plane trees, and even during the day there is insufficient light. Light — that great Biblical word — was clearly essential. "Let there be light" Diccon seemed to be saying; but at first that seemed just a practical problem. I had no idea I should find myself being taught to revalue light. A dull day meant a different painting; and I became aware in the two-hour sitting how the light could and would change, virtually every minute. One moment, through Diccon's Brixton skylight, light would flood his studio; at another, clouds would shroud and darken the room. From where I sat I might see white clouds scudding across a blue sky, but in seconds there might be an entirely different sky with quite different light. I began to realise I had hardly valued light at all before: certainly I had never realized how essential it is to seeing and not seeing, and to seeing in detail. I don't think I shall ever again take light for granted.

But, of course, not only light but seeing is of the essence of painting, not least of painting a portrait. I had never seen anyone gaze at one object for two hours — let alone gaze at that object for two hours week after week — for a dozen weeks. I began to realize how cursory and slipshod was most of my observation of anything, and to wonder whether I had ever really looked at anything. I had always assumed I was not bad at observing people and am quite experienced at it; but Diccon's observation put my observation as a pastor to shame. "You must look and look until your eyes bleed" one artist had said. Here was another area of theology which having my portrait painted was literally illuminating. It is of the Pharisees that St. John, in his Gospel, says: "Ye say 'we see'".

"Contemplation" is a very religious word. Diccon is, strictly speaking, a contemplative. And "whereas I was blind..." I will not say "now I see", but now I see a little more what is involved in seeing.

In religion, contemplation is often allied to loving. St. Augustine said: "We shall see and we shall love". I was soon astonished by how much loving went into Diccon's contemplation — "astonished", because he was able to love what I myself had never been able to find particularly lovable: my own body!

One day I was admiring one of the many canvases of finished or half-finished portraits that lay about Diccon's studio. "How wonderfully

171

you have painted that chap's hair!" I exclaimed, as I sat looking at it while
Diccon was painting me. Back came Diccon's immediate enthusiastic
reply: "I can't tell you how much I'm longing to paint *your* hair!" *My* hair!
My all but bald head with its grey and white strands of nondescript sporadic
growth! Diccon's contemplation seemed to contain a degree of detailed
acceptance and love which was neither easy for me to believe or to accept.

On another occasion, not being able to see from where I was sitting
anything but the back of the portrait, I asked Diccon: "What are you
working at this morning?" "Well, I'm trying to get the flesh of your face
right" he replied. Again, I was astonished. "Oh God" I involuntarily
exclaimed, "poor you, having to do *that*!" The gentle, and usually
unruffleable Diccon was, I thought, somewhat irritated, and as near to
anger as I have yet seen him. "I have these colours here" he said, pointing
to his palette, "and I'm trying to get the wonderful colours in your face.
You might give me a little more encouragement." But I had never myself
seen the "wonderful colours" in my face. "Open thou mine eyes that I may
see the wondrous things ..."

It was not long before I began to see that having one's portrait painted
is akin to some aspects of psychotherapy, and that the work of the portrait
artist is one of the caring professions. That does not mean that the artist
has only kind things to say in a portrait. It means that he cannot paint well
unless he cares — not least for the truth. He paints what he sees to be true
and paints with caring eyes. Concentration and contemplation are forms
of caring.

The portrait artist is trying to "do the truth" — another Johannine phrase:
"He that doeth the truth cometh to the light". That may have something to
say about more than mere accuracy and detail. It will certainly have
something to do with the search for identity.

It was Picasso who said: "Art is a lie which makes us realize the truth."
A portrait is obviously not identical with its subject. It is clearly not true
in that sense. It is a perceptive selection, so to speak, which gives an
interpretation of the truth. A portrait images reality.

After about half a dozen sittings, a disconsolate Diccon greeted me one
morning. "I may have done something that will shock you" he said, with
manifest embarrassment. "I've discarded what I've done so far and started
again. I simply wasn't getting you". He clearly expected me to be annoyed,
or, at the least, dismayed. I was not. I couldn't be glad that he had set aside
what he had worked at with such care, but I could only admire his
determination to pursue this elusive identity — which I found as impossible
to penetrate as he. It was an exploration into truth of a kind with which I
was unfamiliar but recognised its kinship with other sorts of exploration.

Of course, the sitter — and his friends — may not always like what the
artist sees and does. It is notorious how Lady Churchill hated what Graham
Sutherland made Sir Winston Churchill look like — and what his wife did

with his portrait. In ecclesiastical circles it is almost as notorious that when Sir William Orpen painted the portrait of Cosmo Gordon Lang, then Archbishop of York, Lang angrily confided to Hensley Henson, then Bishop of Durham, that people said the portrait made him look "proud, prelatical and pompous". "To which of those epithets does your Grace take exception" enquired his sardonic fellow prelate. Actually Lang thought it a fine portrait, but it has to be said that when Orpen came to paint it he said: "I see seven Archbishops: which am I to paint?" And when Nathan Söderblom, Archbishop of Uppsala, was shown the portrait he said: "That is what the devil meant him to be, but, thanks be to God, it is not so."

When you ask for your portrait to be painted, you not only ask for truth but for judgment. Inevitably, inescapably, sitting for a portrait is a kind of training exercise in "loving your judge" — which some maintain lies at the very heart of Christian spirituality.

When Henry Luke Paget, Bishop of Stepney and, later, of Chester had his portrait painted (he was, it must be said — like others I could name — "no oil painting") a friend said to him: "Well, the artist has done you justice". "Justice?" exclaimed the bishop "it's not justice I need, but mercy!"

Diccon Swan resorts to photographs to help him with some of his portraits — not least because many of his sitters — like John Major, whom he has just begun to paint — are too busy to manage all the sittings he would so much prefer. But Diccon maintains that a photograph — or even a few photographs — is no substitute for a painted portrait. A portrait requires a depth of intimacy with the subject which a photograph most often does not. A photograph is literally — usually — a 'snap' judgment. I was bound to recognise that the failure of Diccon's first attempt to paint me was probably in large part my own fault. At the beginning, I was apprehensive and suspicious of the whole exercise, somewhat afraid of the judgment it might involve, and perhaps of the intimacy and mutuality in relationship which soon seemed indispensable. The result was a portrait of a frightened subject.

I have said: "A portrait is inescapably involved with identity". Perhaps one word more is needed that might otherwise too easily be taken for granted. A portrait is inescapably involved with a person's *unique* identity. It is that emphasis on the uniqueness of each sitter that gives to the portrait artist what I can only call a gift of ministry. It is a gift allied to the very act of divine creation which brings each one of us uniquely to birth. That fact of our uniqueness can, of course, be a source of arrogance when it is not seen as the gift from God — "What hast thou which thou hast not received?". That fact can also be a source of loneliness if our uniqueness is not seen as set within a fellowship beyond the individual.

While Diccon was painting my portrait he made an incidental remark — he talks while he paints, maintaining that it is "like listening to music when you're driving a car." "What other art" he asked "draws to the artist

173

such frequent and immediate disapproval and criticism — even obloquy?" "A concert pianist" he said "is rarely greeted with immediate disapproval. First comes the applause, and then, maybe on the way out of the hall, people may say that the artist made rather a mess of, say, the second movement. But it's rare for a portrait artist not to have someone at the very first showing — when you have done your best, for good or ill — say: 'I don't think you've got the nose quite right — or the mouth' — or even: 'I'm afraid it just isn't him.'" Sargent said: "Every time I paint a portrait, I lose a friend." A portrait artist has to have huge confidence and courage and yet be well aware what a precarious task is his: to portray another unique human being. In other words he has to have humility.

I will suggest that perhaps that very sense of precariousness and fallibility which must be the portrait artist's gift alongside his confidence and courage when he approaches another subject, another person, is something which all of us could profitably covet.

Sargent, I've just quoted, as saying that every time he painted a portrait he lost a friend. I'm rather glad that by having my portrait painted I have *gained* a friend.

I have found that having it painted has in fact refreshed the way I look at *other* people — in trains, in newspapers, those near to me and those I only see on TV — this week, for instance, Kurds on the mountains of the Turkish border. They seemed each of them unique subjects for a portrait.

Sometimes portraiture is thought of as the preserve of the rich — of top people and wealthy patrons. But besides the portraits of Reynolds — in the Grand Manner — there have been, thank God, the paintings of Hogarth — "The Rake's Progress" for instance. I suspect it's in that *genre* that my portrait belongs. That "progress" will, of course, go on beyond *this* life, so I shall tack on to the end of my sermon the text I tacked on to the beginning: "When I awake up after *thy* likeness, I shall be satisfied with it."

But I must say a final word about that word "*likeness*". Since my portrait was finished, people have talked rather easily about it being a "very good likeness", without, I think, always recognising just what technical competence that has required — in terms of application of paint, composition, colour, knowledge of anatomy, and so on. There's theology *there*. Whatever else portraiture requires, it all depends on very down-to-earth technical skill — though that isn't *enough* in itself. There have been others who — I think as a kind of "leg-pull" — have said the portrait flatters me.

I am reminded that when Velasquez painted Philip IV he turned a rather unglamorous individual into quite a convincing candidate for the divine right of Kings. I don't think Diccon Swan has attempted that sort of thing with me! But perhaps there's something theological there. When we "awake up after his likeness", it won't be that we are all "look-alikes" of the Jesus of the New Testament — clones of Jesus: it will be that, given our unique raw materials and, above all, the work of grace upon them — upon our nature, we shall have been changed, as St. Paul says "into his likeness from glory to glory". That's the rake's *progress*. And because of that alone, "when I awake up after thy likeness, I shall be satisfied with it".

38

ST. GEORGE AND THE RED CROSS

The Bedfordshire Red Cross Annual Service of
Dedication;
The Priory Church of St. Peter, Dunstable;
May 19th 1991

It was over five hundred years ago that the Red Cross, on a white
background, first became a uniform for soldiers and sailors in England.
Certainly by the year 1347 the Red Cross was to be seen flying from the
Chapel of St. George's Windsor; for St. George had become the patron of
what we call in Britain the Order of the Garter, and the Chapel at Windsor
was the Chapel of the Order; and the Red Cross on a white background
was then the badge and emblem of St. George.

We hardly know anything about St. George except that he was a martyr,
and probably suffered and died at Lydda, in Palestine, before the time of
the Roman Emperor Constantine: that's to say before the middle of the 4th
Century. But not until a couple of hundred years later did the cult of St.
George become popular, and it took another six centuries for the dragon
to make its appearance. (I say carefully "its" appearance: for in these days
it would be unwise for a preacher to say for certain in public whether the
dragon was male or female.)

The circumstances in which St. George became Patron Saint of England
are what the historians call "obscure"; but, as I say, from the 14th Century
the Red Cross on a white background was to be seen flying all over the
country. William Caxton's translation and printing in 1483 of *The Golden
Legend*, which contained a life of St. George, did much to popularise his
story, and, soon, wherever there was a St. George's Church, there was the
flag of the Red Cross on white.

I begin my sermon for your Red Cross Service here in this lovely Priory Church of Dunstable, with St. George, because, when St. George was made the Patron Saint of England, out from this very Abbey, to Toddington, six miles away, some monks were sent to found a church; and they called it the Church of St. George, and there is no more ancient church in all of England with the name of St. George than the church at Toddington, founded in 1222 to mark the making of St. George as England's Patron Saint. So you can be sure that the Red Cross has been flying in these parts for over 750 years.

So much for St. George and the Red Cross and ancient England and ancient Bedfordshire.

But what has St. George and the Red Cross to say to us today?

I should perhaps tell you that from 1959 to 1964 I was vicar of a church in south London called St. George's Camberwell, and each year I had to ask myself that question: "What has St. George and his Red Cross to say to us today?"

If you become the Vicar of a church dedicated to St. George you have at least to pretend to be rather a fan of his; and one of the first things I ever did when I became Vicar of St. George's Camberwell was to nip smartly down to East Street Market, near the Elephant and Castle, and buy a roll of white satin and half a roll of red, and get my long-suffering housekeeper to run up a dozen or so St. George's flags, which, hanging from the gallery of our vast Victorian edifice, were calculated to bring tears to the eyes of our congregation, when they set eyes on those Red Crosses on white satin. But the question remains: "What has St. George and his Red Cross to say to us today?"

Well, clearly St. George was, for reasons known to people in his day, a saint, and, of course, he was a martyr.

George — George Carey, our new Archbishop of Canterbury, not Saint George — in his enthronement sermon a month ago, reminded us that a martyr is a witness; for our word "martyr" comes directly from the Greek word *marturos*, a witness. A martyr witnessed in a particular way to what he believed. He put his life on the line. He put his life where his mouth had been. He did that most contradictory and paradoxical thing: he said that what he believed in this world was so important to the people of this world that he was willing to have his existence in this world terminated. Speaking out caused him — again paradoxically — permanently to be put to silence. But since he was a saint, his example would go on speaking long after he was dead: which clearly it did long after St. George was dead. His actions spoke louder than his words, which is a phrase which I believe typifies those who follow the Red Cross.

Again, as the Archbishop said in his enthronement sermon, it's a curious fact, and not an unimportant one, that there have probably been more Christian martyrs in our day than in any time since the birth of Christ:

177

martyrs in Russia, and in other countries that used to be behind the "iron curtain"; martyrs in Nazi Germany; martyrs in Africa — in places like Uganda; martyrs in South and Central America, like Archbishop Romero, and so on.

Martyrdom — witness unto death — is so dramatic, even romantic — particularly to those who don't have to undergo it themselves — that the subject of the down-to-earth details of witness-unto-death, or what might lead to death, rarely gets the attention it deserves.

We think of those who died as martyrs in Nazi Germany; but we seldom reflect that most people in Nazi Germany who were Christians simply became Nazis; just as in more recent years most white people in South Africa who were Christians simply became supporters of apartheid: much of their holiness, much of their specifically Christian witness, simply evaporated under pressure. And who dare say that we Christians here in England would have done much better had we suffered similar circumstances? Indeed, many of the white supporters of apartheid in South Africa in recent years have been fairly recent immigrants from England who have gone out since the War to follow the sun, and a more affluent society, with servants a-plenty, black, and on the cheap.

St. Paul says something rather important in his great hymn of love — his letter to the Corinthians — which we do well to remember this Whit Sunday. He says: "If I give my body to be burned and have not charity, it profiteth me nothing." It's possible to give even your life — to be a martyr — for an unworthy cause: to crash your aircraft as a kamikaze pilot in the cause of a country like, say, Iraq, with unjust aims and goals. Martyrdom by itself does not make you worthy of the Red Cross.

One of the greatest sayings that came out of the First World War was the "famous last words" of the English nurse Edith Cavell. The daughter of a country vicar, she tended friend and foe alike, but was ruthlessly executed. Her last words were unforgettable and unforgotten: "Patriotism is not enough". "I realize" she said "that patriotism is not enough. I must have no bitterness towards anyone." Those words, I suggest, are worthy of the Red Cross.

You may have thought when I began my sermon with St. George and England and the Red Cross that I was going to preach a very patriotic sermon — well, Nurse Cavell did not say there was anything wrong with patriotism, just that it is "not enough".

And I think the Red Cross in England has never, and must never be concerned only with England and the English and the British Red Cross. It is right that we should see our roots going back to our ancient past; but in 1859 the Red Cross was, so to speak, born again. You will most of you know very well how in that year a young Swiss businessman saw something which was to change his life, and influence the course of history. That young man was Henry Dunant. What he saw was the carnage at the

Battle of Solferino in Italy. And worse even than the killing and maiming on the battlefield was the dreadful suffering of the wounded from both sides who were left largely uncared for. And this appalling scene gave birth to a magnificent humanitarian idea, which transcended the separate nations. Patriotism, for Dunant, was not enough. He saw every country creating a body of trained volunteers who would care impartially for the wounded of all sides under the protection of international agreement.

His vision led directly to the founding of the Red Cross, the signing of the first Geneva Convention, and the adoption of the Red Cross as an international symbol of protection.

Today, the International Red Cross can be proud of the fact that it is the world's largest voluntary organisation. It has a global membership of close on a quarter of a million.

I don't need to tell you today of the role the Red Cross has recently played in the Gulf War, or the help it is giving to the victims of the major famines which are now threatening various parts of Africa.

But I want to come back home again; indeed, I want to come back to Bedfordshire.

I want to say that I read very carefully your most recent report, and I want to congratulate you on all the variety of voluntary work the Red Cross here in Bedfordshire is doing — all the time and care you are giving, week in week out.

I was reading earlier this week a Report concerning the North Bedfordshire District Health Authority and its Department of Community Medicine. I noticed that there are 130,000 people in that area of Bedfordshire alone, and that one in five of them are what that report calls "a minority culture": Asian, West Indian, Italian, and so on; and I said to myself: "Next Sunday, I must be sure to ask how the Red Cross is doing amongst those Bedfordshire minorities." The Red Cross is an international organisation which can probably do more than most organisations to weld into one community people who come here from distant parts of the globe: for all our elderly, wherever they come from, need caring for — I speak as one now myself nearer seventy than sixty — and all young people, whatever their colour or country of origin, have the same possibilities of caring for the rest of the community. Each year, I noticed, over a hundred new immigrants come from other parts of the world to live in Bedford alone. You will know well that the Red Cross can do so much to make them feel cared for and to know what health care is available to them — for, for instance, their babies — when they come as strangers to a strange land.

One of my friends — alas, no longer living — wrote a book some years ago called *The Gift Relationship*. It's about blood-doning. Richard Titmuss didn't believe in God as much as he wanted to, but he said that nothing brought him nearer to belief in God than this study of his. "What is it" he

179

kept asking himself "which gives people such a deep-seated desire to help others? — people they have never met: anonymously, and without a financial reward?" Those who were questioned in his study came up with different answers: "I do it to help the hospitals" some said. "It's a way of saying 'thank you' for my own good health" said others. And others: "You never know: you might be saving someone's life"; and others: "It might be you next time."

I should emphasize that Richard Titmuss found this "altruism", as it's called, this concern to help others, in people of different races, of different religions, and none.

Titmuss' study included a comparison of different ways of procuring blood in different societies. They varied from complete reliance on voluntary donors to accepting the free play of market forces: procuring the blood at the price it could command. It was from this comparison that Titmuss concluded that the commercialization of blood-donor relationships represses and suppresses the expression of this capacity we all have voluntarily to help others.

I find it important today, at your Red Cross Service of Rededication, simply to reflect on that fact, and to reflect thankfully, that we each of us have this capacity. I'd want to suggest that any human being who does not take it seriously is neglecting a very important part of themselves. And I'd go further, and say that if we take time and care about this deep-seated desire and capacity — which is part of us by our very creation — we may discover parts of ourselves we hardly knew existed.

If I were asked to put what the Red Cross, in Britain and world-wide, stands for, I think I'd say simply: "The Gift Relationship". And for that I give thanks this day to almighty God.

39

MOTIVATION

Malvern College Commemoration Service;
June 29th 1991

"Motivation": that is the subject of my Commemoration Sermon for you today.

Recently, I received a letter from the son of a judge: "Could I come and talk with you?" he wrote. "To put my problem briefly: I've been working in the City for a couple of years now; I'm motivated enough now to get out of it, but I'm not motivated enough to get into the more needy parts of the world."

The young man had been studying to be a Chartered Accountant, and his exams were not far off; so I told him I'd see him after he'd sat his exams. As a Cambridge Chaplain I became familiar with an affliction which a tutor used to refer to laconically as a "touch of the change of subject", which occurred invariably about examination time, especially among those who thought they had a good chance of failing.

But this young man wasn't facing failure, though he didn't enjoy the work involved in preparing to be a Chartered Accountant. And it wasn't hard work that he minded.

When I saw him, needless to say I let him talk about himself first of all, and listened for quite a time. Then I played, to some extent, Devil's Advocate. I said that I thought that Chartered Accountants were very necessary to the world; that someone had to do that kind of work, and that I had little sympathy with people who run away from the bread and butter jobs. I said that I'd never seen anything wrong in people making money: it's what they do with it when they've made it that counts. I agreed with him that most people who make money aren't all that keen on parting with it once they've made it. But in the early stages of Chartered Accountancy I could presume that wasn't his problem — yet.

I then switched to a different tack. I asked him when he'd last fallen in love. Because it's my experience that it really is love that "makes the world go round". If you don't love anybody, and you don't love your job, that's a pretty good recipe for depression, and, indeed, for feeling that a place like the City has nothing to be said for it.

He said he didn't think he had fallen in love — yet, and he rather hoped he wouldn't — yet; because if he fell in love, the City might seem more attractive because it was more useful, and might provide the kind of way of life for his wife and — in due course — his kids that would probably seem appropriate. And he'd really come to the conclusion that the City was "Mammon-with-a-capital-M", and he didn't want to be seduced into staying with it.

I didn't immediately move away from that area of questioning: having a look at his emotional life; because very often I find that what looks like a rational process on the top surface has behind it some emotional blockage. And I still think I may be right: that the unsatisfactoriness of my young friend's emotional life — he has many acquaintances but few strong friendships, either male or female — may in large part be responsible for his particular view of the City.

I could see that he didn't like my digging around in this area — people rarely do; and he blurted out suddenly: "Why aren't you taking me more seriously? Why can't you accept that I think that the City is bloody awful? I thought I would at least find you in sympathy with me, and that we could start there." "No", I said. "It's because I'm trying to take the whole of you seriously that I can't just take all that you say at face value."

He continued to look rather aggrieved, and said: "But I thought any Christian was bound to sympathise with what I've said — and you in particular."

"Yes" I said. "A Christian will sympathise with you; but he may not agree with all you have to say".

And I reiterated what I'd said earlier, in a slightly different way: that a Christian believes God created the world, indeed, that He loves the world; and therefore the things that carry it on — buying and selling, farming, marketing — and the things that order it, are very much God's work. The City, or a good deal of it, is therefore, of God.

"Of course", I said, "the Christian takes sin seriously; and there's a lot of it about. But I'm not aware that the church is all that less sinful than the world; and I don't have much respect for people who want to run away from the world because of its sin." I said that I find those Christians who run away from the world not to my liking at all. There are some who seem to spend their time pulling people into what they think of as the 'pure' church, out of the swamp of the world; and you can almost hear the sound of the suction as they pull them out! But I don't believe the Christian Gospel is primarily about taking people out of the world: in part, it's about getting rid of their sin while they're in the world — in families, friendships, businesses, governments, political parties, social work, the priesthood, the teaching profession, the theatre, the law — and," I added, "in Chartered Accountancy. But as a Christian I daren't say that Chartered Accountancy — particularly Chartered Accountancy in the City — is specially evil, or that the City is a particular slough of sin."

I was obviously getting nowhere fast, and we sat in a kind of frustrated silence for a while. And then he said: "So you think I ought really to be enjoying the City".

"Oh, no" I said. "That's quite a different matter; and let's go into that. But I could name a couple of hundred people straight away who work in the City, and who are Christians — and some of my best friends are Chartered Accountants — in the City; and in order to be a friend to you I daren't say that the City — which includes many of my friends — is all wrong."

"If you are saying that there's a lot of heartless money-making going on in the City at the moment" I continued "— and fraud — I'm with you. If you're saying that riches are a terrible seduction, of course I'm with you. Didn't Jesus say 'It is easier for a camel to go through the eye of a needle than for a rich man to enter the Kingdom of Heaven?' And who am I to disagree with Him? And He told one young man — like you — to go and sell all that he had; but it was too much for him, and he went away sorrowful, for he was clearly possessed by his possessions, as many people are — not least in the City; and the City is within sight and sound of areas of extreme need and poverty, which is why I said there's a lot of heartless money-making going on in the City.

But *abusus non tollit usum*. The abuse of money-making in the City is no reason for getting out of it. You need a better reason than that for getting out. So let's discuss whether and why you feel you're a 'square peg in a round hole' in the City, and whether it's the discomfort of that position that makes you dislike the City itself."

We might at this stage have turned to the question of that young man's particular gifts, and where they might better be used; and we did, in fact, some time later. But at that point, he again said, rather forcefully: "You know, you haven't yet referred to the second of my questions: How do I get motivated to get into the more needy parts of the world?"

I said that we had to some extent tackled that when we looked a little at his emotional life; because most people have some contact with some people in need: need of one sort and another crosses most of our paths, and we don't actually have to make a particular effort to enter the world of need. It's in our newspapers, or on TV, or in our neighbourhood, or in our family. And if what he had been saying was that he did not feel the needs of others — which were in front of him and around him — I was right to query whether he had some emotional blockage.

"Have you ever met someone in great need?" I asked. He was silent for quite a long time, and then said "No. Not as far as I know"; and added:

"Of course, I've seen them on TV and on the streets. But that's the problem." And then he was silent again.

And then he said something that I thought was particularly interesting and important. "You know" he said "I don't feel I belong to anyone". "I belong to my mother, of course. She's marvellous. But I don't feel I belong to the real world....."

"Your mother" I said "would probably like you to think of her as part of the real world".

Again there was silence, and I said: "Do you believe with your mind, intellectually, that you belong to anyone or anything?" "In a rather cold, theoretical way I suppose I do" he said. "I know I belonged to the school I went to and belong now to the firm I work for. But that's what I mean: that now all seems so unreal, such a waste of precious time."

"Well" I said "there's no way in which *I* can help you *feel* you belong; though I could put you in touch with someone who could help you in that area of your feelings. And there are ways in which I might hope to persuade you intellectually that you belong to, say, the church, and to the human race, and so to those in need. But from what you've been saying I don't feel that what you're asking me to do is to persuade you simply to believe something intellectually."

"So" I said "I think I'd like to suggest two things to you: First, that you go somewhere where you can see very clearly that you're needed. There are hospices, like St. Joseph's in Hackney and St. Christopher's Sydenham, and, nowadays, all round the country, where they desperately need volunteers, not least at night; and there are AIDS victims who need 'Buddies'. And when you've done something like that for a little while we might talk again. I do assure you" I said "the world is full of people in need." "Yes" he said "I do believe that; but I've been brought up, I've discovered, school and family, in such a world apart. And I suppose I may be rather frightened of a world I simply don't know."

"Well, my second suggestion" I said "is that you should book up a week-end, or the inside of a week, at a monastery: either with the Franciscans or the Benedictines. I think a few days there should teach you something — I don't know what. You may find at either place God has something to say to you." "A monastery!" he exclaimed. "That doesn't sound like the real world."

"No" I added "it doesn't to many people. And I think you should be clear — as I've said — that God speaks to most people in their everyday job and in their everyday world. That's where most of us have to learn to meet Him and serve Him: in our marriages, friendships and our bread and butter occupations. But monasteries for *some* people are as close to reality as, say, marriage." "And" I said "I think you really should take seriously my suggestion that your problem may at least in part be emotional. We all need some kind of healing; and our wounds are often in the end our best gifts. God speaks to us through our wounds as much as through our gifts." He smiled — for the first time that evening. So I thought I would introduce just one more line of thought before we brought our conversation to a close. "Margaret Simey" I said "Lady Simey, who wrote a very good book called *Charitable Effort in Liverpool*, said in it, of people at the end of the last century: "There was a yearning to do good to the poor in person...Guilt sought relief in contact with the injured."

"You say you haven't any motivation to work with the needy. I wonder whether you have any guilt? I don't see why people shouldn't feel guilty if they have been part of a wrong done — or a good not done — to, say, the poor or the hungry, or the homeless. Most of us are right to feel some guilt in that area."

He thought, and said: "No. I don't think I feel any guilt. Perhaps I should do: perhaps I would do if I felt I belonged to the rest of society; but, as I said, I don't feel I really do belong..."

We had almost agreed to leave things there for the moment, when I decided to add just one more thought. "I haven't mentioned your sexuality" I said — at which point he looked like a frightened rabbit caught in a headlight. "Lots of people find their sexuality quite a help in deciding their vocation"."Whatever d'you mean?"he asked. "I mean what I said"I replied "but I don't think I want to talk much about that now. I'll just say that I regard my sexuality as one of God's best gifts in my ministry as a priest; and it's a huge mistake to ignore it or pretend it's not there." I could see that the respectable rather frightened part of him was much relieved that I quickly finished what I had to say on that point.

I have told you what I remember of that conversation as best as I can, and roughly as I remember it. I could not pretend I'd coped with my young friend's important questions in one meeting; but I hope to meet him again soon.

As he got up to go, he pointed to a pile of papers on my living room floor — where I keep a good many things. (They can't fall any further!) "Busy?" he asked. "Yes" I said "I'm writing the biography of Bishop Trevor Huddleston who's just returned to South Africa after thirty-five years absence from it. He worked there for thirteen years, from 1943 to 1956, with a parish of 80,000 black people"."Tell me how *he* knew that's what he'd got to do" my friend asked. "Oh" I said "that'd take hours and hours, and will take pages and pages"."Could you put it in just a sentence or two for me now?" he asked.

"Well" I said "the young Trevor Huddleston, when he'd finished at Lancing and Christ Church, knew he simply had to test his vocation as a monk; and, in 1939, at the outbreak of War, when every other able-bodied young man was joining up, he went away to a monastery in Yorkshire for four years, and it was they who sent him to the slums of Johannesburg for thirteen years. After a spell back here, he was eight years in Tanzania; then ten years as a bishop in Stepney, East London, back home again; then eight years in Mauritius and Madagascar. He's been 'retired' eight years, heading up the Anti-Apartheid Movement. He's seventy-eight now, frail, but full of courage; and when Nelson Mandela asked him to go back to South Africa, he was clear he must go."

"It was clear for *him*" said my young friend. "Yes" I said "But you're very different people, with different gifts. Your job is to go on working hard at what God wants you to do — with your gifts. And remember: Trevor Huddleston wrestled with the question for four years — and more."

My friend stood there ruminating; and I knew I had to show him the door — the door on my London, Lambeth world.

As I say: we're meeting again soon.

The question "What does God want me to do in his world?" has not left him in peace — I'm happy to say.

40

IN MEMORIAM: EVELYN UNDERHILL

Gray's Inn Chapel; July 21st 1991

"I pray not that thou shouldest take them out of the world, but that thou shouldest keep them from the evil....That they all may be one; as thou, Father, art in me, and I in thee, that they also may be one in us...."

The Gospel according to St. John: Chapter 17 verses 15 and 21

The first line of my sermon today might well be "She was only a barrister's daughter", though it might equally be "She was only a barrister's wife". And the daughter and the wife were one and the same: someone I want to commemorate: Evelyn Underhill, who died fifty years ago this year.

Many of you will remember, with much affection, Michael Underhill — so recently taken from us, and commemorated by the glass opposite; and you'll not be surprised he was a sort of second cousin to Evelyn. Others of you will know of Evelyn's father, Arthur, as *Underhill on Torts* and *Underhill on Trusts*. Evelyn's husband, Hubert Stuart Moore, was a member of the Inner Temple.

But why should I *want* to *commemorate* Evelyn Underhill?

Not least, in private duty bound, because she was the first woman to be made a Fellow of King's College, London; and, as myself a Fellow of King's, I particularly delight in that.

But there are, of course, more, and greater, reasons.

In 1907, Evelyn had an experience of religious conversion, and in her spiritual struggles turned to the study of the mystics. The first *literary* fruit of that experience was her very considerable study, simply called *Mysticism*, which was published in the Spring of 1911. In that same year she came under the influence of the Catholic layman the Baron von Hügel, who was renowned as a spiritual director. About the same time, Evelyn herself began to undertake individual spiritual direction. Books began to flow from her pen, such as:

The Mystic Way 1913
Practical Mysticism 1914
The Life of the Spirit and the Life of Today 1922

and the spring of her writing never ran dry until she died, as I've said, in 1941. She prepared editions of the English Mystics — *The Cloud of Unknowing*; Walter Hilton's *Scale of Perfection*, the writings of Richard Rolle, and so on.

At first, her mysticism was somewhat vague and pantheistic, and she was attracted to the occult; but more and more it became Christocentric: "In the depth of reality revealed by the cross" she wrote "Christianity stands alone"; but she encouraged people of different faiths and different Christian denominations to discover what they had in common.

She was not only a writer; she began to conduct retreats, mostly at Pleshey, in Essex, to which she and her friends came to have a special devotion; and the whole retreat movement in England owes a great deal to her. The addresses she gave at retreats were often published, and undoubtedly contain some of the most enduring parts of her life's work. Archbishop Michael Ramsay wrote of her: "In the Twenties and Thirties there were few, if indeed any, in the Church of England, who did more to help people grasp the priority of prayer in the Christian life and the place of the contemplative element within it."

I have suggested that in her earlier years Evelyn Underhill veered towards a vague mysticism. She also veered towards the Roman Catholic Church, but consideration for her barrister husband persuaded her to remain in the Church of England, and so, too, did the liberal heart and mind of the Catholic Baron von Hügel.

In 1936, Evelyn produced what was probably her finest book, with again a simple title: *Worship*. It witnesses both to Evelyn's increasingly deep ecumenism, which was nevertheless fed by her life as an Anglican worshipper, and her profound understanding of corporate liturgical worship.

I preach this sermon today not least because a close friend of mine — who, alas, died young — gave me *Worship* for a Christmas present in 1941, when I was nearing my seventeenth birthday. I still treasure it, and count it one of the books which have most influenced my life.

In her preface to *Worship*, Evelyn Underhill writes: "This study of the nature and principles of Worship, and the chief forms in which they find expression in Christianity, is not the work of a liturgical expert, and is not intended as a handbook to that difficult science. My object has been rather to explore those primary realities of man's relation to God which our devotional action is intended to express. Worship is here considered in its deepest sense, as the response of man to the Eternal: and when we look at the many degrees and forms of this response, and the graded character of human religion, its slow ascent from primitive levels and tendency to carry with it relics of its past, we need not be surprised that even within the Christian family there is much diversity in the expressive worship which is yet directed towards a single revelation of the Divine."

It was W.R. Matthews who suggested to Evelyn that she should write *Worship*. Walter Matthews had been Dean of King's College, London, and, indeed, for twelve years, Preacher to Gray's Inn, until 1932, and was, later, Dean of St. Paul's.

It's often difficult to select a single passage which characterises the thought of a writer like Evelyn Underhill; but in quite a small book, *The Mystery of Sacrifice*, she wrote, in 1938:

> In our religion, and in the worship which is the expression of our religion, we look out towards Eternity; and bit by bit, in various ways and degrees, we discover in ourselves a certain capacity for Eternity — and more than this, a deep thirst for the Unchanging, a need of God. But because we have lost purity of heart, we cannot recognise the way in which that capacity can be filled, that thirst satisfied, that profound need of our nature met. Indeed, this self-opening of the creature to the Eternal, this breaking down of the barriers of self-love, is not an obvious nor an easy process: it makes demands upon the half-grown and half-awakened human spirit which, in its solitude, it can hardly meet. The soul is responding, it is true, to a call, a demand which comes from the very heart of Reality and speaks to something within itself which already has kinship with that Reality.

Evelyn Underhill was a surprising person. A woman keen on mysticism and always conducting retreats might be expected to be a bit of a blue-stocking. Evelyn was, of course, an intellectual, but she was also a serene and lovely person, gifted with a sense of fun. She was religious editor of *The Spectator* for several years from 1928 onwards and gave several series of talks on the BBC in the Thirties.

It cannot be right simply to *accuse* a person of living in Campden Hill Square — which Evelyn Underhill did all her married life. (Successive bishops of Kensington have lived there!) But her biographer, Margaret Cropper, does have this worrying paragraph in her biography:

> The year 1926, which was to be such a turbulent one to many people in England, was another year of growing for Evelyn. I do not feel as if the crux of the General Strike touched her very deeply. Politics never possessed her. I do not remember her talking about them. When the Strike came it meant a hold up to work and plans, but nothing fundamental.

One reviewer of Miss Cropper's biography, Valerie Pitt, commented acidly on that passage, in the radical Anglican monthly *Prism*:

189

Nothing fundamental: just a small matter of social justice and the livelihood of millions of people. There were other little things of this kind occurring while Evelyn Underhill was giving her retreats: unemployment, for instance, and the rise of Hitler. I cannot believe that anyone of any sensibility, let alone of prayer, could cut these things so completely out of their consciousness; yet Miss Cropper's book certainly gives us a picture of a lady whose sole contact with the stirring events of her time was through the Anglican Pacifist Fellowship. It is an impression which Evelyn Underhill's own letters seem to confirm.

That is surely somewhat severe. Evelyn Underhill was well aware of the wide-spread poverty of her time; indeed, Baron von Hügel advised her, for the sake of her soul, to visit the poor. His letter is recorded in Miss Cropper's biography. He wrote:

> I believe you ought to get yourself, gently and gradually, interested *in the poor*; that you should visit them, very quietly and unostentatiously, with as little incorporation as possible into Visiting Societies, etc. You badly want de-intellectualizing, or at least developing homely, human sense and spirit dispositions and activities. Gradually you may be able to draw out, perhaps even to help, some of these poor religiously. But the good *you yourself* will gain, long before this, and quite apart from this, will be very great. For it will, if properly entered into and persevered with, discipline, mortify, soften, deepen and quiet you: it will, as it were, distribute your blood — some of your blood — away from the brain, where too much of it is lodged at the present. And if and when religion does appear on the scene you will find how homely, how much sense as well as spirit it has and had to be. Again, how excellent for you! For what is a religion which cannot mean anything to the uneducated poor?....I should be quite satisfied with two afternoons a week given to such visiting. But pray strive to spread the spirit derived from these two days over the other five days....
>
> I would carefully give the preference to the two weekly visitations of the poor against everything else, except any definite home and family duties, or any express wishes of your husband...

Valerie Pitt worked herself into a lather over this letter — which I must confess seems to me full of sound common sense. Miss Pitt wrote:

> I've no doubt at all that her "families" benefited from Miss Underhill's care; but that von Hügel could advise, and Miss Underhill undertake this kind of work from such a motive is, to me, outrageous. This cultivated lady visited those in need not because she loved them, nor because her conscience was hurt by their sufferings, but as a help to her own soul. And the curious thing is that neither she nor her director nor Miss Cropper seems to realise that this is to make use of people for one's own profit as surely as sweated labour makes use of them. That the profit is spiritual does not alter the facts. But this unawareness is of a piece with the unawareness of an outside world of politics and social disturbance. For in this magic circle nothing matters besides the cultivation of the soul; and in consequence nothing, nothing, nothing, is seen apart from its possible use in spirituality. The chaffinch becomes a spiritual adventurer;

toothache invokes the mystery of the Cross; the most ordinary deprivation of human life, old age, or storing one's books in wartime, are spiritual "stripping". In such an atmosphere ordinary things and real people recede. The world is never seen as it is...

Miss Pitt, I notice, does not record that by the summer of 1922 Evelyn Underhill was writing to the Baron:

Visiting the poor. This prescription has been a complete success. I realize now I was starving for something of the kind. It is an immense source of interest, often of a heart-breaking kind; for they are always in some trouble and misery...often actually hungry.

Terry Tastard, a Roman Catholic writer living in the East End of London, in a recent book *The Spark in the Soul* has a much more sympathetic account of Evelyn Underhill's attitude to social justice in a chapter "Evelyn Underhill and God in the present".

But perhaps that overheated altercation between Miss Pitt and Miss Cropper — eighteen years after Evelyn Underhill had departed this life — may be of some profit to us if it serves to remind us that not everyone of us has precisely the same Christian vocation. It may not have been Evelyn Underhill's vocation to be as active in politics as is the vocation of some, just as it may not be the vocation of others to be as frequently involved in retreats as she. But if the private prayer and the prayer we offer in retreat houses and in churches and chapels is to be in tune with the Gospel we have all somehow to be *alongside the poor* — and not only in prayer. Of this Baron von Hügel seems to me to have been aware, and did his best to make Evelyn Underhill aware: and she did her best to follow his advice. The Baron was aware that the *Christian* mystic cannot separate himself or herself from the multitude: that Campden Hill must always be aware of the realities of Notting Hill; that the the well-heeled lawyer — and his wife — must always somehow bear and share the realities of, say, Brixton and Broadwater Farm; for the prayer of Christ is not that we should be taken *out* of the world but that we should be kept from the evil one, and that we all may be one.

And surveying the variety and multiplicity of vocations that God has given to people in the last half century, I think we are right to give special thanks at this fiftieth anniversary of her death for the vocation of Evelyn Underhill whose vocation it was to remind each one of us that "in our religion, and in the worship which is the expression of our religion, we look out towards Eternity; and bit by bit, in various ways and degrees, we discover in ourselves a certain capacity for Eternity.